T0400148

STRATEGIC REDUNDANCY IMPLEMENTATION

Redundancy, restructuring, downsizing. There are few, if any, other management books on this important topic, and yet the pace of redundancies has only accelerated in recent years. Coupled with this, many companies that implement redundancies as a cost-cutting exercise often fail to achieve their goal.

Whilst viewed as an uncomfortable topic by many, guidance on how to implement a redundancy programme that is fair, proportionate and ultimately leads to improved organisational performance, has never been more needed. This book fills this important gap. It takes the reader through a redundancy implementation strategy – Re-Focus, Re-Organise and Re-Build – that incorporates the key aspects of planning and analysis, fairness and justice, and prepares management for redundancy implementation through training. What will your communications include? What will be your strategy for implementation? What training does your management need? Various helpful template examples are included for employee consultation, communication and training.

The book will be invaluable for business managers, HR professionals, employee representatives and HR students.

Madeleine Stevens is a senior lecturer in Human Resource Management at Liverpool John Moores University. She has published a number of articles for the CIPD on redundancy implementation and how to mitigate the negative impact of redundancies for individuals and organisations. Prior to joining academia, Dr. Stevens worked as a HR practitioner for over 20 years, holding various roles internationally with extensive experience in business restructuring and improvement. She has won several awards for her research and innovative teaching from the Academy of Management and Association of Business Psychologists. Dr. Stevens is a Fellow member of the Chartered Institute of Personnel and Development (FCIPD), Higher Education Academy (FHEA) and Paralegal Society (Specialist Employment Law). She is also a Chartered member of the British Psychological Society.

"Madeleine Stevens has produced an important book for teachers, learners and professional practitioners of HR. The book provides an original and comprehensive guide on all aspects of redundancies, and supplements this with practical examples and templates of associated documents. This is in my view an unmissable resource for everyone with an interest and role in managing redundancies."

Professor Jim Stewart, Professor of Human Resource Development,
Liverpool Business School

"Restructures and redundancies are often an unavoidable part of a HR professional's working life, but knowing how to carry them out with compassion is vital. Madeleine is an expert on limiting the negative effects of such programmes and brings a fresh perspective on the impact on all individuals involved in the process. This book is sure to be a must-read for HR professionals."

Katie Jacobs, Senior Stakeholder Lead, CIPD and business journalist

"Dr. Madeleine Stevens' book offers a fresh and much-needed rethink on the issues around how companies approach and implement redundancies. It explores positive alternatives to redundancies that limit the emotional impact on employees and the detrimental effect redundancies can have on businesses."

Colin Gosling, Senior Unite Rep and European Siemens representative,
Siemens ITS Poole

"At last a book about this difficult topic that is both practical about the process but also deals with the emotional rollercoaster for all participants. Maddy Stevens' compassionate approach is no soft touch, and has the authenticity of hard-won experience."

Toby Peyton-Jones, OBE, Former HR Director Siemens UK and
Northwest Europe

STRATEGIC REDUNDANCY IMPLEMENTATION

Re-Focus, Re-Organise and Re-Build

Madeleine Stevens

LONDON AND NEW YORK

Cover image: © Matthias Kulka / Getty Images

First published 2022
by Routledge
4 Park Square, Milton Park, Abingdon, Oxon OX14 4RN

and by Routledge
605 Third Avenue, New York, NY 10158

Routledge is an imprint of the Taylor & Francis Group, an informa business

British Library Cataloguing-in-Publication Data
A catalogue record for this book is available from the British Library

Library of Congress Cataloging-in-Publication Data
A catalog record has been requested for this book

ISBN: 978-0-367-46570-4 (hbk)
ISBN: 978-1-032-17052-7 (pbk)
ISBN: 978-1-003-03041-6 (ebk)

DOI: 10.4324/9781003030416

Typeset in Joanna
by codeMantra

This book is dedicated to:

Dave Pickles – the smiling assassin of redundancies

Ke'ala and Kai – my children who put the purpose of life into context

Ron and Betsie Stevens – my 'oracles'

Ronnelie Nieuwenhuis – a superhero, always there to make things better

CONTENTS

FIGURES

TABLES

ABBREVIATIONS

BEIS	Department of Business, Energy and Industrial Strategy
BOHICA	"bend over, here it comes again"
CA	Court of Appeal Judge, Court Appeal
EAP	employee assistance programmes
EAT	Employment Appeal Tribunal
ECJ	European Court of Justice
ERA	Employment Rights Act
ERC	employee representative committee
FAQ	frequently asked questions
HR	Human Resources
ICE	Information and Consultation of Employees Regulations 2004
IRLR	Industrial Relations Law Reports (UK)
PESTLE	Political, Economic, Technological, Legal and Environmental
PILON	pay in lieu of notice
RPS	redundancy payments service
RRR	Re-Focus, Re-Organise and Re-Build
TUL(C)RA	Trade Union and Labour Relations (Consolidation) Act

TUPE	Transfer of Undertaking (Protection of Employment)
SMP	statutory maternity pay
STEEEPLE	Social, Technological, Economic, Environmental, Political, Legal and Ethical
SWOT	strengths, weaknesses, opportunities and threats

ABOUT THE AUTHOR

Madeleine (Petzer) Stevens is a Senior Lecturer in Human Resource Management at Liverpool John Moores University. Prior to joining academia, Dr. Stevens worked as an HR practitioner for over 20 years, having worked in South Africa, England, Channel Islands and France.

Formerly, Dr. Stevens was Divisional HR Business Partner and Head of HR Zone North Europe where she had responsibility for eight countries in Europe in Siemens before taking the reigns as HR Director at City Fibre in London.

She has also worked as HR policy and projects manager in Dubai Ports World, Southampton and HR Manager and Learning and Development Manager in various hotels internationally.

Dr. Stevens received her PhD from Solent University, Southampton in 2019 with her thesis focusing on 'Developing effective interventions for mitigating the psychological impact experienced by redundancy envoys during redundancy situations'. She holds a master's degree (merit) in Personnel and Development from Solent University, focusing on Occupational Stress after studying Industrial, Applied and Developmental psychology in South Africa (distinction).

She is a Fellow member of the Chartered Institute of Personnel and Development (FCIPD), Higher Education Academy (FHEA) and Paralegal

Society (Specialist Employment Law). She is also a Chartered member of the British Psychological Society and a Chartered member of Business Educators (CMBE).

Dr. Stevens and Prof Claire Hannibal were awarded the prestigious 2022 Professor Ian Beardwell Prize for applied research on behalf of the CIPD, for their paper `The smiling assassin?: Reconceptualising redundancy envoys as quasi-dirty workers', available at: https://doi.org/10.1080/09585192.202 1.1976246.

In 2021, Dr. Stevens received the distinguished 'Innovative Teaching Award' from the HR Division of the Academy of Management and 'Rising Star Award' from the Liverpool Business School. She was a finalist for 'Excellence in Learning and Development' from the Association of Business Psychologist's Workforce Experience Awards 2020.

In 2014, she won 'Outstanding student achievement' and 'Excellence in employee wellbeing' at the Association of Business Psychologist's Workforce Experience Awards for her PhD research in mitigating the negative impact of implementing redundancies and was finalist in the categories of 'Excellence in change management' and 'Employee engagement'. She won the 'Best HR professional leading strategic and operational change' in 2013 through Bond Williams/CIPD. Her first recognition in HR commenced in South Africa, where she designed a bespoke training programme for the 5 star, Relais and Chateau Property, Hunters Country House Hotel in Plettenberg Bay that led to the recognition of 'Best fine dining restaurant in 2002'.

Dr. Stevens' research passion is about mitigating the negative impact of redundancies for individuals and implementing redundancies successfully for organisations. She has published various articles for the CIPD on redundancy implementation.

For further information or to get support with redundancy implementation or general queries, please visit www.madeleinestevens.com.

ACKNOWLEDGEMENTS

Professional thanks to my brilliant editor Jijendrakumar Paulraj Thomas.
Toby Peyton-Jones and Claire Hannibal – invaluable mentors
Research participants – none of this was possible without your valued contributions
And finally, all 'redundancy envoys' – I know how hard your job is

PREFACE

I am not sure if it is worse to implement redundancies or to be at risk of redundancy yourself. I have done both. I have implemented several redundancy programmes. I have also been put at risk of redundancy. Twice. I consider myself to be lucky. Redundancies have peaked as a result of COVID-19 at the highest rate of 14.2 redundancies in every 1000 people in the UK (ONS, 2021). The International Labour Organization's (ILO, 2021) statistics suggests that the labour market was disrupted to an unprecedented scale during 2020 with working-hour losses equalling 255 million full-time jobs globally.

All things considered, I definitely consider myself lucky and I unquestionably anticipate more redundancies to come in my career. Further, to the two 'at risk' events; I had two very unique and contrasting experiences. The first was horrendous, while the second experience is completely the opposite. It was driven to make the best of an unpleasant situation.

The first time, I was on maternity leave with my second child, nine months old, whilst caring for his sister, then three years old. He caught a vomiting and diarrhoea bug whilst in Greece on holiday and was very ill. I received a phone call whilst on holiday from my line manager, who asked if I could come into the office to discuss my imminent return to work and some exciting promotional opportunities. I explained that my youngest was ill, but as this was an opportunity not to be missed, I will get someone to come and look after him. My line manager was keen for me to come in as soon as I was back in the UK. In fact, so keen, he wanted me to come in at 8:00 am the first day after I returned from holiday. Being the main bread winner in the family, I was super excited about the prospect of a promotional opportunity, and with my return to work being less than three months away, the timing was great. Enthused by the news, despite having had very little sleep after arriving back in the UK the night before with a sick baby and a toddler, I left home at 6:30 am to get to the office for 8:00 am. I arrived early, and no one was in the office yet, and thus I waited at my desk like a coiled spring. 8:00 am came and went, and around 45 minutes later, my line manager showed up and apologised for being late. He then shortly apologised again as he had a board meeting at 9:00 am. The next 5–10 minutes left me in a state of shock. I was expecting a conversation around a promotion opportunity, but instead, it turned out to be a very blunt message of redundancies. I was informed that my role was placed at risk of redundancy as of the previous day and we have already entered 30-day consultation. I was handed a standard letter with the wrong date, referring to the announcement I attended the day before where the rationale for redundancies were explained. That day I was supposed to have attended the announcement meeting, I was actually in Greece on holiday, so none the wiser what the announcement contained. I asked about the 'promotion opportunities' and was told I would need to look at the vacancy board, as there may be some positions available to apply for. No details were provided. It then sunk in, I had to be there early enough, probably to avoid embarrassment before other colleagues arrived. Not for my benefit, for my line manager. I had to come in as quickly as possible, as he had a target date to complete consultation and my absence was causing a delay and was clearly an inconvenience. The 'promotion opportunities' was in fact one opportunity between 18 staff members being made redundant and in a different location. I lost complete and utter respect for my line manager, and my psychological contract was broken. I could and I never worked for him again. Even if I kept by job, I could not work for him or ever trust him again.

This unethical and insensitive manner of communicating my job was as risk and may end in less than a month, has taught me a lot about how 'not' to implement redundancies. This episode was just the beginning of a myriad of poor practice throughout the consultation process. Lesson 1 learned; treat people with honesty, respect, empathy and dignity. Manage expectations credibly.

The second time, I had a distinctively different experience. The announcement of redundancies was received whilst in hospital with my son, then aged five, who was diagnosed with Type 1 Diabetes only a few days prior to the call. Recently divorced, working in hospital was not only a necessity, but also a delightful distraction from my new reality of a lifetime of insulin dependence, working out carbs, injections, finger pricks to read blood glucose levels and a little boy in a hysterical state when a needle pierced him every two hours to keep him alive. Every time he needed an injection or finger prick, it took four hospital employees to hold him down to administer the injection or finger prick whilst his screaming pierced every cell in my body. He screamed so much; he was transferred into a private room.

Losing my job was the last thing I wanted to worry about. The timing was not great, but when is the time ever right for someone to lose their livelihood? This time, I was treated with utmost respect, dignity, sensitivity and empathy. I was not thrown into 'your job is at risk' shock. Instead, an approach was adopted by a 'different' line manager that reflected that of being treated as a human being, not a process, not a tick box exercise and I will always be entirely grateful.

Consultation was effective and carefully considered. The timing of phone calls and live meetings were considerate and thought through. My line manager had all the time in the world to listen to my thoughts for the future. Or maybe he did not, either way, he treated me as if I was a priority. This was not part of the role of the consultation tick box exercise. This was someone who cared and showed it. This was someone who advocated humanity in the process of redundancy implementation and who wanted to help me make the best decisions for the future of my family. He applied this approach to all his team. Thank you, again.

Whether you are at the receiving end of redundancies (victim), a witness to your colleagues being made redundant (survivor) or the messenger (redundancy envoy), the role is unpleasant for all parties involved. The opportunity to minimise the unpleasant experience where possible is in the supremacy of the employer and the redundancy envoys.

Whether you label a workforce reduction as 'redundancies', 'restructuring', 'retrenchment' or 'downsizing' the requirements to implement a successful programme that meets its intended purpose is challenging. By intended purposes, it could include achieving a sustainable future for the organisation, improving effectiveness, reducing costs and/or enhancing performance and profitability.

This book will guide you through the critical stages of implementing a redundancy programme underpinned by the Re-Focus, Re-Organise and Re-Build (RRR) strategy and is intended to support HR professionals, directors and managers, lecturers, students, employee representatives and anyone who feel they can learn from the process.

This book is divided into three clear sections to help the reader navigate depending on where they are in the process of implementing a workforce reduction.

I. **Re-Focus**: Understanding the challenge

II. **Re-Organise**: Redundancy implementation planning and strategy

III. **Re-Build**: Re-building the organisation

Without careful planning and consideration of your organisational strategy, the intended objectives are hard to achieve, and the literature indicates that most organisations implementing workforce reduction strategies fail to achieve economic success and can end up in expensive tribunals. It is this challenge, along with implementation that is responsible and compassionate that led to the writing of this book.

References

ILO. 2021. *ILO Monitor: COVID-19 and the world of work*. Seventh edition [Online]. Available: https://www.ilo.org/wcmsp5/groups/public/@dgreports/@dcomm/documents/briefingnote/wcms_767028.pdf [Accessed 28 May 2021].

ONS. 2021. *ILO redundancy rate* [Online]. Office of National Statistics: ONS. Available: https://www.ons.gov.uk/employmentandlabourmarket/people-notinwork/redundancies/timeseries/beir/lms [Accessed 28 May 2021].

Part I

RE-FOCUS

Understanding the challenge

1

THE REDUNDANCY PHENOMENON

This chapter explores the main definitions of redundancy, including the terms redundancy, restructuring, downsizing, retrenchment, rightsizing and reengineering. This is followed by a discussion covering the drivers of redundancies, including external, internal, social and miscellaneous factors.

Introduction to the redundancy phenomenon

Redundancy is not a new phenomenon; however, it should be recognised that the scope and pace of redundancies have accelerated in recent years (Baruch and Hind, 1999). The management strategy of restructuring, often resulting in redundancies, has been used globally for more than two decades (Williams, 2004, Gandolfi, 2009) and more frequently deployed as a human resource management strategy (Orlando, 1999, Allen et al., 2001, Tourish et al., 2004).

DOI: 10.4324/9781003030416-2

The economic crisis that began in 2008 impacted on numerous companies that faced tough trading circumstances, posing a direct threat to their survival in some cases (Schoenberg et al., 2013). To cope with increased competitive pressure, demand for cost savings and high performance, many organisations have come to rely on the strategy of implementing redundancies. With the outbreak of the global pandemic: COVID-19, redundancies have become an inevitable part of living in a global economy with continual organisational adjustments to ensure sustainability. In the business lexicon, we refer to this phenomenon as living in a VUCA world: a world of volatility, uncertainty, complexity and ambiguity.

The objectives of downsizing are to promote organisational efficiency and productivity, and to improve market competitiveness by making changes that impact on costs, such as the size of the workforce (Cameron, 1994; Allen et al., 2001). Workforce reduction rationale also typically includes benefits such as reducing costs, improving productivity, better service and aligning the business with the changing economy (Gervais, 2014). In addition, companies also restructure to lower overhead costs and improve communication (Burke, 1998). Despite these reported organisational benefits, implementing redundancies have a severely negative impact on an organisation's workforce. Many organisations still are of the view that the pain of large redundancy payouts in the short term is a worthy compromise to increase profitability over the longer term; however, the evidence of the success of redundancies to achieve this aim is unreliable at best. The pandemic of COVID-19 has had a further significant impact on the global scale of redundancies (Petzer, 2020).

Various definitions

The terms 'redundancy', 'downsizing', 'workforce reductions', 'reengineering', 'rightsizing', 'organisational decline', 're-organising' and 'restructuring' are used interchangeably in literature, and various definitions apply that refer to dismissal of employees or a head count reduction in some context, with each having its own distinction in meaning.

Typically, the terms 'downsizing', 'rightsizing' and 'layoff' are used in the USA, whereas 'redundancy' is more aligned to language used in the UK and Europe. 'Retrenchment' is often used in the southern hemisphere, such as Australia and South Africa. 'Restructuring' is also frequently found in the UK lexicon, and although a restructure may not necessarily lead to a reduction of employees, it can still have implications similar to those caused by redundancies.

Associated with the language of downsizing and redundancy is the language that refers to those employees impacted by the process. They are referred to in numerous ways; 'laid off' is typically used in the USA, and 'dismissals' or 'terminations' are more often used in Europe and the UK. In South Africa and Australia, the term 'retrenched' is often favoured. For the purpose of this book, I will use the terminology 'dismissal'.

Some definitions have slight variations in meaning, whereas others may not refer to headcount reductions at all and could cause misinterpretation if used incorrectly. To highlight the differences, the definitions of the main redundancy lexicon are explained in the next section.

Definition of redundancy

Redundancy, as demarcated in the UK's legalistic interpretation Employment Rights Act, 1996, section 139:1, is defined as a reason for dismissal of an employee attributable wholly or mainly to:

- **Business closure**

Ceasing or intending to cease to carry on the business for the purposes for which the employee was employed.

- **Workplace closure**

Ceasing or intending to cease to carry on that business in the place where the employee was so employed.

- **Reduced requirement for employees**

Having a reduced requirement for employees to carry out work of a particular kind or to do so at the place where the employee was employed.

Definition of restructuring

Corporate restructuring is defined as a major change in the configuration of an organisation's resources coupled with a major change in the organisation's corporate strategy (Hoskisson and Turk, 1990). There are three different types of corporate restructuring: Portfolio, financial and organisational restructuring. This book focuses on organisational restructuring, which could result in changes in functions, with the ultimate aim to improve efficiency and productivity. Restructuring is usually implemented as a result of an organisation's ambition to adapt their staffing requirements to best suit their changing needs for sustainability or ultimately growth. Consequently, employees are 'reshuffled' according to their strengths and best match to organisational departments. This could include the harmonisation of two departments, such as Marketing and Communication, which will become one department. The intentional outcome would be a more streamlined function with enhanced collaboration between employees with the aim to be more aligned with the organisation's strategic goals. Organisations choose to restructure for reasons other than implementing redundancies such as the ones similar to driving efficiency or effectiveness. Restructuring often occurs as a result of a change in the organisation's portfolio offering. Such organisational changes in the strategic structure will lead to corresponding changes in the organisation's authority and decision-making hierarchies. Restructuring, however, does not always have to lead to a head count reduction; however, it often does lead to the implementation of redundancies.

Definition of downsizing

Downsizing presents itself with various meanings, often dependent on the country where downsizing takes place. Shaw and Barrett-Power (1997:109) define downsizing as a 'constellation of stressor events centering around pressures toward workforce reductions which place demands upon the organisation, work groups, and individual employees and require a process of coping and adaptation.' Freeman and Cameron (1993) complements this definition of downsizing as an intentional reduction in the number of people in an organisation. It is accomplished via a set of managerial actions, which may include the use of hiring freezes, layoffs, and normal or induced attrition.

An interesting challenge to the definition of downsizing suggests that downsizing refers to a reduction of size and costs of an organisation and that head count reduction is a strategy within the downsizing process (Kets De Vries and Balazs, 1997), whilst Cameron (1994) agrees that downsizing often involves a reduction in personnel. In Germany, definitions of downsizing exist linked to the percentage of employees being made redundant with a typical threshold of a minimum of 3%. Nonetheless, downsizing refers to management's reduction in human capital. Literature also refers to 'rightsizing', which is the application of organisational downsizing to cut costs through reducing human resources to get to the 'right organisational size'. A key distinction between downsizing and redundancies is that downsizing incorporates a strategy to not only reduce the employees, but also the work requirement. This may be realised through outsourcing, divesting unrelated businesses, eliminating functions or the selling of capital assets.

Definition of retrenchment

Retrenchment has been defined in Australia as a termination of employment that is not on account of any personal act of the employee dismissed or any consideration peculiar to him, but because the employer no longer wishes the job the employee has been doing to be done by anyone. The word 'retrenchment' is used as the expression that stipulates an employee's status when their employment is terminated because their job has become redundant.

The following circumstances can amount to an employee being retrenched:

- where the employer has introduced new technology resulting in the employee no longer being needed to work in their job
- the employer restructures the organisation, and the job is no longer needed to be done by the employee
- the employer by reason of financial necessity, has to reduce the size of its workforce
- the employer dismisses a worker and redistributes their work to those who remain
- the employer, being a company, has failed and receivers have been appointed.

Definition of reengineering

The concept of reengineering was founded by Professor Michael Hammer (Hammer, 1990). Reengineering suggests the process of reviewing the different aspects of an organisation's operation with consideration of opportunities for improvement. The objectives of reengineering are aligned with the objectives of previous definitions discussed earlier and include the improvement of the organisation's competitive advantage, increased profitability and improved productivity. Similar to restructuring and redundancies, the concept of reengineering is not a new phenomenon, but rather a reconceptualisation for the contemporary world of business. A key distinction to the definition of reengineering is the inclusion of information technology when it comes to forecasting the organisation's goals with the support of databases and networks to improve business processes. One criticism against reengineering is that it often leads to large-scale workforce reduction, which focuses on lower-level departments without addressing upper management.

Definition of rightsizing

Rightsizing is often associated with concepts such as 'creative decline' (Swope, 2006), 'controlled shrinkage' (Aeppel, 2007) or 'smart decline' (Hollander, 2011). These concepts are typically associated with population shrinkage of a city's infrastructure, which is associated with a reduced population. Whilst applying these concepts to organisations, what is essentially implied is the process of bringing an organisation to its optimal size. The process of rightsizing includes the phenomenon of restructuring, which may include workforce reduction with the aim of reducing costs and improving profitability. Quite often the senior management team is included in the re-organisation of staff. What sets rightsizing apart in the organisational context from downsizing, redundancies or retrenchments is that in theory, rightsizing could also involve the increase of the workforce. In other words, downsizing implies a workforce reduction, whilst rightsizing is the adjustment of the workforce to its right size, which could be a reduction or an increase in the workforce. Notably, the latter is rare.

Other terms associated with redundancies

It is not necessarily advantageous to delve into the distinctions between various arguable euphemisms for redundancies; however, in the interest of being inclusive, the following terms are also used in literature:

- delayering
- excess reduction
- leveraging synergies
- organisational decline
- recursion
- redeployment
- reduction in force (RIF)
- smartsizing
- workforce optimisation
- workforce simplification.

Drivers of redundancies

Many organisations anticipate outcomes of redundancy programmes to be that of cost savings, lower overhead costs and associated expenses, greater entrepreneurship and quicker decision-making due to reduced organisational hierarchies.

Both redundancy programmes, as well as restructuring, present problematic consequences for the organisation and the workforce.

Redundancies typically lead to an intended reduction in headcount, driven by organisational factors such as a decline in business, and therefore, the role of the employee carrying out that task no longer exists. This may be due to internal or external factors that drive the need to gain a competitive edge.

Redundancies can be categorised into three contexts:

- market
- organisational
- individual.

Market

The market context includes redundancy drivers as a result of mergers and acquisitions, joint ventures or employment trends (Cameron, 1994) such as automation and the use of technology.

Organisational

The organisational context is centred around the specific strategy or circumstances unique to the organisation and their rationale for the reduction in workforce. The organisational strategy contemplates how and when redundancies will be implemented and what are the anticipated outcomes and economic benefits.

Individual

The individual context centres around everyone in the organisation that is impacted. This will include the impact on their psychological and physiological well-being.

Organisations struggling with debt, increased competitive pressure and automation amongst a few factors, all tempt organisations to cut costs and often the first consideration is to achieve cost cuttings through the implementation of redundancies. Implementing a redundancy programme as a strategy to optimise business performance should always be a consideration for any business operating in a VUCA world; however, it should be done with the right strategy and careful planning. When considering a redundancy programme, especially as a cost-saving strategy, the consequences to the organisation and the workforce are significant. To mitigate the negative impact as best as possible, implementing a redundancy should be carefully planned and executed avoiding any knee-jerk reactions.

The objectives of redundancies are to promote organisational efficiency and productivity, and to improve market competitiveness by making changes that impact on costs such as the size of the workforce. Many organisations use redundancy programmes with the aim of getting a 'leaner' workforce or one fit for the purpose.

The rationale also typically includes benefits such as reducing costs, improving productivity, better service and aligning the business with the changing economy. Companies also restructure to lower overhead costs and improve communication (Burke, 1998). On some occasions, organisations implement redundancies as a method to 'clean up' their existing workforce. In such circumstances, organisations may implement redundancies to get 'new blood' in the organisation or create an opportunity for graduates to move up on the career ladder. This can normally be identified by the scale of redundancies, where an indicator of such activities is when a large organisation with over a thousand employees has a redundancy programme impacting two or three individuals only. Tribunal judges are somewhat astute in identifying such cases and typically find it hard to accept that a large organisation could not retrain or redeploy two or three employees. It is not the intended objective of redundancies as demarcated by law, to be used for the purpose of promoting talent management or as a method to get rid of underperformers, yet this quite often realises in the workplace. Not surprisingly, many of these cases do lead to tribunal cases. On some occasions, managers argue a case of redundancy to get a certain employee removed 'legitimately' from an organisation, when quite often, the employee should be subject to performance management. In such instances, the human resources (HR) department needs to be robust enough to identify the real cause of the manager's wish to terminate the employee's contract. In organisations where finances are not a concern, redundancies are sometimes unfortunately used irresponsibly by way of 'chequebook management' (Petzer, 2019), where essentially the organisation does not wish to follow redundancy law or protocol, and therefore 'buys' the silence of employees with settlement agreements. Although this is highly unethical, the reality is that these practices do exist. When any redundancy is proposed, it is critical that HR test the reason for redundancy by asking these critical four questions:

1. Does the role of the employee cease to exist after they are terminated?
2. Is the employer intending to stop (or has stopped) to carry on with the business for the purpose of which the employee was hired?

Or

3. Does the role of the employee cease to exist after they are terminated at the location where they were employed?
4. Is the employer intending to stop (or has stopped) to carry on the business in the place where the employee was employed?

If the answer is a definitive yes, then the case is more likely to be a genuine redundancy as demarcated by the Employee Rights Act 1996. Despite the test of legitimacy of a redundancy, there are several other factors organisations need to consider, whilst demonstrating how they have attempted to avoid redundancy, such as exploring redeployment for a suitable alternative role within the same location or suitable alternative locations. These factors will be discussed in further detail in Chapters 4 and 5.

Most organisations implement workforce reductions with the anticipation of increased organisational and financial benefits (Cascio, 1993, Freeman, 1999). Senior management is regarded as very capable of predicting future costs than predicting future revenues and thus cost-cutting is advantageous to increase the organisation's income (Cascio, 1993).

Some popular justifications for implementing redundancies:

External factors:

- decreased market shares
- lack of orders
- decline in customer demand
- production complications; suppliers unable to produce critical components
- advances in technology, resulting in obsolete products
- market crashes
- product being outsourced
- reductions in capacity
- new competitors with a competitive advantage
- changes in legislation resulting in less funding
- government deregulation
- consumer habits, i.e. where and how they shop
- loss of a major customer
- increased foreign competition.

Internal factors:

- internal harmonisation after a merger or acquisition and removing duplication of roles
- organisational redesign of hierarchical structures
- re-organisation of departments to improve staff utilisation
- improvement of operating efficiencies

- location mergers
- outsourcing or relocation to other countries.

Miscellaneous factors:

- appease shareholders
- appease headquarters
- provide reassurance for security analysts.

Social factors:

- constraining
- cloning
- learning.

McKinley et al. (1995) categorise the social factors as follows.

Constraining

Constraining is the exertion of pressure on an organisation to comply to company rules. Targets of workforce reduction are often set to achieve a specific model; i.e. for every 1,000 customers, the organisation's operation requires one customer service call handler, and therefore, if the customer service call handlers are more than the target customers, a reduction in workforce will take place.

Cloning

Cloning is the exertion of pressure to copy companies that are successful and highly regarded in the industry for providing excellence and being brand leaders. If these brand leaders implement redundancy programmes, other organisations may feel they have to follow the example and also implement redundancy programmes. Little consideration is given to the intended benefit of workforce reduction (McKinley et al., 1995).

Learning

Learning involves redundancy decisions made based on our learning through education, universities and professional bodies. Theories being taught on redundancy implementation are then used as a rationale for decisions made.

Whatever the rationale may be for implementing redundancies, the requirement for careful workforce analysis, planning, training and responsible implementation should not be underestimated.

This chapter explored various definitions of workforce reductions as well as the different drivers of redundancies. With the aim of limiting the various potentially convoluted definitions, which is not entirely indistinguishable in meaning, my preference is to use the term 'redundancy' in the remaining chapters.

The next chapter will focus on the likely success of redundancies as a business strategy and explore why organisations fail to achieve their intended objectives.

References

Aeppel, T. 2007. Shrink to fit: As its population declines, Youngstown thinks small; rather than trying to grow, Ohio city plans more open space. *The Wall Street Journal*. ISSN 00999660.

Allen, T. D., Freeman, D. M., Russel, J. E., Reizenstein, R. C. & Rentz, J. O. 2001. Survivor reactions to organizational downsizing: Does time ease the pain? *Journal of Occupational and Organizational Psychology*, 74, 145–164.

Baruch, Y. & Hind, P. 1999. Perpetual motion in organizations: Effective management and the impact of the new psychological contracts on 'Survivor Syndrome'. *European Journal of Work and Organizational Psychology*, 8, 295–306.

Burke, R. J. 1998. Downsizing and restructuring in organizations: Research findings and lessons learned--introduction. *Canadian Journal of Administrative Sciences*, 15, 297.

Cameron, K. S. 1994. Strategies for successful organizational downsizing. *Human Resource Management*, 33, 189–211.

Cascio, W. F. 1993. Downsizing: What do we know? What have we learned? *Academy of Management Perspectives*, 7, 95–104.

Freeman, S. J. 1999. The gestalt of organizational downsizing: Downsizing strategies as packages of change. *Human Relations*, 52, 1505–1541.

Freeman, S. J. & Cameron, K. S. 1993. Organizational downsizing: A convergence and reorientation framework. *Organization Science*, 4, 10–29.

Gandolfi, F. 2009. Sustaining innovation during corporate downsizing. *SAM Advanced Management Journal (07497075)*, 74, 42–54.

Gervais, R. 2014. Measuring downsizing in organizations. *Assessment and Development Matters*, 6(3), 2–5.

Hammer, M. 1990. Reengineering work: Don't automate, obliterate. *Harvard Business Review*, 68, 104–112.

Hollander, J. B. 2011. *Sunburnt cities: The great recession, depopulation and urban planning in the American Sunbelt. Choice (Middletown)*, 49(10), 4949–5954.

Hoskisson, R. E. & Turk, T. A. 1990. Corporate restructuring: Governance and control limits of the internal capital market. *Academy of Management Review*, 15, 459–477.

Kets de Vries, M. F. & Balazs, K. 1997. The downside of downsizing. *Human Relations*, 50, 11–50.

Mckinley, W., Sanchez, C. M. & Schick, A. G. 1995. Organizational downsizing: Constraining, cloning, learning. *Academy of Management Perspectives*, 9, 32–42.

Orlando, J. 1999. The fourth wave: The ethics of corporate downsizing. *Business Ethics Quarterly*, 9(2), 295–314.

Petzer, M. 2019. *Developing effective interventions for mitigating the psychological impact experienced by redundancy envoys during redundancy situations.* PhD, Solent University.

Petzer, M. 2020. Coronavirus and the workforce: How can we limit redundancies? CIPD LAB. Available: https://www.cipd.co.uk/news-views/ changing-work-views/future-work/thought-pieces/coronavirus-workforce-redundancies

Schoenberg, R., Collier, N. & Bowman, C. 2013. Strategies for business turnaround and recovery: A review and synthesis. *European Business Review*, 25(3), 243–262.

Shaw, J. B. & Barrett-Power, E. 1997. A conceptual framework for assessing organization, work group, and individual effectiveness during and after downsizing. *Human Relations*, 50(2), 109–127.

Swope, C. 2006. Smart decline. *Governing*, 20(2), 46–52.

Tourish, D., Paulsen, N., Hobman, E. & Bordia, P. 2004. The downsides of downsizing: Communication processes information needs in the aftermath of a workforce reduction strategy. *Management Communication Quarterly*, 17, 485–516.

Williams, S. M. 2004. Downsizing–intellectual capital performance anorexia or enhancement? *The Learning Organization*, 11(4/5), 368–379.

2

SUCCESS OF REDUNDANCIES AS A BUSINESS STRATEGY

This chapter addresses the likely economic success of implementing redundancies, the anticipated outcomes and how this compares to the reality and likely aftermath. The positive and negative implications of implementing redundancies and why most organisations fail to reap economic success are discussed. Rationale is provided for the difficulty in demonstrating cost savings. This chapter also discusses the anticipated and unforeseen cost of implementing redundancies.

The economic success of implementing redundancies

Organisations facing competitive pressures use redundancies as a business or human resource management strategy in an attempt to reduce costs and increase profitability (Waraich and Bhardwaj, 2011). The strategy of implementing redundancies is described as a way of life (Filipowski, 1993), with Datta et al. (2010) contending that redundancies are a complicated, multidimensional business phenomenon.

DOI: 10.4324/9781003030416-3

Essentially, the economic logic that drives the decision to implement redundancies comes from the notion that a business is based on two basic principles, increase revenue and/or decrease your costs with the latter being the more predictable element (Cascio, 2002).

Organisations implementing redundancies ultimately expect that the cost savings by the reduction in human capital will lead to financial and organisational benefits. Unfortunately, redundancy programmes are often implemented as a short-sighted, knee-jerk reaction rather than deserving of a full strategic plan for a business turnaround situation. With careful planning and consideration, workforce reductions can lead to the intended organisational benefits and improve the long-term sustainability of an organisation.

The findings on the success of redundancies as a cost-saving initiative are wide-ranging and inconsistent. Redundancy programmes have pro-found consequences to individuals and the organisation and relevant litera-ture includes numerous examples where organisations fail to demonstrate an improvement of financial performance, organisational effectiveness, profitability and productivity, as a result of implementing redundancies (Macky, 2004; Gandolfi, 2009; Gandolfi and Hansson, 2011; Cascio, 2012). Furthermore, multiple changes of managers, structures, performance indicators, targets and policy can have a negative impact on productivity and profits (Harter et al., 2002). Market perception can also be negatively impacted by redundancies such as in the study by Nixon et al. (2004) who found that market perception of implementing redundancies to reduce costs are viewed negatively due to the concerns that losing valuable skills, talent and knowledge pools will outweigh the benefits of reduced costs. Various studies on the success of redundancies as a strategy to improve productivity and profitability demonstrate heterogeneous results. Baumol et al. (2003) found that redundancies can lead to improved profitability; however, no evidence of increased productivity, whilst Burke and Nelson (1998) found that 85% of organisations reported a reduction in costs and 63% reported increased profit. Studies have also indicated that by reducing the workforce, the human asset reduction strategy may actually attenuate the competitive advantage of the organisation due to inflexibility and the inability to expand (Luan et al., 2013). Research, however, indicates that some organisations enjoy an initial increase in productivity immediately after the workforce reductions are implemented (Appelbaum et al., 1987).

As summarised in Table 2.1, literature demonstrates contradictory views on the research conducted on the impact of redundancies. A possible reason for the opposing views is the requirement of detailed information from organisations that is not always readily available. This typically includes the detail of key performance indicators that need to be measured against human assets. To demonstrate the complications in obtaining suitable data to draw such conclusions, it is worth noting that a recent study (Goesaert et al., 2015) involved analysing operational and financial performance of 500 organisations, coupled with the analysis of approximately 50,000

Table 2.1 A summary of the economic results post redundancy implementations

Researcher	Organisational context	Results
Zemke (1990)	Right Associates conducted a study of 500 organisations that reduced the workforce in 1989 and repeated the study in 1990	No financial gains reported Negative economic impact Significant aftershocks
Henkoff (1990)	Society of Human Resource Management surveyed 1468 organisation that restructured	More than 50% reported productivity remained the same or worsened
Bennett (1991)	*Wall Street Journal* surveyed 1005 organisations that reduced workforce	46% reduced expenses 32% increased profits 22% reduced bureaucracy 22% increased productivity
Worrell et al. (1991)	194 organisations implemented workforce reductions between 1979 and 1987	Negative market reaction to the announcements, prior to reductions with a loss in stock value of 2% Reports of declining stock values post reductions
Baumohl (1993)	Consulting firm reported on organisations that reduced workforce in the 1980s	By 1990s, the stock prices were lower than the industry average
Cameron (1994), Cascio (1993)	Wyatt Associates – studied 1005 organisations that reduced workforce between 1986 and 1991	46% reduced expenses 32% increased profits 22% increased productivity 17% reduced bureaucracy
Cameron (1994), Cascio (1993)	Society for Human Resource Management surveyed 1468 organisations that reduced workforce	Over 50% reduction in productivity

De Meuse et al. (1994)	Studied 52 Fortune 100 companies over a five-year period, of which, 17 organisations made workforce reductions, whilst 35 made none. They compared and analysed the results two years prior to the workforce reduction announcement, the year of the announcement and the two subsequent years	No improved financial performance for the organisations that implemented workforce reductions Organisations that implemented workforce reductions continued to lag afterwards
Mabert and Schmenner (1997)	American Management Association conducted two surveys: one in 1993 and the other in 1995 to assess workforce reduction experiences	1993 Survey Operating profits decreased 22.8% Worker productivity decreased 23.5% Employee morale decreased 84.1% 1995 Survey Operating profits decreased 20.4% Worker productivity decreased 30.1% Employee morale decreased 86%
Kirby (1999)	Conducted longitudinal studies in Australia on organisations implementing workforce reductions	Organisations failing to cut costs − 60%. Organisations failing to increase productivity − 60%
Morris et al. (1999)	Studied organisation's financial performance of the S&P 500 Index between 1981 and 1992 after employment changes. Their study posits empirical evidence to suggest that workforce reduction was unlikely to lead to improved financial performance	No reported relationship between workforce reduction and improved financial performance Organisations with stable employment demonstrated better performance than organisations that reduced workforce
Goesaert et al. (2015)	Studied the performance of 500 of Germany's largest organisations during downsizing	The study demonstrated little evidence of an improvement in organisational productivity or profitability with indicators leaning towards a decline in organisational performance

media articles to establish redundancy volume and timescales. Another challenge is the time frame to measure the impact before, during and after a redundancy programme has been completed. In addition, many organisations that implement redundancy programmes, do not necessary want to be associated with 'perceived' failure and therefore hesitant to share their data due to fear of reputation damage (Zyglidopoulos, 2005).

Redundancy costs

Quite often the initial cost and post-implementation costs are not fully considered before a redundancy programme is considered. Underestimating the costs could also result in organisations not achieving their intended aims. Costs to consider include:

Anticipated costs:

- severance packages
- outplacement services
- relocation costs
- early retirement packages
- training for employees being redeployed
- new systems being implemented to accommodate fewer staff
- period of time that 'employee overheads' may be carried despite exit date.

Unforeseen costs:

- contractors/consultants
- recruitment costs
- tribunal costs
- costs of building up morale post workforce reduction
- overtime costs to help accommodate increased workload
- missed business opportunities as a result of lack of resources and skills
- retention bonuses
- employee benefits or salary increases.

Unforeseen costs often creep in when the organisation requires some of the skills that were 'let go' back in the organisation and a typical reaction is to bring employees back as 'contractors' or 'consultants'. The costs of deploying contractors and consultants are typically much higher than employee costs. These unintended costs can cause a significant erosion in the intended cost (Mabert and Schmenner, 1997). Another cost quite often not fully considered is recruitment cost of replacing staff that may be required to secure a specific new revenue stream, or if organisations cut too deep, they may have to rehire with recruitment and training costs associated with new hires being very high. Mabert and Schmenner (1997) found in their study of several organisations that implemented workforce reductions, including Cyprus Amax, Allison Engine, Amoco, general Electric, Eli Lilly and towers Perris, Cummins Engine and Inland Steel that some organisations reported increased costs in respect to 'quality' essentially due to quality being compromised as a result of work demand, wastage and inspections.

Evidence also suggests that the time frame for organisations to demonstrate economic success ranges from six to 18 months (Petzer, 2019). The reason for the delay in demonstrating cost savings is due to some organisations having to carry overhead costs per employee until the end of the contract year, even if employees left the organisation months before. Such costs may typically include utility costs per employee, such as cost per phone, IT accounts, cost per desk space or parking space allocation. Companies may also have a cost assigned to employees, paid per annum such as employee assistance support or medical benefit, which essentially, the organisation must honour until the end of the contract period. In such cases, the financial benefit of the employee's exit may only be realised once contract periods related to all such employee overheads are cleared.

Initially, organisations also struggle to demonstrate cost savings due to the significant cost of redundancy packages that is likely to hit the organisation at once. Many private sector organisations may offer enhanced redundancy packages and when long-serving employees are part of the workforce reduction, the redundancy costs could easily equate to the equivalent of an employee's full year's salary. In the case of a large-scale redundancy programme, the costs can thus be significant and impact the organisation's profitability for a while. There are several other costs associated with workforce reductions that organisations need to include, when considering redundancies, such as outplacement services, relocation costs, early retirement packages, new systems often associated with workforce reduction, training for redeployed employees to name a few. Unforeseen costs often not anticipated with workforce reductions could potentially be the costs of consultants, contractors or overtime to compensate for too few staff if a new contract is unexpectedly acquired and skill shortage presents itself. Other unplanned costs could include recruitment costs, legal fees, and costs to Re-Build the organisation such as team building.

Positive implications of implementing workforce reductions

Economic theory stipulates the advantages and disadvantages of implementing redundancies. One of the advantages anticipated is an increase in productivity through Schumpetarian creative destruction (Schumpeter, 1942) whereby less productive workers are replaced with more productive ones and productivity increases accordingly. Some organisations report economic benefit as a result of redundancy programmes such as the increase in value for shareholders. Another reported benefit is decentralised organisational structures, and streamlined and reduced management hierarchies. Should a redundancy programme be implemented successfully, organisations can expect economic benefits such as:

- reduced expenses and overhead costs (Cascio, 1993, Kets De Vries and Balazs, 1997)
- higher return on investment (Cascio, 1993, Kets De Vries and Balazs, 1997)
- improved organisational health (Freeman and Cameron, 1993)
- enhanced efficiency and productivity (Cascio, 1993, Kets De Vries and Balazs, 1997)
- increased competitive advantage (Cascio et al., 1997).

For redundancy programmes to be successful, internal processes need to be aligned to increase the chances of organisational survival and quite often this does not happen during the implementation of workforce reductions, due to lack of planning and careful analysis of the workforce skills and organisational requirements.

Why organisations fail to achieve intended outcomes of workforce reductions

Medium- to long-term losses are often caused by a focus on short-term profitability (Thanassoulis, 2013). Literature indicates that a short-term focus where the aim is to improve the organisation's financial position, typically by reducing personnel, is short-sighted and does not reap sustainable results. 'Short-termism' is an overly short-term focus where the organisation's strategy is focused on immediate successes, not necessarily complementing the long-term sustainability of an organisation (Sudarsanam and Lai, 2001). Barker and Mone (1994) warn, however, that solely focusing on cost-cutting during a turnaround is likely to reduce employee morale and commitment, resulting in higher staff turnover. Redundancies are also often seen to have a major negative impact not only on the organisation, the employees, the government and its survival, but also on society overall (Labib and Appelbaum, 1993). Cameron (1994) postulates that the implementation of redundancies has derived from the objective to obtain a new organisational structure that allows for a competitive edge. To achieve the continued competitive edge in the global and local markets, quite often organisations reduce their headcount in multiple phases (Labib and Appelbaum, 1993), which can have a further compounded negative impact on the organisation.

Despite the known negative impact of redundancies (Labiband Appelbaum, 1993, Clair and Dufresne, 2004, Gandolfi, 2008, Gandolfi and Hansson, 2011), there are prevalent expectations that organisations will continue to implement redundancies as a human resource strategy, especially during times of economic downturn, such as caused by COVID-19 restrictions. It is of paramount importance for organisations to succeed in achieving their aims of implementing redundancies, as they need to maintain their position locally and globally and promote a positive corporate image (Labib and Appelbaum, 1993). Some research indicates that negative consequences of redundancies can be reduced by proper management (Waraich and Bhardwaj, 2011, Petzer, 2019).

Some of the most frequent reasons why organisations fail when implementing workforce reductions are:

- knee-jerk/panic reaction
- poor planning and preparation
- poor implementation
- lack of leadership and poor management
- failure to adopt the 3C approach (Command, Control and Compartmentalisation)
- lack of involvement and consultation
- resistance to change
- poor rationale for the workforce reduction

- lack of retraining
- underestimation of the human impact
- underestimation and poor planning for anticipated cost.

Despite the known likely impact of implementing redundancies, it remains a popular strategy for organisations to adopt. There may be a perception that the implementation of redundancies suggests that action is being taken to address the challenging financial position and action relates to acknowledgement and awareness; however, without due planning and consideration for the people implications, redundancy programmes are likely to fail.

Overall impact of implementing redundancies

Despite some positive outcomes reported, one of the most underestimated negative consequences of redundancies is the damage to the employees' psychological contract and the relationship factors between employers and employees. Aspects such as trust, motivation, employee morale, commitment and productivity are all known to be negatively impacted by the implementation of redundancy programmes.

Redundancies have a significant negative impact on the psychological and physical well-being of employees and impacts on the entire workforce, including those who implement the redundancies.

The anticipated outcomes of implementing workforce reductions and the likely success of such strategies have now been discussed with an explanation why organisations fail to reap economic success. This chapter also discussed the anticipated and unforeseen cost of implementing redundancies. The following chapter will explore the negative impact on the workforce, by focusing on each impacted group.

References

Appelbaum, S. H., Simpson, R. & Shapiro, B. T. 1987. The tough test of downsizing. *Organizational Dynamics*, 16 (1), 68–79.

Barker, V. L. & Mone, M. A. 1994. Retrenchment: Cause of turnaround or consequence of decline? *Strategic Management Journal*, 15, 395–405.

Baumohl, B. 1993. When downsizing becomes dumbsizing. *Time*, 141, 55–55.

Baumol, W. J., Blinder, A. S. & Wolff, E. N. 2003. *Downsizing in America: Reality, causes, and consequences.* New York: Russell Sage Foundation.

Bennett, A. 1991. Downsizing doesn't necessarily bring an upswing in corporate profitability. *Wall Street Journal,* 6, B1. ISSN 00999660.

Burke, R. J. & Nelson, D. 1998. Mergers and acquisitions, downsizing, and privatization: A North American perspective. In Gowing, M. K., Kraft, J. D. & Quick, J. C. (Eds.), *The new organizational reality: Downsizing, restructuring, and revitalization* (21–54). Washington, DC: American Psychological Association. Available: https://doi.org/10.1037/10252-001.

Cameron, K. S. 1994. Strategies for successful organizational downsizing. *Human Resource Management,* 33, 189–211.

Cascio, W. F. 1993. Downsizing: What do we know? What have we learned? *Academy of Management Perspectives,* 7, 95–104.

Cascio, W. F. 2002. Strategies for responsible restructuring. *Academy of Management Perspectives,* 16, 80–91.

Cascio, W. F. 2012. How does downsizing come about. In Cooper, C.L., Pandey, A. and Quick, J.C. (Eds.), *Downsizing: Is Less Still More* (51–75). Cambridge: Cambridge University Press.

Cascio, W. F., Young, C. E. & Morris, J., R, 1997. Financial consequences of employment-change decisions in major US corporations. *Academy of Management Journal,* 40, 1175–1189.

Clair, J. A. & Dufresne, R. L. 2004. Playing the grim reaper: How employees experience carrying out a downsizing. *Human Relations,* 57, 1597–1625.

Datta, D. K., Guthrie, J. P., Basuil, D. & Pandey, A. 2010. Causes and effects of employee downsizing: A review and synthesis. *Journal of Management,* 36, 281–348.

De Meuse, K. P., Vanderheiden, P. A. & Bergmann, T. J. 1994. Announced layoffs: Their effect on corporate financial performance. *Human Resource Management,* 33, 509–530.

Filipowski, D. 1993. Don't rush downsizing: Plan, plan, plan. *Personnel Journal,* 72, 64–76.

Freeman, S. J. & Cameron, K. S. 1993. Organizational downsizing: A convergence and reorientation framework. *Organization Science,* 4, 10–29.

Gandolfi, F. 2008. Reflecting on downsizing: What have managers learned? *SAM Advanced Management Journal,* 73, 45.

Gandolfi, F. 2009. Unraveling downsizing: What do we know about the phenomenon? *Revista de Management Comparat Internaţional,* 10, 414–426.

Gandolfi, F. & Hansson, M. 2011. Causes and consequences of downsizing: Towards an integrative framework. *Journal of Management & Organization*, 17, 498–521.

Goesaert, T., Heinz, M. & Vanormelingen, S. 2015. Downsizing and firm performance: Evidence from German firm data. *Industrial and Corporate Change*, 24, 1443–1472.

Harter, J. K., Schmidt, F. L. & Hayes, T. L. 2002. Business-unit-level relationship between employee satisfaction, employee engagement, and business outcomes: A meta-analysis. *Journal of Applied Psychology*, 87, 268.

Henkoff, R. 1990. Cost cutting: How to do it right. *Fortune*, 121, 40.

Kets De Vries, M. F. & Balazs, K. 1997. The downside of downsizing. *Human Relations*, 50, 11–50.

Kirby, J. 1999. Downsizing gets the push. *Business Review Weekly*, 21, 50–51.

Labib, N. & Appelbaum, S. H. 1993. Strategic downsizing: A human resources perspective. *Human Resource Planning*, 16(4), 69–93.

Luan, C.-J., Tien, C. & Chi, Y.-C. 2013. Downsizing to the wrong size? A study on the impact of downsizing on firm performance during an economic downturn. *The International Journal of Human Resource Management*, 24, 1519–1535.

Mabert, V. A. & Schmenner, R. W. 1997. Assessing the roller coaster of downsizing. *Business Horizons*, 40, 45–53.

Macky, K. A. 2004. Organisational downsizing and redundancies: The New Zealand workers experience. *Journal of Employment Relations*, 29, 63–87.

Morris, J. R., Cascio, W. E. & Young, C. E. 1999. Downsizing after all these years: Questions and answers about who did it, how many did it, and who benefited from it. *Organizational Dynamics*, 27, 78–87.

Nixon, R. D., Hitt, M. A., Lee, H. U. & Jeong, E. 2004. Market reactions to announcements of corporate downsizing actions and implementation strategies. *Strategic Management Journal*, 25, 1121–1129.

Petzer, M. 2019. *Developing effective interventions for mitigating the psychological impact experienced by redundancy envoys during redundancy situations.* PhD, Solent University.

Schumpeter, J. 1942. Creative destruction. *Capitalism, Socialism and Democracy*, 825, 82–85.

Sudarsanam, S. & Lai, J. 2001. Corporate financial distress and turnaround strategies: An empirical analysis. *British Journal of Management*, 12, 183–199.

Thanassoulis, J. 2013. Industry structure, executive pay and short-termism. *Management Science*, 59, 402–419.

Waraich, S. B. & Bhardwaj, G. 2011. Coping strategies of executive survivors in downsized organizations in India. *SAM Advanced Management Journal*, 76, 26.

Worrell, D. L., Davidson III, W. N. & Sharma, V. M. 1991. Layoff announcements and stockholder wealth. *Academy of management Journal*, 34, 662–678.

Zemke, R. 1990. The ups and downs of downsizing. *Training*, 27, 27–34.

Zyglidopoulos, S. C. 2005. The impact of downsizing on corporate reputation. *British Journal of Management*, 16, 253–259.

3

THE NEGATIVE IMPACT OF REDUNDANCIES ON THE WORKFORCE

This chapter is an extension of the previous chapter that discussed the challenge of achieving organisational success by way of redundancies and the overall negative impact on the whole organisation. In this chapter, I highlight the severe negative impact of implementing redundancies on each of the three groups impacted: victims, survivors and redundancy envoys and introduce a new group: semi-survivors. The importance of redundancy envoys in the success of redundancy implementation is also discussed.

Impacted groups in the organisation

During the implementation of a redundancy programme, the entire workforce is impacted, whether the individual exits the organisation or not.

Three clear groups of employees that are impacted have been identified in literature with an emerging new group. The three known groups are:

DOI: 10.4324/9781003030416-4

- victims
- survivors
- redundancy envoys.

The new group is:

- semi-survivors.

Victims

'Victims' are the ex-employees who have been unsuccessful in remaining employed by the organisation, and, as a result, have left their positions of employment. Victims experience a myriad of feelings including that of anger towards employers, sadness at leaving colleagues and staff, fear of not finding future employment and financial worries (Parris and Vickers, 2010). Some of the key implications for victims are:

- psychological stress
- ill health
- family and personal problems
- reduced self-esteem
- depression
- helplessness and anxiety
- feelings of social isolation
- damage to career
- loss of earning power
- feelings of cynicism
- uncertainty
- decreased loyalty in future employment (Paulsen et al., 2005, Vickers and Parris, 2007, Waters, 2007, Gandolfi, 2008, Parris and Vickers, 2010).

The psychological impact experienced is influenced by a range of factors, unique to each individual, such as age, gender, career status, social support, financial position, previous occupational level, education level, length of employment, individual ability to cope with stress and job satisfaction with the most recent employment (Leana and Feldman, 1988). Findings on the uniqueness of the impact are supported by Waraich and Bhardwaj (2011) who state that organisations must remember that each employee is affected differently based on their personal characteristics or their ability to manage the situation. Parris and Vickers (2010) found that victims of redundancy reported a feeling of shock at the point of being made redundant. Victims of redundancy experience a similar emotional rollercoaster as portrayed by the grief change curve (Kubler-Ross, 1969) commencing with shock (Vickers and Parris, 2007) and transitioning through the changes, moving from denial, shock and anger through to negotiation and depression, which is the lowest point. Once victims pass the stage of depression, victims can move on towards acceptance and relief as per Figure 3.1 that demonstrates the likely experience and associated behaviour of redundancy victims.

For victims, the feeling of assault on their identity has a significant impact on their psychological well-being, as their ability to demonstrate achievement through work and showing competence and capability are being removed. Furthermore, the impact of lowered self-esteem experienced due to their job loss is linked to their feelings of loss of control, shame, a sense of failure and feelings of rejection (Kates et al., 1990). Vickers and Parris (2007) also claim that the respondents in their study who were victims of job loss experienced alienation; however, it represented itself individually as feelings of social isolation, powerlessness, betrayal, shock, shame and humiliation. The negative impact on redundancy victims is often exacerbated when individuals do not find new jobs, which impacts on their confidence in addition to the known repercussions of depression and hardship (Appelbaum et al., 1987).

There are a few rare cases where victims have reported their job losses as a positive outcome. In these cases, the redundancy had given them the opportunity to re-evaluate their career goals and make changes in a more gratifying direction (Labib and Appelbaum, 1993). Employers can help mitigate the negative impact by offering the necessary support to victims to transition through the stages of change as swiftly as possible. Chapter 10 provides insights into recommended organisational support for each impacted group.

Survivors

Survivors are the individuals that remain in the company during and after the implementation of the redundancy programme (Brockner, 1992,

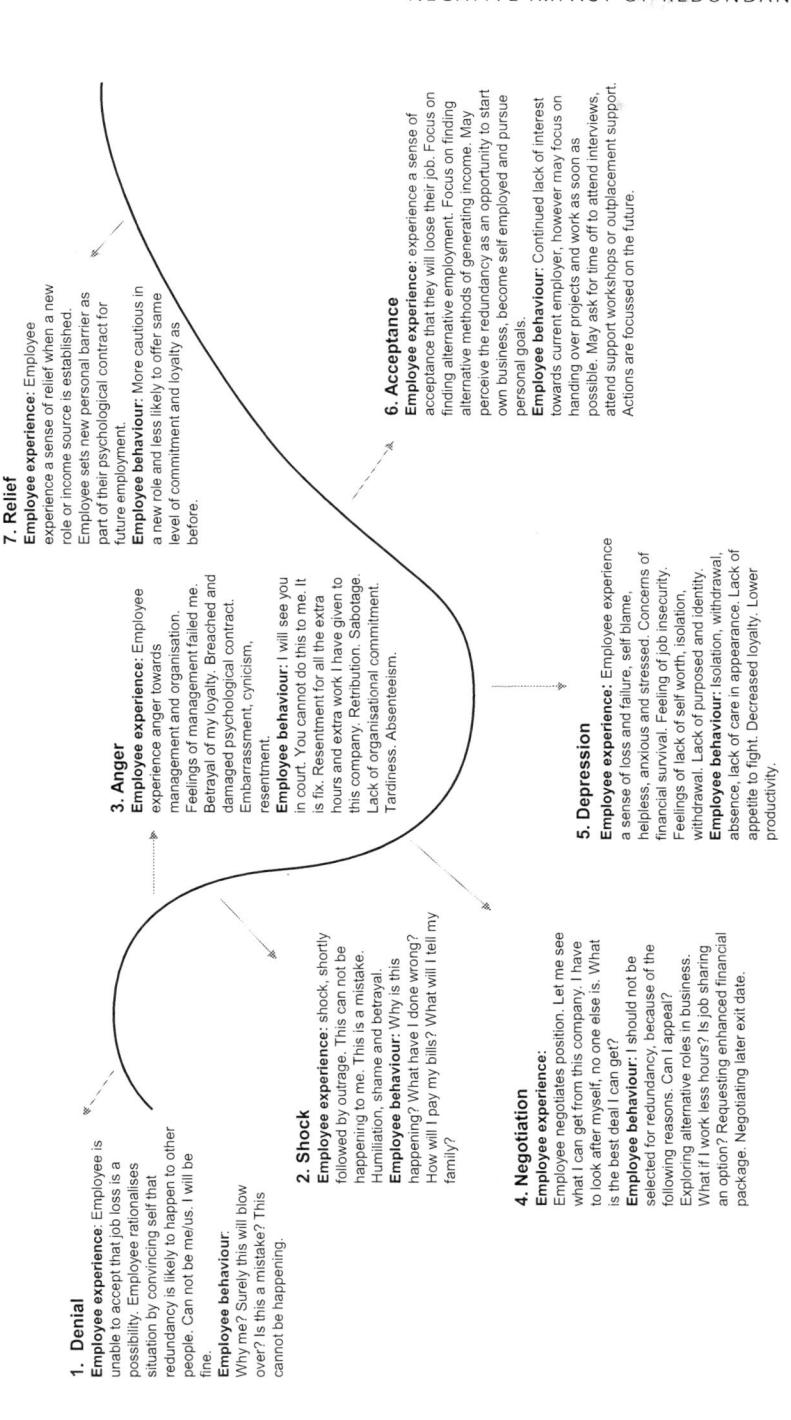

1. Denial

Employee experience: Employee is unable to accept that job loss is a possibility. Employee rationalises situation by convincing self that redundancy is likely to happen to other people. Can not be me/us. I will be fine.

Employee behaviour:
Why me? Surely this will blow over? Is this a mistake? This cannot be happening.

2. Shock

Employee experience: shock, shortly followed by outrage. This can not be happening to me. This is a mistake. Humiliation, shame and betrayal.
Employee behaviour: Why is this happening? What have I done wrong? How will I pay my bills? What will I tell my family?

3. Anger

Employee experience: Employee experience anger towards management and organisation. Feelings of management failed me. Betrayal of my loyalty. Breached and damaged psychological contract. Embarrassment, cynicism, resentment.
Employee behaviour: I will see you in court. You cannot do this to me. It is fix. Resentment for all the extra hours and extra work I have given to this company. Retribution. Sabotage. Lack of organisational commitment. Tardiness. Absenteeism.

4. Negotiation

Employee experience:
Employee negotiates position. Let me see what I can get from this company. What I can get from myself, no one else is. What is the best deal I can get?
Employee behaviour: I should not be selected for redundancy, because of the following reasons. Can I appeal? Exploring alternative roles in business. What if I work less hours? Is job sharing an option? Requesting enhanced financial package. Negotiating later exit date.

5. Depression

Employee experience: Employee experience a sense of loss and failure, self blame, helpless, anxious and stressed. Concerns of financial survival. Feeling of job insecurity. Feelings of lack of self worth, isolation, withdrawal. Lack of purposed and identity.
Employee behaviour: Isolation, withdrawal, absence, lack of care in appearance. Lack of appetite to fight. Decreased loyalty. Lower productivity.

6. Acceptance

Employee experience: experience a sense of acceptance that they will loose their job. Focus on finding alternative employment. Focus on finding alternative methods of generating income. May perceive the redundancy as an opportunity to start own business, become self employed and pursue personal goals.
Employee behaviour: Continued lack of interest towards current employer, however may focus on handing over projects and work as soon as possible. May ask for time off to attend interviews, attend support workshops or outplacement support. Actions are focussed on the future.

7. Relief

Employee experience: Employee experience a sense of relief when a new role or income source is established. Employee sets new personal barrier as part of their psychological contract for future employment.
Employee behaviour: More cautious in a new role and less likely to offer same level of commitment and loyalty as before.

Figure 3.1 Redundancy victim's experience of change.

Baruch and Hind, 1999, Astrachan, 2004). The survivors of a redundancy programme often experience the adverse effects of being subject to the process as profoundly as those who exit the organisation. This may include feelings of anger, anxiety, cynicism, resentment, resignation and retribution often referred to as the survivor syndrome (Brockner, 1992, Baruch and Hind, 1999).

Survivor syndrome is experienced by survivors of the redundancy programme as well as by redundancy envoys. Survivor syndrome includes feelings of guilt, where, for example, colleagues feel guilty that they kept their jobs, when they may believe that employees that were more able or who needed the finance more, should have stayed in the role. Survivor syndrome also include feelings of job insecurity, fear and anger towards the organisation for being put in this position, essentially systematic from a perceived breach of their psychological contract. Others experience a feeling of relief that they have kept their jobs. High levels of mistrust are often experienced between colleagues, but also towards the organisation.

Survivors report the following elements as a result of redundancy programmes:

- increased workload
- survivor guilt
- survivor envy
- anger
- relief
- job insecurity
- managing higher levels of stress, absenteeism and mistrust
- working in an environment with possible decreased work quality, morale and productivity
- decreased employee involvement
- decreased trust towards management (Gandolfi, 2008).

Vickers and Parris (2007) contend that survivors are often left emotionally damaged from witnessing colleagues lose their jobs and it is argued by some authors that survivors experience more stress than the victims, who inevitably moved on (Devine et al., 2003). Kets de Vries and Balazs (1997), however, found that both survivors and victims report high levels of stress. Sometimes survivors may have feelings of envy towards the victims (Campbell-Jamison, 2001). This is due to the perception that victims may be receiving generous retirement incentives, generous settlement packages or new jobs with attractive compensation.

Survivors' intention to quit their jobs poses the biggest threat to organisational survival (Ugboro, 2006). This occurs due to survivors' experience of job insecurity as soon as redundancy intentions are announced. As a result, survivors pursue an element of safeguarding in case they lose their jobs by starting to explore suitable alternative positions in the market. The more capable and qualified employees find alternative employment easiest and may decide to leave the current organisation due to the element of job insecurity. This could have very negative consequences for the organisation as they could lose talented and valuable skills. Furthermore, survivor performance is often negatively impacted during redundancies as a result of low levels of job security and role clarity.

Survivor behaviour also includes increased levels of absenteeism (Campbell-Jamison, 2001) and a decline in innovation (Cascio, 1993). If the attitudinal and motivational issues facing survivors are understood, organisations will be able to manage the processes better to enhance the performance of the organisation during and after a redundancy programme (Doherty and Horsted, 1995).

A helpful theoretical model of survivor's responses to workforce reduction describes the responses as either constructive or destructive (Mishra and Spreitzer, 1998) as per Table 3.1.

One of the reasons that organisations do not achieve the anticipated success after a redundancy programme is that it is not beneficial to the company to have survivors remain who experience negative emotions and

Table 3.1 Theoretical model of survivor responses (Mishra and Spreitzer, 1998)

Constructive: hopeful	Constructive: obliging	Destructive: fearful	Destructive: cynical
Hope	Calm	Anxiety	Disgust
Excitement	Relief	Fear	Anger
Demonstrating	Committed	Helplessness	Moral outrage
initiative	Loyal	Procrastination	Retaliation
Optimism	Following order	Withdrawal	Cynicism
Problem solving	Routine behaviour	Worry	

behaviours (Cross and Travaglione, 2004); typically, this includes cynicism, demotivation and decline in organisational commitment (Baruch and Hind, 1999, Gandolfi, 2008). Employers should thus focus on how to mitigate the negative implications on the workforce when implementing redundancies, which is discussed in Part II.

Redundancy envoys

'Redundancy envoys' are the individuals with the responsibility of implementing redundancies, which includes directors, managers, HR professionals and employee representatives. Their role typically involves activities such as strategic decision-making that lead to the redundancy implementation, planning stages, consultation, communication as well as dealing with the aftermath. Many authors refer to this role as 'grim reapers' (Folger and Skarlicki, 1998, Clair and Dufresne, 2004), 'executors' (Downs, 1995), 'downsizers' (Burke, 1998) 'downsizing agents' (Clair and Dufresne, 2004) and 'executioners' (Kets De Vries and Balazs, 1997, Gandolfi, 2005). Personally, I have even been called 'Darth Vader' in my role of redundancy envoy, seen as the bearer of bad news. All the above labels refer to the individuals who plan and implement redundancies with the main focus on the role of consulting and the dismissal of employees.

The role of a redundancy envoy has been compared with that of 'death tellers', where doctors inform others about the death of a loved one (Clark and LaBeff, 1982). It is thus no surprise that redundancy envoys report finding it difficult to deal with the emotional trauma of the victims and survivors (Gandolfi, 2009). The anxiety experienced with these intense, negative situations impacts on how an individual emotionally engages with their responsibility within the role.

Redundancy envoys are survivors themselves and thus have similar concerns for their own job security, experiencing a range of conflicting emotions such as anxiety, fear, anger, frustration, relief, hope and regret. Research supports this notion that managers who are part of a redundancy programme, quite often experience some of the same feelings as the survivors and victims (Noer, 1993). Furthermore, quite often redundancy envoys know in advance that they will be victims of redundancy themselves; however, they have to remain in their role for an extended period of time to see the organisation through the final stages of the redundancy programme. This scenario is quite typical of business closures or mergers and acquisitions. This extended period adds to the pressure on redundancy envoys during tumultuous times.

When managers get asked to fire an individual, some managers undergo a personal crisis (Deems, 1995). Gandolfi (2009) postulates that redundancy envoys felt anxious and uncomfortable when they were pursuing executioners' responsibilities supported by Clair and Dufresne (2004), who describe the responsibility of making people redundant as professionally challenging and emotionally taxing.

The decision to make people redundant is one of the hardest to make and to live with, the reason being that redundancies are often seen as personal failure with potentially disastrous psychological and mental consequences for the redundancy envoy and the victim (Torres, 2011). Sometimes managers experience burnout after the implementation of a redundancy programme, which could be due to a lack of qualifications or experience and skill to cope with the demands of the job when it comes to implementing redundancy programmes (Moran, 2001).

Middle management in particular have a challenging role during redundancy implementation as they are often responsible for managing and enforcing the dismissals but are rarely involved in making the initial decisions (Dugan, 1996). In addition, middle management staff are quite often concerned with their own job insecurity and whilst having to manage their own survivor syndrome, they have to assume a leadership role in managing the redundancy programme. Redundancy envoys may thus have concerns about their own positions' tenure as survivors, which can add to their stress (Appelbaum et al., 1999).

Redundancy envoys themselves rarely admit to experiencing suffering during redundancies, as arguably this could be regarded as a weakness (Torres, 2011). Torres (2011) argues that redundancy envoys suffering during the process of redundancies is ignored by specialists in the field on the basis of their theoretical preconception that because the employer is dominant, they are unable to experience suffering, and, thus, their suffering is unheard. The suffering of redundancy envoys is however very real, despite coming across as being deceptive as redundancy envoys appear insensitive to employees, due to their own fear of rejection (Moran, 2001). The role of a redundancy envoy during redundancies is unique, underestimated and extremely stressful, yet the importance of their well-being is of utmost importance as these are the individuals who need to lead the organisation through its transition into the future.

Idiosyncrasy of redundancy envoys

The impact of redundancy on the employees is typically shown in a loss of loyalty and commitment, an impact on continuity (Hitt et al., 1994, Luthans and Sommer, 1999, Gandolfi, 2008) and a decline in employees' attitudes (Petzall et al., 2000). This places a burden of responsibility on redundancy envoys to lead disgruntled employees through a period of tough times.

Torres (2011) refers to the emotion of 'laying off' people as almost always painful. Research suggests that the work of implementing redundancies places considerable professional demands on redundancy envoys and provokes long-term emotional effects (Wright and Barling, 1998). Kets De Vries and Balaz (1997) argue that during redundancy implementation programmes, redundancy envoys use 'emotional numbing' as a coping technique, which is a direct result of dealing with persistent, major stressful tasks.

The importance of the role of the redundancy envoy and the significant impact they can have on the success of a redundancy programme is critical based on the following dimensions:

(a)   Redundancy envoys have different roles and experiences.
(b)   They can positively influence victims and survivors.
(c)   This can positively impact the success of the business.

(Petzer, 2020)

It is invaluable to understand the experiences of redundancy envoys as their experiences are different and distinct (Clair and Dufresne, 2004); they largely adopt more than one role, that of survivor and change agent (Dewitt et al., 2003).

Organisations that understand the impact of implementing redundancies on the attitudes and motivation of their employees are in a better position to manage the process to enhance the performance of their survivors and thus, ultimately, the business (Doherty and Horsted, 1995). Redundancy envoys are unsung corporate heroes who has the capacity to limit the negative impact on victims during major change programmes (Frost, 2003). The role of the redundancy envoy can help to enrich jobs and keep people motivated during restructures by helping employees develop a more positive approach to lateral career development (Holbeche, 2009). Redundancy envoys have the capacity to influence employees' perceptions of fairness and justice and can thus influence employee morale during the process of redundancy implementation (Brockner, 1992). The anxiety experienced with these intense, negative situations impacts on how an individual emotionally engages with their responsibility within the role, thus the benefit of reducing the anxiety will be beneficial for the redundancy envoy, as well as the organisation.

Redundancy envoys are thus important as their experiences are distinct and their methods can positively influence the success of a redundancy programme (Wright and Barling, 1998, Clair and Dufresne, 2004).

Main stressors for redundancy envoys
Psychological contract and trust

'Psychological contract' refers to an individual's belief regarding the terms and conditions of a reciprocal exchange agreement between an individual and another party. A belief exists that a promise has been made and in return, a commitment is offered, binding the parties to a set of reciprocal obligations, as defined by Rousseau (1989). The concept of the 'psychological contract' was first presented by Levinson et al. (2013) and later developed by Kotter (1973), Nicholson and Johns (1985), Robinson et al. (1994) and Rousseau (1996). When employees' psychological contracts are impacted due to insecurity of tenure, the organisation is less likely to be successful than with a stable workforce (Rousseau, 1995, Rousseau, 1996, Harter et al., 2002).

Survivor reaction to redundancies often results in a breach of the psychological contract (Mishra and Spreitzer, 1998). When rationale for change is not understood by employees, their psychological contracts become reformulated and that makes them more cynical about further organisational change proposals (Connell and Waring, 2002). Without appropriate and targeted interventions to help employees to see rationale for change, this phenomenon, described as the 'BOHICA syndrome', may significantly reduce employee preparedness to consider new change proposals (Connell and Waring, 2002). 'BOHICA' is an acronym that stands for "Bend over, here it comes again" which is used to indicate that an adverse scenario is about to repeat itself (Connell and Waring, 2002) such as redundancy implementation.

The typical psychological contract implies that employees offer loyalty, conformity and commitment to their organisation. In return, employers offer career prospects, employment security and training and development

(Baruch and Hind, 1999). The psychological contract relationship is based on 'trust'. In a redundancy situation, it is often perceived that the 'contract' and 'trust' has been breached due to the potential of loss of employment. Many survivors feel that their contract with the organisation is broken or damaged after a redundancy programme was implemented. The risk and stress caused by lack of commitment leads to a high propensity to leave the organisation (Ugboro, 2006). The risk is even further compounded if younger, possibly more creative individuals choose to leave the organisation, as this could have an impact on the organisation's competitive edge (Gandolfi, 2013).

The Reina Trust and Betrayal Model (Reina and Reina, 2016) looks at betrayal as a breach of trust or the perception of a breach. A redundancy resulting in loss of employment is classified as a major form of betrayal, albeit unintentional, according to the Reina Trust and Betrayal Model. When the relationships between employer and employee were respectable prior to the redundancy situation, the perception of betrayal by the employee is even greater (Torres, 2011).

With deteriorating psychological contracts and a perceived breach of trust, emotional attachment is often impacted as well. Employees tend to detach themselves emotionally from the organisation, often due to their perception that the people in charge have a disregard for their concerns (Gervais, 2014). Managing a breached psychological contract is thus a significant challenge for redundancy envoys to deal with during and after redundancy implementation.

Job insecurity and motivation

One of the consequences of redundancies and re-organisations is a significant negative impact on employees' sense of security and well-being (Baptiste, 2008). Survivors and victims reported a similar level of job insecurity and uncertainty in a study conducted by Tourish et al. (2004). This is nothing that should surprise us if we refer to Maslow's (1943) classic hierarchy of needs which states that the foundations of an individual's needs are physiological, including security and safety, and only once these needs are met can we strive to meet the higher levels of motivation. A redundancy situation can strip an individuals' needs from self-actualisation right back to the basic level of requiring physiological needs of having to provide a roof over a family's head, clothing, heating, water and food.

If the redundancy programme impacts all levels of the organisation, that in itself can cause significant disruption. The level of ambient uncertainty that comes when an organisation's management structure is under review can have a profound, detrimental impact on motivation and job security within the organisation, irrespective of the remuneration on offer (Ryan and Deci, 2017). The threat of further workforce reductions adds to the levels of job insecurity as found by Hartley et al. (1990).

Morale and performance

During a redundancy programme, the survivors are less likely to give their unconditional commitment to the organisation and this is likely to reduce morale, and subsequently performance. Brockner (1992) found an inverted-U relationship with regard to work effort and the threat of redundancies in their study. Besides the experience of low morale, there is a possibility of a further consequence: behaviours of sabotage (Dugan, 1996). Furthermore, employees also experience increased resistance to change during a redundancy, a behaviour that is counterproductive for achieving success during a redundancy programme (Macky, 2004).

Employee satisfaction

The use of terms such as 'shake out', 'getting rid of dead wood' or 'housekeeping' evokes a sense of inferiority for the victim that impacts on employee satisfaction with the overall redundancy programme (Tyson and Doherty, 1991). A study on the impact of redundancies in hospitals demonstrated a negative impact on the employees who reported greater internal conflict and lower employee satisfaction (Wagar and Rondeau, 2000). Research further supports that even employees who are not subject to the full impact of a redundancy programme, report a decline in commitment and job satisfaction and vicariously feel its effects (Hitt, 1994, Mullaney, 1989, Petzall et al., 2000).

Blame and guilt

Literature clearly recognises the correlation between guilt experienced by the redundancy envoy and the impact this has on their emotions during a redundancy programme (Tomasko, 1987, Noer, 1993, Moran,

2001). Managers are often blamed for redundancies due to the perception that the management has made poor decisions about the organisation's management (Moran, 2001). Noer (1993) supports this by stating that even though the implementation of a redundancy programme may be successful, a great deal of pain and guilt is still felt by many managers over what they think they have done to the employees. The perception and feeling that the managers are harming others, provokes not only guilt but also anger and denial (Moran, 2001). The guilt is often derived from having to dismiss employees who are productive and employees who have long tenure with the organisation which often correlate with being more senior in years. Guilt has been found to be the most destructive consequence for redundancy envoys to deal with (Petzer, 2019, Petzer, 2020).

Workload and pressure

One of the causes of major stress that survivors experience in relation to redundancy implementation is job demand, where the demand exceeds their ability to cope, which can easily lead to overworking (Waraich and Bhardwaj, 2011). Managers who are already responsible for a large remit including multiple functions, large employee numbers and smaller units, experience an increased workload with a more significant area of responsibility during and after redundancies (Cameron et al., 1991). The most pressure in relation to workload was felt by middle-level executives in a study conducted by Waraich and Bhardwaj (2011). Workload and pressure are attributable to factors such as managing the redundancy programme whilst having to continue with the day job, as well as potentially picking up additional work due to fewer resources.

Besides the normal pressures of the job, redundancy envoys have to put extra effort into managing employees who experience low morale, commitment and job satisfaction. In addition, employees who are at risk of losing their jobs might be inclined to exhibit unethical behaviour that could be detrimental to the organisation's long-term survival (Ghosh, 2017). Dugan (1996) found that disgruntled employees may even be tempted to deliberately sabotage the success of the organisation. This puts additional pressure on redundancy envoys to be vigilant in managing people during a redundancy situation.

Decision-making

Another key challenge that redundancy envoys are faced with is making tough decisions about whom to make redundant (Clair and Dufresne, 2004). Redundancy envoys report it is particularly difficult to make decisions around who should exit the organisation when there is no clear indication of who is a less effective employee, among equally effective employees. The decisions and selection of whom to make redundant is described as complex, confusing and chaotic and is exacerbated as names of those selected to be made redundant could change at a moment's notice (Clair and Dufresne, 2004).

Proximity

Several studies agree that the proximity of the redundancy envoy to the employee could influence the redundancy envoy emotionally (Gandolfi, 2009). The closer redundancy envoys are to the redundancy situation, the more significant the emotional impact, whereas with a certain distance, the dimensions and implications are not as significant. Redundancy envoys that had deeper connections with employees and insights into employees' private lives found it harder to make the redundancies (Bandura et al., 1996). Torres (2011: 286) refers to a well-known metaphor used in the military to describe the impact of proximity very effectively: "it is always more traumatic to kill someone with a blade than with a rifle." For some redundancy envoys, proximity meant that they knew personal facts about the employees at risk and whether they were facing hard times (such as financial difficulties or divorce), and this made the process of redundancy even more stressful (Clair and Dufresne, 2004).

Torres (2011) explains that the emotional challenge of proximity during redundancies quite often occurs in small and medium-sized enterprises (SME) due to the close proximity of relationships, whereas in large companies, the redundancy envoy may potentially not even know the employee or employees being made redundant. Potentially, redundancy envoys and the employees at risk of redundancy are less likely to know each other in larger organisations. The additional burden on the person making the decision to implement redundancies in an SME is thus even more challenging, as they cannot pass on the blame and must accept responsibility for the redundancy decisions as the owner or director in charge (Torres, 2011).

Depending on the proximity to the employees, the approach to the implementation of redundancies should be adapted accordingly (Petzer, 2019). Torres (2011) refers to the difficulty of making redundancies in a small village or community where the organisation implementing the redundancies is the main employer in the town. The employer becomes a notable figure in their community, and this puts even more pressure on their social responsibility and symbolic status. Additional pressure to manage potential reputation damage is thus placed on redundancy envoys (Zyglidopoulos, 2005). A situation like this can damage the status of the person/employer in and out of the work context.

Lack of communication and information

Survivors are often faced with challenges of poor communication such as being misinformed about issues, such as their role in the newly restructured organisation and information about key people leaving or changing roles (Isabella, 1989). Tourish et al. (2004) support these findings in their research that found that middle managers received less information during the redundancies than senior managers in all aspects. The lack of convergence between the implementation of a redundancy programme and the communication plan is often a cause of stress for the employees (Labib and Appelbaum, 1993), which places pressure on redundancy envoys to deal with rumours and misinformation.

Miscellaneous stressors

The stressors previously discussed are the most frequent causes of stress for redundancy envoys; however, there are a few additional stressors that are recognised to explore. The impact and extent of these stressors specific to redundancy situations have received very little attention in the literature. Although the emotional component of work is almost certainly relevant to work stress, it should not be considered as the only explanation for high stress levels and that other stressors will undoubtedly play an important role in the experience of work stress (Johnson et al., 1996). Torres' (2011) study suggests that isolation for the redundancy envoy during redundancies should be recognised as having a significant impact as well. He explains that directors often find themselves alone with regard to making difficult decisions around redundancies but also alone in the sense of whom they can trust and talk to about their feelings and the situation.

Another significant stressor that has received limited recognition in the literature in the context of redundancies is poor leadership. Poor leadership or lack of leadership during a redundancy programme can lead to an increased level of resistance to change, individualism and disconnectedness, which have a negative impact on teamwork (Cameron, 1994, Hansson, 2008). Regardless of the numerous implications on individuals and the organisation, it is the very same redundancy envoys that have to pick up the pieces during the redundancy programme and especially in the aftermath of redundancies. Chapter 11 provides useful guidance on how to Re-Build and Re-Focus the organisation post redundancy implementation.

Semi-survivors

More recently, during the outbreak of COVID-19, organisations have also come to rely on fire and rehire techniques to support organisational survival. This had led to a new group of impacted employees, semi-survivors that potentially experience the negative impact of redundancy-related actions even more so than survivors. These employees were essentially first victims when 'fired' and then 'rehired' becoming survivors. There is a distinction between employees that were at risk of redundancy who secured alternative employment internally and employees who were dismissed and rehired.

This group thus experienced the negative impact of both groups, but with the additional burden of long-term damage caused by being 'rehired' subject to less favourable conditions such as reduced wages and benefits. Symptoms associated with survivor syndrome are likely to be more severe when it comes to a breached psychological contract, breakdown in trust, loyalty and commitment.

This chapter summarised the strong evidence that corroborate that the impact of implementing redundancies is profound, leading to serious negative implications for the entire workforce and the organisation. The next chapter will focus on exploring alternative solutions to implementing redundancies, including how to limit or avoid redundancies.

References

Appelbaum, S. H., Close, T. G. & Klasa, S. 1999. Downsizing: An examination of some successes and more failures. *Management Decision*, 37(5), 424–437.

Appelbaum, S. H., Simpson, R. & Shapiro, B. T. 1987. The tough test of downsizing. *Organizational Dynamics*, 16(1), 68–79.

Astrachan, J. H. 2004. Organizational departures: The impact of separation anxiety as studied in a mergers and acquisitions simulation. *The Journal of Applied Behavioral Science*, 40, 91–110.

Babchuk, N., Price, C. R., Munden, K. J., Mandl, H. J. & Solley, C. M. 2013. *Men, management, and mental health. American Sociological Review*, 28(6), 1050–1051.

Bandura, A., Barbaranelli, C., Caprara, G. V. & Pastorelli, C. 1996. Mechanisms of moral disengagement in the exercise of moral agency. *Journal of Personality and Social Psychology*, 71, 364.

Baptiste, N. R. 2008. Tightening the link between employee wellbeing at work and performance. *Management Decision*, 46(2), 284–310.

Baruch, y. & Hind, P. 1999. Perpetual motion in organizations: Effective management and the impact of the new psychological contracts on "Survivor Syndrome". *European Journal of Work and Organizational Psychology*, 8, 295–306.

Brockner, J. 1992. Managing the effects of layoffs on survivors. *California Management Review*, 34, 9–28.

Burke, R. J. 1998. Downsizing and restructuring in organizations: Research findings and lessons learned--introduction. *Canadian Journal of Administrative Sciences*, 15, 297.

Cameron, K. S. 1994. Strategies for successful organizational downsizing. *Human Resource Management*, 33, 189–211.

Cameron, K. S., Freeman, S. J. & Mishra, A. K. 1991. Best practices in white-collar downsizing: Managing contradictions. *Academy of Management Perspectives*, 5, 57–73.

Campbell-Jamison, F. 2001. Downsizing in Britain and Its effects on survivors and their organizations. *Anxiety, Stress & Coping*, 14, 35–59.

Cascio, W. F. 1993. Downsizing: What do we know? What have we learned? *Academy of Management Perspectives*, 7, 95–104.

Clair, J. A. & Dufresne, R. L. 2004. Playing the grim reaper: How employees experience carrying out a downsizing. *Human Relations*, 57, 1597–1625.

Clark, R. E. & Labeff, E. E. 1982. Death telling: Managing the delivery of bad news. *Journal of Health and Social Behavior*, 366–380.

Connell, J. & Waring, P. 2002. The BOHICA syndrome: A symptom of cynicism towards change initiatives? *Strategic Change*, 11, 347.

Cross, B. & Travaglione, A. 2004. The times they are a-changing: Who will stay and who will go in a downsizing organization? *Personnel Review*, 33(3), 275–290.

Deems, R. S. 1995. *Fear of firing*, Wayne, NJ: Career Press.

Devine, K., Reay, T., Stinton, L. & Collins-Nakai, R. 2003. Downsizing outcomes: Better a victim than a survivor? *Human Resource Management*, 42, 109–125.

Dewitt, R.-L., Trevino, L. K. & Mollica, K. A. 2003. Stuck in the middle: A control-based model of managers' reactions to their subordinates' layoffs. *Journal of Managerial Issues*, 15(1), 32–49.

Doherty, N. & Horsted, J. 1995. Helping survivors to stay on board. *People Management*, 1, 26–30.

Downs, A. 1995. *Corporate executions: The ugly truth about layoffs – How corporate greed is shattering lives, companies and communities.* New York: AMACOM.

Dugan, R.D. 1996. Corporate executions: The ugly truth about layoffs--how corporate greed is shattering lives, companies, and communities. *Personnel Psychology*, 49(4), 998–1001.

Folger, R. & Skarlicki, D. P. 1998. When tough times make tough bosses: Managerial distancing as a function of layoff blame. *Academy of Management Journal*, 41, 79–87.

Frost, P. J. 2003. Toxic emotions at work: How compassionate managers handle pain and conflict, Boston, MA: Harvard Business Review Press.

Gandolfi, F. 2005. How do organizations implement downsizing? An Australian and New Zealand study. *Contemporary Management Research*, 1, 57–68.

Gandolfi, F. 2008. Reflecting on downsizing: What have managers learned? *SAM Advanced Management Journal*, 73, 45.

Gandolfi, F. 2009. Unraveling downsizing: What do we know about the phenomenon? *Revista de Management Comparat Internaţional*, 10, 414–426.

Gandolfi, F. 2013. Workforce downsizing: Strategies, archetypes, approaches and tactics. *Journal of Management Research*, 13, 67.

Gervais, R. 2014. Measuring downsizing in organizations. *Assessment and Development Matters*, 6(3), 2–5.

Ghosh, S. K. 2017. The direct and interactive effects of job insecurity and job embeddedness on unethical pro-organizational behavior an empirical examination. *Personnel Review*, 46(6), 1182–1198.

Hansson, M. 2008. *On closedowns: Towards a pattern of explanations to the closedown effect.* Doctoral dissertation, Örebro University.

Harter, J. K., Schmidt, F. L. & Hayes, T. L. 2002. Business-unit-level relationship between employee satisfaction, employee engagement, and business outcomes: A meta-analysis. *Journal of Applied Psychology,* 87, 268.

Hartley, J., Jacobson, D., Klandermans, B. & Van Vuuren, T. 1990. *Job insecurity: Coping with jobs at risk.* London: Sage Publications Ltd.

Hitt, M. A. 1994. Rightsizing: Building and maintaining strategic leadership and long-term competitiveness. *Organizational Dynamics,* 23, 18–33.

Hitt, M. A., Keats, B. W., Harback, H. F. & Nixon, R. D. 1994. Rightsizing: Building and maintaining strategic leadership and long-term competitiveness. *Organizational Dynamics,* 23, 18–33.

Holbeche, L. 2009. *Aligning human resources and business strategy.* 2nd ed. Amsterdam; Boston, MA: Butterworth-Heinemann.

Isabella, L. A. 1989. Downsizing: Survivors' assessments. *Business Horizons,* 32, 35–41.

Johnson, J. R., Bernhagen, M. J., Miller, V. & Allen, M. 1996. The role of communication in managing reductions in work force. *Journal of Applied Communication Research,* 24(3), 139–164. doi:10.1080/00909889609365448

Kates, N., Greiff, B. S. & Hagen, D. Q. 1990. *The psychosocial impact of job loss.* Washington, DC: American Psychiatric Association.

Kets De Vries, M. F. & Balazs, K. 1997. The downside of downsizing. *Human Relations,* 50, 11–50.

Kotter, J. P. 1973. The psychological contract: Managing the joining-up process. *California Management Review,* 15, 91–99.

Kubler-Ross, E. 1969. *On death and dying.* Sydney: Travistock Publications.

Labib, N. & Appelbaum, S. H. 1993. Strategic downsizing: A human resources perspective. *Human Resource Planning,* 16(4), 69–93.

Leana, C. R. & Feldman, D. C. 1988. Individual responses to job loss: Perceptions, reactions, and coping behaviors. *Journal of Management,* 14, 375–389.

Luthans, B. C. & Sommer, S. M. 1999. The impact of downsizing on workplace attitudes: Differing reactions of managers and staff in a health care organization. *Group & Organization Management,* 24, 46–71.

Macky, K. A. 2004. Organisational downsizing and redundancies: The New Zealand workers experience. *Journal of Employment Relations,* 29, 63–87.

Maslow, A. H. 1943. A theory of human motivation. *Psychological Review,* 50, 370.

Mishra, A. K. & Spreitzer, G. M. 1998. Explaining how survivors respond to downsizing: The Roles of trust, empowerment, justice, and work redesign. *The Academy of Management Review,* 23, 567–588.

Moran, M. 2001. *Managers coping mechanisms and job satisfaction while implementing downsizing.* PhD, Kent State University.

Mullaney, A. D. 1989. Downsizing: How one hospital responded to decreasing demand. *Health Care Management Review,* 14, 41–48.

Nicholson, N. & Johns, G. 1985. The absence culture and psychological contract: Who's in control of absence? *Academy of Management Review,* 10, 397–407.

Noer, D. M. 1993. *Healing the wounds: Overcoming the trauma of layoffs and revitalizing downsized organizations.* San Francisco, NC: Jossey-Bass.

Parris, M. A. & Vickers, M. H. 2010. "Look at Him ... he's failing": Male executives' experiences of redundancy. *Employee Responsibilities and Rights Journal,* 22, 345–357.

Paulsen, N., Callan, V. J., Grice, T. A., Rooney, D., Gallois, C., Jones, E., Jimmieson, N. L. & Bordia, P. 2005. Job uncertainty and personal control during downsizing: A comparison of survivors and victims. *Human Relations,* 58, 463–496.

Petzall, B. J., Parker, G. E. & Stoeberl, P. A. 2000. Another side to downsizing: Survivors' behavior and self-affirmation. *Journal of Business & Psychology,* 14, 593–604.

Petzer, M. 2019. *Developing effective interventions for mitigating the psychological impact experienced by redundancy envoys during redundancy situations.* PhD, Solent University.

Petzer, M. 2020. Don't shoot the messenger: The enigmatic impact of conveying bad news during redundancy situations and how to limit the impact. 2020 Applied Research Conference. CIPD.

Reina, D. S. & Reina, M. L. 2016. *Trust and betrayal in the workplace.* 3rd ed. Oakland: Berrett-Koehler, 2015.

Robinson, S. L., Kraatz, M. S. & Rousseau, D. M. 1994. Changing obligations and the psychological contract: A longitudinal study. *Academy of Management Journal,* 37, 137–152.

Rousseau, D. 1989. Psychological and implied contracts in organizations in Farmer, S. & Fedor, D. (1999). Volunteer participation and withdrawal: A psychological contract perspective on the role of expectations and organizational support. *Nonprofit Management & Leadership,* 9, 349–367.

Rousseau, D. M. 1995. *Psychological contracts in organizations.* Thousand Oaks, CA: Sage.

Rousseau, D. M. 1996. Changing the deal while keeping the people. *Academy of Management Perspectives,* 10, 50–59.

Ryan, R. M. & Deci, E. L. 2017. *Self-determination theory: Basic psychological needs in motivation, development, and wellness*. New York: Guilford Publications.

Tomasko, R. M. 1987. *Downsizing: Reshaping the corporation for the future*. New York: AMACOM/American Management Association.

Torres, O. 2011. The silent and shameful suffering of bosses: Layoffs in SME. *International Journal of Entrepreneurship and Small Business*, 13, 181–192.

Tourish, D., Paulsen, N., Hobman, E. & Bordia, P. 2004. The downsides of downsizing: Communication processes information needs in the aftermath of a workforce reduction strategy. *Management Communication Quarterly*, 17, 485–516.

Tyson, S. & Doherty, N. 1991. Redundant executive: Personality and the job change experience. *Personnel Review*, 20(5), 3–10.

Ugboro, I. O. 2006. Organizational commitment, job redesign, employee empowerment and intent to quit among survivors of restructuring and downsizing. *Journal of Behavioral and Applied Management*, 7, 232.

Vickers, M. H. & Parris, M. A. 2007. "Your job no longer exists!": From experiences of alienation to expectations of resilience – A phenomenological study. *Employee Responsibilities and Rights Journal*, 19, 113–125.

Wagar, T. H. & Rondeau, K. V. 2000. Reducing the workforce: Examining its consequences in health care organizations. *International Journal of Health Care Quality Assurance Incorporating Leadership in Health Services*, 13(3), 1.

Waraich, S. B. & Bhardwaj, G. 2011. Coping strategies of executive survivors in downsized organizations in India. *SAM Advanced Management Journal*, 76(3), 26.

Waters, L. 2007. Experiential differences between voluntary and involuntary job redundancy on depression, job-search activity, affective employee outcomes and re-employment quality. *Journal of Occupational and Organizational Psychology*, 80, 279–299.

Wright, B. & Barling, J. 1998. "The executioners' song": Listening to downsizers reflect on their experiences. *Canadian Journal of Administrative Sciences/ Revue Canadienne Des Sciences De l'Administration*, 15, 339–354.

Zyglidopoulos, S. C. 2005. The impact of downsizing on corporate reputation. *British Journal of Management*, 16, 253–259.

4

LIMITING REDUNDANCIES – ALTERNATIVE STRATEGIES

The previous chapter highlighted the negative impact of redundancies on organisations and individuals, and in response to this information, it is meaningful to consider alternative strategies to prevent or limit redundancies. This chapter will explore various strategies to save costs including 'pull' strategies in more depth. Reducing the workforce may not always be preventable, but there are undoubtedly actions that should be considered to limit or even avoid redundancies. Fire-and-rehire strategies discussed at the end of this chapter are not condoned.

Knee-jerk reaction to financial difficulties

Many organisations suffer financial difficulties. In the first instance, it is important to have a thorough understanding of the reasons behind the financial challenges. For many organisations, the reasons may be obvious, i.e., as a result of COVID-19 restrictions, the organisation was unable to trade for many months.

DOI: 10.4324/9781003030416-5

Redundancies can be very expensive to an organisation as discussed in previous chapters, especially if enhanced packages are offered. Before jumping to 'redundancy conclusions', consider the following questions:

- Is the situation short-lived?
- What are the chances of recovery?
- If recovery is possible, when is it going to realise?
- How are the organisation's competitors coping and adapting?

Ensure comprehensive market research is undertaken to inform the decision-making process (Petzer, 2020). Deciding to implement redundancies can have catastrophic consequences for an organisation and due consideration should be given if this is the right strategy for your organisation. Loosing valuable employees as a result of a knee-jerk reaction is counterproductive as the organisation will need them when the crisis is over and not only would their loyalty be lost, so would the organisational knowledge that they have. Contemplate the implications of losing employees with valuable skillsets that are already very challenging to find and retain. If rash decisions are made, how feasible would it be for an organisation to hire talented employees back? Would they join a company that has a reputation for redundancies and that may appear to have lost credibility in the business world?

Another reason to not overreact or implement redundancies hastily is that once an organisation has made someone redundant, their role cannot be filled for a fixed period of time, depending on your country's specific regulation. This ratifies the point that the implementation of redundancies should always be considered as a long-term strategy. When an organisation opts for redundancies, the reality is that the organisation will likely be without that role for a minimum of at least 12 months. The consultation process itself could take several months, depending on the scale of the redundancy programme. Carefully consider if the redundancy costs and potential recruitment cost to replace the person in future, combined with the disruption and negative impact, balance out against the potential cost savings. If not, it probably is not worth considering the redundancy.

If making the decision to implement a redundancy programme, ensure contingency plans are made to continue to deliver to customer needs and that medium- and long-term plans are in place to protect the organisation and its people.

Adapt your product or service line

Think about how you can adapt your service or products to generate income through alternative means. A workshop or focus group that includes representatives from all levels in the organisation, usually works best to encourage these brainstorming sessions.

During the coronavirus pandemic, many organisations had to rethink their business proposition and service offering. Some highstreets retail stores allowed for customers to 'window shop' and if a customer were interested in purchasing a product, they could call, reserve and arrange a collection time or get the item delivered. Some manufacturers changed their product line; for example, a company that produced gin, adapted their production processes to make hand sanitisers in response to market needs. Many classes and courses that were taught face to face in studios, gyms or classrooms adapted their offering to online classes. The point is simply, that before considering redundancies, consider what else can be done and how can things be done differently during challenging times to keep sustaining the business, instead of simply shutting the doors.

Another option to reduce redundancies is to only address a closure in the area of business that is not producing results. For example, if there is a specific product line that is not selling but affecting the overall profit and loss of business, address the manufacturer, distributor or retailer of that product only. It may have a small, short-lived impact to save the overall organisation.

Exhaust all other measures of saving costs

Demonstrating other means of saving costs prior to considering redundancies is advocated by UK employment law and supports a collaborative approach to redundancy consultation.

It is easy to fall into the trap of letting senior management make all the tough decisions on how to address a business's financial problems.

An approach that reaps improved results is to be transparent with business challenges and share the problems that may impact the success of the organisation's future with employees. There are two key benefits to this approach. First, you are managing employees' expectations in case a redundancy programme is inevitable. Second, an opportunity is created to feed into the ideas of cost savings as well as creating innovative ideas around adapting new services or products (Petzer, 2020). Establishing trust in the workforce drives a sense of ownership by focusing on a shared goal. If the business survives, so will the roles within the organisation.

Organisations can be creative when it comes to saving costs when the going gets tough, such as the reduction of non-essential travel, reviewing the need for company vehicles and relocation to cheaper premises. If a redundancy programme is inevitable, the management team will gain more understanding and employee buy-in if they can genuinely demonstrate they considered measures to reduce costs and that reducing headcount was truly the last option available.

Insourcing

Insourcing (Warner and Hefetz, 2012) is essentially the opposite of outsourcing. Outsourcing is defined as a strategic decision to transfer organisational activities to external suppliers, typically administrative services, information systems, payroll and delivery services (Brown et al., 2009). Outsourcing is often implemented with the aim to save organisational costs and it often drives redundancies. Some scholars have highlighted the unintended consequences of outsourcing (Boyne, 1998, Entwistle, 2005), which can lead to retuning the outsourced activities back 'in-house' (Damanpour et al., 2020). Insourcing utilises an organisation's own resources to perform tasks, complete a project or achieve organisational goals, instead of hiring an external company or person to perform the duties. During challenging times, creative thinking such as insourcing, where bringing activities in-house, may help job creation and limit redundancies. Bringing outsourced activities in-house may be completely impractical for some organisations and the decision should be made based on skillsets, facilities and employee aptitude, subject to each individual organisational context. Think more broadly about insourcing by establishing the known and hidden skillsets of the organisation's workers.

What else can they do? What else are they qualified for that you could utilise? What are they passionate about that may help drive revenue and income streams? One example of this situation realised in an advertising firm in Cape Town, South Africa that specialised in selling advertisement space in various council-related publications. The organisation essentially specialised in sales and marketing. When going through a process of re-evaluating their business model, they realised that most of their profits were consumed by paying high costs to reproduction houses to produce the artwork for the advertisements. As a result, they adjusted their business proposition, by reducing the sales focus and re-focusing the business by setting up their own in-house design house. The consultation process with employees resulted in several sales personnel transitioning into completely different roles in a creative environment, some becoming graphic designers.

Saving costs by reducing the wage bill

Limiting the use of contractors

Reviewing an organisation's use of contractors is a requirement as part of the collective consultation process in the UK context. There is a general assumption that the costs of contractors are substantially higher than permanent staff and thus work can be created for existing employees by replacing contractors with employed personnel. When considering the replacement of contractors, a due diligence analysis is thus recommended to establish if it is indeed a cost-effective decision.

Analysis should include the on-cost of a permanent staff member compared with a contractor rate and should include:

- annual salary
- the cost of paid holidays and bank holidays
- pension
- National Insurance contribution
- training costs
- utility costs (desk hire, IT account, phone line, parking space, etc.)
- additional benefits (healthcare, life insurance, EAP packages, etc.)
- miscellaneous costs (sick pay, redundancy packages, administrative costs, etc.).

Despite just looking at costs, a skills analysis would help drive the decisions in line with organisational goals. Depending on the organisation's business model, contractors may be a more suitable option if, for example, the business is project-focused with specific start and end dates. Depending on the length of projects or current progress against completion dates, it may be more pragmatic to retain the contractors until project completion. Contingent on the organisational needs, a hybrid approach of using contractors and permanent employees may be suitable to balance the organisational risks during tumultuous times.

Finally, understanding your cost and skill base of your contractors would put you in a great position to answer potential future questions from employee representatives or the workforce, should redundancies become inevitable.

Recruitment freezes

There is little benefit in hiring new employees, whilst having to make others redundant, unless the vacancies are addressing specific skill shortages. Recruiting new employees is not only expensive, but needs to be carefully considered when redundancies are looming, as it may cause resentment or create the perception of poor management amongst employees.

Recruitment agency fees tend to range from 15% to 20% of annual salaries and can go as high as 30% for hard-to-fill positions. The average cost-per-hire in the UK is £3,000 for a new worker, without using agencies (Glassdoor, 2020).

The following external and internal recruitment costs need to be contemplated:

External recruitment costs:

- background checks and work eligibility
- pre-employment medical or health screening
- capability or personality assessments
- costs of advertising on job boards and marketing
- recruitment technology
- job sourcing
- travel expenses.

Internal recruitment costs:

- in-house or full-time internal recruitment staff
- internal recruitment systems such as an Applicant Tracker System (ATS)
- referral rewards
- management time spent on interviewing.

Only in rare circumstances, where there is a robust argument for the requirement of a specific skill set that cannot be fulfilled by a reasonable amount of training of an existing staff member is it advisable to recruit. Adopting a responsible approach to recruitment would allow the organisation to retain credibility should a redundancy situation be inevitable.

Salary freezes and salary cuts

With appropriate consultation, some organisations agree to salary cuts and/ or the freezing of annual salary reviews as a method of collective cost-cutting (Petzer, 2020). During the COVID-19 pandemic, some organisations chose to specifically reduce salaries within the senior leadership team with the aim of demonstrating commitment to the workforce. This is a delightful shift in approach, where traditionally, the senior team is often regarded as 'excluded' from redundancies, whilst lower levels of employees were taking the 'brunt' of cost-saving implications. Although this approach may go some way to protect the majority of the workforce's morale and levels of job security, the impact on the senior management team should still be carefully considered to avoid alienation and withdrawal. At a senior level, these behaviours could be very destructive. Agreeing to salary cuts across the whole organisation may drive a collective aim of organisational survival and a perception that all the employees are 'in the same boat'. On the contrary, the introduction of salary cuts can have a major negative impact on morale and cause deep emotional scars, which will present itself in different problems such as lower productivity (Cascio, 2010). The key to the successful implementation of these initiatives is to do so with thorough transparent consultation and communication. The participation and involvement of employee representatives, whether unionised or not, are essential in the successful implementation of these change initiatives.

Chapter 9 discusses the advantages of employee participation and representation. In addition, or instead of salary reductions, some organisations opt to stop or reduce the payment of bonuses and incentives, which is normally paid based on set targets and management discretion.

Job sharing and reduced working hours

Introducing the options of job sharing and or reducing working hours is a useful strategy to limit redundancies. Effective individual consultation is a critical factor of a successful outcome of such changes to employment terms and conditions.

For some employees, the preference to move to temporary work has been a preferable option (Marler et al., 2002) rather than being made redundant. The myriad of implications of becoming a temporary worker should not be ignored, including increased job insecurity, less control over shifts and hours of work (Cohen and Mallon, 1999). It is thus important to recognise that this option may suit some employees, but for others, it will still have a negative impact on morale and commitment. If employees who opt for these solutions are, however, fully engaged and desire the change, the risk can be reduced for the organisation as well as the individual. A key part of the success in these initiatives is open and honest communication. Arrangements could be put in place for a trial or temporary period and reviewed after an agreed period of time, which could allow for more employee uptake.

Limiting overtime

Reducing overtime costs, where possible, could meaningly contribute to cost savings. Some organisations pay 1.5 times or double normal wage for overtime worked or work completed on bank and public holidays. Revisit workforce planning to optimise working hours around limiting or avoiding the payment of higher rates. Alternatively, investigate if overtime rates are billable to clients directly where contracts allow. The overtime bill can thus be reduced by looking at when and how people work through strategic workforce planning. This can be achieved by having open conversations with the workforce and working collaboratively on reducing costs with a clear rationale of the value and impact of these compromises.

Alternative working arrangements to reduce hours

Alternative working arrangements with the aim to reduce the salary bill could include a range of different options. One option would be to introduce reduced hours, such as a reduction from 40 to 30 hours over five days. An alternative offering could include working fewer days per week, such as Monday to Thursday, instead of Monday to Friday, which will have a similar effect. The benefit of this situation is that subject to customer demand and the organisation's requirements, a solution can be tailored to the employee's needs, resulting in a win-win situation for both parties. When considering flexible working or reduced hours, offer this across the board to non-essential roles. Offering flexible working or reduced hours does not have to exclude senior members of the organisation. If directors adopt this approach, the role modelling will reinforce the seriousness of an organisation's financial position and could help to build a community spirit of 'we are in this together'.

Unpaid sabbaticals

When the business is unsure of the longevity or uncertainty of their position, yet hesitant to make employees redundant, unpaid sabbaticals is a great option and may suit the needs of both the employees and the organisation.

Making employees redundant when the period of economic uncertainty is short-lived could be unnecessarily expensive. From an organisational perspective, if the business picks up again later, the organisation will need to rehire employees, and it would, therefore, be counterproductive to firstly pay a redundancy package, followed in short succession with recruitment cost. From an employee's perspective, they may be at a stage in their lives where a few months unpaid break may be affordable and yet convenient, such as grandparents wanting to help with a new grandchild around or a newlywed couple who wants to travel the world for a few months.

If unpaid sabbaticals are agreed, the risks need to be transparent to both sides and the terms of the sabbatical needs to be agreed in writing to protect both parties. Employers could offer promotional incentives such as a continued service record when employees return from their sabbaticals or a guarantee to return to the same/similar role, subject to unique organisational circumstances.

Removing or freezing benefits

Another method to save costs is to revisit organisational benefits. Many organisations offer a range of benefits such as discount schemes, fuel allowances, private medicals, life insurance, employee assistance programmes, enhanced pensions, will writing services, online GP services, pet insurance, and phone insurance just to name some of the more popular ones. Some benefits are available through a benefits platform that carries a cost to the employer. It may be more difficult to negotiate a reduced or more cost-effective offering for the organisation if tied into long, contractual terms than individual agreements. Thus, if redundancies are a likely future prospect, a proactive approach should be undertaken to reduce the anticipated membership levels with due notice.

Organisations can explore creative ways to reduce costs where contractual terms are not necessarily applicable. During the COVID-19 pandemic, some organisations for example reduced company pension contributions with the agreement to repay the money back into employee's pensions when the organisation moved to a more stable position. Alternatively, consider a temporary freezing of benefits. Most employees would prefer a temporary 'loss' of benefits as opposed to the risk of losing employment. The cuts could be a temporary measure until the organisation is in a more stable and financially secure position. Some benefits could be put on freeze for new starters and reinstated at a later stage when the business operates under greater financial stability.

Short-term working and lay-offs

During the COVID-19 pandemic, many organisations relied on short-term working and lay-offs to help address lack of work and to limit redundancies. 'Laid off' in this context should not be confused with US lexicon where 'laid off' implies being made redundant. Being 'laid off' in the UK context means that the employer does not require an employee to work for a short period of time due to diminished work demand and such an employee will not get paid whilst being 'laid off'. The short-term working refers to the period when the employee is required to work for a short term, such as part of a week instead of the normal contractual hours. Employers can only implement lay-offs or short-term working, subject to employees having an implied or express term within their contracts of employment. Besides the damage caused to the employee relationship such as lack of commitment, loyalty and trust, employers should be conscious of a high risk of employment tribunal claims based on unauthorised deduction from wages.

Employees may be able to claim a redundancy payment whilst being laid off or on short-term working in accordance with the Employments Rights Act 1996. Statutory guarantee payments for any complete day of being laid off apply to most employees. Statutory guarantee payments are limited to a maximum of five days' payment in any three-month period.

Pull strategies

If all options are exhausted to save costs and prevent the implementation of redundancies via 'push' strategies, the next step is to consider 'pull' strategies to encourage voluntary resignations. This approach is less aggressive than 'push' strategies and thus also helps maintain better morale by empowering employees to make their own decisions about their future, leading to a less damaged psychological contract. Ultimately, 'pull' strategies are aimed to entice employees to put their hand up for voluntary redundancies as well as to protect victims from having no income as a result of job loss. Loss of income has a bigger impact on individuals than loss of job, especially if job satisfaction was not prevalent (Kets De Vries and Balazs, 1997).

Early retirement interventions

Early retirement interventions are a popular strategy to encourage voluntary leavers; however, the benefits need to be carefully weighed up against the risks. Early retirement can be successful with the intention of reducing headcount and potentially could allow for career advancement opportunities for the remaining employees. For early retirement interventions to be successful, it is of utmost importance that applicants meet qualifying criteria and is subject to an application process, bound by legal terms and conditions. If this process is not managed with due care, it can backfire on organisations who could lose their most talented employees (Cascio, 1993). Organisations should anticipate that employees that are habitually eligible for early retirement are most likely going to employees with more firm-specific knowledge (Flint, 2003). Although early retirement interventions could be a successful method of reducing headcount, it is hard to control (Hitt et al., 1994). Without the necessary controls in place for the application and qualifying process, early retirement practices could be counter-productive. It is essential that the selection of who remains and who leaves the organisation is focused on skills and value to the organisation to ensure future sustainability and to prevent the loss of talent.

Prior to considering early retirement interventions, it is recommended that organisations undertake detailed analysis of their workforce age demographics, including employees with key skills and knowledge pools. Analysis may help identify potential employees in the catchment of such an offering, which may help to dictate restrictions on who are eligible to apply. Once restrictions are in place, resentment may present itself amongst employees who are out of scope to apply.

If early retirement interventions are the right solution for the organisation, consideration can be given to what incentives to include in the offer. Organisations typically offer a cash payment or ex gratia bonus to entice employees to take this option. A popular arrangement is the '5-5-4' early retirement plan, which involves the following method:

+ add five years to the employee's current age
+ add five years to the employee's service record (impacting retirement benefits)
+ four weeks additional pay for each year of service (Tomasko, 1991).

Redeployment

Another strategy to help limit redundancies is to drive redeployment; essentially providing alternative employment for employees that may be at risk of losing their jobs. Redeployment offered could be a new or adapted role or a similar role in a different branch or location. Offering employees at risk of redundancy suitable, alternative employment is a requirement of employment law in the UK. This approach also demonstrates a willingness to be agile and find solutions that help build trust across the organisation. Quite often employees have qualifications or experience in another field that is unknown to the employer. In this instance, redeployment can be extremely beneficial to both parties, can boost productivity and might align with organisational goals. Redeployed employees may be grateful to retain employment but are still subject to emotional turmoil. Redeployed employees experience part of the impact of being made redundant combined with that of survivors and thus occupy a unique intermediate space, where their individual needs should not be discounted (McLachlan et al., 2020).

Although redeployment is largely beneficial for both organisation and individuals, it could cause the redundancy implementation to be protracted due to the process involved, which requires skills analysis, interviews and trial periods (Ashman, 2015). Organisations should thus be mindful to ensure that sufficient resources are available to ensure the process of redeployment can be conducted as time-efficiently as possible.

To boost redeployment whether internally or externally, various actions can be adopted by organisations to build confidence and skills in the process. Chapter 10 builds on this section by providing more detailed guidance on how to support each impacted group through the turmoil of redundancy implementation.

Fire-and-rehire techniques

Despite 'fire-and-rehire' techniques being rife through the COVID-19 pandemic, it is a strategy that is deemed to have poor organisational ethics, causing a significant negative impact on employee relations. Employers use redundancy as a method to dismiss employees and rehire them on worse conditions, such as less pay and reduced benefits. This is a permanent change and different from the temporary measures discussed earlier in this chapter. Ten percent of workers in England and Wales were subject to 'fire-and-rehire' strategies since the start of the first lockdown in March 2020 caused by COVID-19 restrictions, as found by a Trade Union Congress survey, and it is anticipated that this 'bully-boy tactics' used by some organisations will continue unless the government changes regulations. Whether governed by employment regulations or not, using fire-and-rehire strategies for organisational survival should be limited or avoided where possible. Besides the immoral argument presented, the likely negative consequences on the well-being of the semi-survivors reinstated are disastrous and not condoned.

This chaptered discussed various interventions organisations can deploy to limit or prevent redundancies. Unfortunately, for some organisations, there may be no alternative other than to close the doors permanently, and they may have little choice in avoiding redundancies. The next chapter focuses on the legal aspects of implementing redundancies.

References

Ashman, I. 2015. The face-to-face delivery of downsizing decisions in UK public sector organizations: The envoy role. *Public Management Review*, 17, 108–128.

Boyne, G. A. 1998. Bureaucratic theory meets reality: Public choice and service contracting in US local government. *Public Administration Review*, 58(6), 474–484.

Brown, T. L., Potoski, M. & Van Slyke, D. M. 2009. Contracting for complex products. *Journal of Public Administration Research and Theory*, 20, 141–158.

Cascio, W. F. 1993. Downsizing: What do we know? What have we learned? *Academy of Management Perspectives*, 7(1), 95–104.

Cascio, W. F. 2010. Employment downsizing and its alternatives. *SHRM Foundation's Effective Practical Guide Series*. Available: https://www.shrm.org/foundation/ourwork/initiatives/resources-from-past-initiatives/Documents/Employment%20Downsizing.pdf

Cohen, L. & Mallon, M. 1999. The transition from organisational employment to portfolio working: Perceptions of 'boundarylessness'. *Work Employ. Soc*, 13, 329–352.

Damanpour, F., Magelssen, C. & Walker, R. M. 2020. Outsourcing and insourcing of organizational activities: The role of outsourcing process mechanisms. *Public Management Review*, 22, 767–790.

Entwistle, T. 2005. Why are local authorities reluctant to externalise (and do they have good reason)? *Environment and Planning C: Government and Policy*, 23, 191–206.

Flint, D. H. 2003. Downsizing in the public sector: Metro-Toronto's hospitals. *Journal of Health Organization and Management,* 17(6), 438–456.

Glassdoor. 2020. *How to calculate your cost-per-hire* [Online]. Web: Glassdoor for Employers. Available: https://www.glassdoor.co.uk/employers/blog/calculate-cost-per-hire/ [Accessed 8 March 2021].

Hitt, M. A., Keats, B. W., Harback, H. F. & Nixon, R. D. 1994. Rightsizing: Building and maintaining strategic leadership and long-term competitiveness. *Organizational Dynamics,* 23, 18–33.

Kets De Vries, M. F. & Balazs, K. 1997. The downside of downsizing. *Human Relations,* 50, 11–50.

Marler, J. H., Woodard Barringer, M. & Milkovich, G. T. 2002. Boundaryless and traditional contingent employees: Worlds apart. *Journal of Organizational Behavior,* 23, 425–453.

Mclachlan, C. J., Mackenzie, R. & Greenwood, I. 2020. Victims, survivors and the emergence of 'endurers' as a reflection of shifting goals in the management of redeployment. *Human Resource Management Journal,* 31(2), 438–453.

Petzer, M. 2020. Coronavirus and the workforce: How can we limit redundancies? CIPD LAB. Available: https://www.cipd.co.uk/news-views/changing-work-views/future-work/thought-pieces/coronavirus-workforce-redundancies

Tomasko, R. M. 1991. Downsizing: Layoffs and alternatives to layoffs. *Compensation & Benefits Review,* 23, 19–32.

Warner, M. E. & Hefetz, A. 2012. Insourcing and outsourcing: The dynamics of privatization among US municipalities 2002–2007. *Journal of the American Planning Association,* 78, 313–327.

5

THE LEGAL ASPECTS OF REDUNDANCIES

When implementing redundancies, organisations have more than just an ethical role of implementing a programme responsibly to protect the future sustainability of the organisation. The legal aspects of implementation need to be fulfilled to prevent subsequent claims against the organisation and its employees. This chapter is situated within the UK legislation and will explore the legal requirements of implementing redundancies with a focus on the following elements of what constitutes a fair redundancy process:

- statutory definition of redundancy
- redundancy warning and notice
- entitlement to redundancy payment
- individual consultation
- collective consultation
- protective awards
- redundancy selection
- suitable alternative employment

DOI: 10.4324/9781003030416-6

- redundancy and maternity
- redundancy and TUPE transfers.

Statutory definition of redundancy

When looking at the legislation pertaining to redundancies, the first question to satisfy is if the dismissal meets the legal definition of redundancy according to Section 139 Employee Rights Act 1996 (s. 139 ERA).

Redundancy, as demarcated in legalistic interpretation Employment Rights Act, 1996, section 139:1 is defined as a reason for dismissal of an employee attributable wholly or mainly to:

(a)   the fact that the employer has ceased, or intends to cease

    (i)   to carry on the business for the purposes of which the employee was employed by him or

    (ii)   to carry on that business in the place where the employee was so employed or

(b)   the fact that the requirements of that business:

    (i)   for employees to carry out work of a particular kind or

    (ii)   for employees to carry out work of a particular kind in the place where the employee was employed by the employer have ceased or diminished or are expected to cease or diminish.

(Employments Rights Act 1996)

The legal definition of redundancy creates two rights to be considered:

- potentially a reason for fair dismissal
- entitlement to a redundancy payment (subject to meeting qualifying criteria).

To establish if the dismissal qualifies as a redundancy, the following tests should be satisfied:

Was the employee dismissed?

- If so, had the requirements of the business for employees to carry out work of a particular kind ceased or diminished (or did one of the other economic states of affairs in section 139(1) exist)?

- Was the dismissal of the employee caused wholly or mainly by the state of affairs identified above?
- Did changes in an organisation lead to changes in terms or conditions due to a restructure or was it due to a genuine redundancy?

From a legal perspective, it is important to meet the test criteria for what constitutes a redundancy as this definition is used for the purposes of determining whether a redundancy is fair and if the employee is entitlement to a statutory redundancy payment. The Employment Rights Act 1996, section 92 (2)(c) sets out the criteria for redundancy to be a potentially fair reason for dismissal coupled with Employment Rights Act 1996, section 98 (4), which sets out the requirement of the employer to act reasonably, which leads to the second part of the test; was the dismissal fair?

The Employment Rights Act 1996, section 105 dictates that any redundancies related to the following elements will be regarded as automatically unfair and there is no requirement for a qualifying period of service to bring a claim:

- whistleblowing
- asserting a statutory right
- trade union membership or activities
- health and safety activities
- exercise of working time rights.

Redundancy selection will all be regarded as automatically unfair, if the reason included any of the following:

- pregnancy
- maternity leave
- parental leave
- paternity leave
- adoption leave
- shared parental leave
- bereavement leave.

Redundancy warning and notice

Redundancy warning entails the legal responsibility of the employer to provide a 'warning' of impending redundancies as soon as possible with the intention for employees that may be impacted to start exploring alternative income sources. The duty to warn employees is separate to the duty to consult.

A **redundancy notice** is the period of time between when the employer informs employees, they will be made redundant and their last working day.

The length of notice depends on the length of service of each individual. Statutory notice periods are determined as per Table 5.1.

Legally, organisations can require employees to work their notice period, unless contractual clauses state otherwise. Some employers prefer to pay employees for the notice period instead and allow the employee to leave immediately. In this case, the employer should add on the minimum statutory notice period to the employee's service as at the date on which the employment ends. This payment is known as 'pay in lieu of notice' (PILON). PILON payments do not generally include payment for holiday entitlement accrued over the notice period; however, some organisations may decide to include this element within the PILON payment.

CASE LAW:

Rowell v Hubbard Group Services Ltd [1995] IRLR 195 EAT
Publicis Consultants UK Ltd v O'Farrell EAT/0430/10
Williams and others v Compair Maxam Ltd [1982] IRLR 83 EAT

Table 5.1 Redundancy notices based on years of service

Years of service	Notice period	Example
Employment between 1 month and 2 years	1 week	1 year's service = 1 week's notice
Employment between 2 and 12 years	1 week for each completed year served	3 years and 4 months service = 3 weeks' notice
Employment of 12 years or more	12 weeks	14 years' service = 12 weeks' notice

Entitlement to redundancy payment

Section 162 of the Employment Rights Act 1996 states how a redundancy payment is calculated. Some employers offer redundancy payments that may be more generous than the statutory minimum and when calculating redundancy payments in this instance, individual contractual clauses need to be honoured.

If an employee qualifies for redundancy in accordance with the legal definition provided in the beginning of this chapter, they are entitled to a statutory redundancy payment. Employees who have been made redundant only pay tax on payments over £30,000. National Insurance is not deducted from redundancy payments. Redundancy payments are subject to meeting the following criteria:

- qualifying time in employment (minimum of two years)
- employer terminates with/without notice
- fixed-term contract expires and is not renewed subject to no break longer than one week, if not continuous service
- employer's conduct entitled employee to resign with or without notice leading to constructive dismissal.

Redundancy pay is calculated based on the following employee aspects:

- age
- length of continuous service
- current salary.

Redundancy pay entitlement based on age are calculated as per Table 5.2.
What should a redundancy payment include?

- redundancy pay: if the employee has worked for the employer for at least two years
- holiday pay: any unused leave the employee was entitled to take between the start of the leave year and the date of termination, as well as any unpaid holiday taken

Table 5.2 Redundancy pay entitlement based on age

Age	Redundancy pay entitlement
Under 22	Half a week's pay for each full year worked
Between 22 and 41	A week pay for each full year worked
Over 41	One and a half weeks' pay for each full year worked
	A maximum of 20 years' employment can be taken into account

- money owed by the employer, for example, unpaid wages, overtime and commission
- statutory notice pay, subject to the employee working for the organisation for at least one month.

Salary, holiday, bonus, commission and other termination payments other than the redundancy payment are all subject to tax and National Insurance contributions.

Enhanced packages may include additional payments depending on contractual clauses and the organisation's redundancy policy.

If a business has declared itself insolvent, then redundancy pay may be provided by the government, and individuals can submit their claims directly through the following link: www.gov.uk/claim-redundancy.

Continuous service is an area to be cautious of when calculating redundancy payments. Any special leave that was agreed between employer and employee such as sabbaticals could be contentions if clarity were lacking regarding it being a break in employment or recognised as continuous service. If an employee were still 'technically' employed, even if not receiving a monthly wage, a sabbatical could be regarded as continuous service, which may impact the eligibility of redundancy pay, if it falls within the two years of service qualifying period. If, however, there was a break in employment and an employee was offered a new contract with no prior agreement of continuous service, the employment relationship was broken, and the employee may not be entitled to claim redundancy pay.

Individual consultation

In every redundancy situation, there is a legal requirement for meaningful and genuine consultation with individuals. Ensuring this requirement is met, helps to limit potential claims of unfair dismissal. Consultation does not have to end in an agreement between parties; however, it must be carried out with the intention of reaching an agreement and include ways of avoiding or reducing redundancies. Consultation should take place prior to any redundancies being finalised. Meaningful consultation requires organisations to have an open mind and to discuss and give due consideration to employee proposals and concerns. Legally, there is no set timescales for individual consultation; however, many organisations have redundancy policies that include the organisation's approach to individual consultations. Consultation should ideally take place early in the process to demonstrate genuine intend by the organisation to fulfil the needs of meaningful consultation. The minimum consultation period indicated by law is seven days; however, many organisations opt for longer to allow for a fair process. Good practice indicates that a period of 30 days individual consultation tends to demonstrate strong ethical practice by the organisation by allowing sufficient time to find alternative solutions.

Consultation should include the following topics for discussion:

- why the organisation needs to make the proposed changes
- how the organisation intends to make the proposed changes
- what the proposed changes are
- methods of avoiding of limiting redundancies (refer to Chapter 4)
- what the organisation's future skills and experience requirements are
- details of the selection criteria used for selecting employees for redundancy
- employee concerns
- support measures in place for employees at risk of redundancy.

The law only requires one individual meeting to discuss redundancy as part of the consultation process; however, I would advise against this approach for two main reasons. First, it is very hard to demonstrate meaningful consultation and second, to allow the employee to deal with the negative impact as discussed in Chapter 3, the negative impact of redundancies on the workforce.

Best practice suggests that two to three individual consultation meetings are recommended before a final dismissal meeting takes place.

CASE LAW:

Williams and others v Compair Maxam Ltd [1982] IRLR 83 EAT

Collective consultation

For the purposes of determining whether the collective redundancy consultation duty applies, the definition of redundancy under the Trade Union and Labour Relations (Consolidation)(TUL(C)RA) Act 1992, section 195 (1) applies: a "dismissal for a reason not related to the individual concerned", which includes the situation where an employer proposes to dismiss and re-engage employees who do not agree to a proposed variation of their contract.

What to consult about:

Consultation must be meaningful, referring to discussions of how to avoid or reduce dismissals where possible. Consultation should take place 'with a view to reach an agreement' and must be undertaken in 'good time'. Consultation should take place for as long as appropriate to reach agreement or exhaust the possibility of agreement.

An employer proposing to make collective redundancies (more than 20 employees) is required by law to enter meaningful consultation prior to any dismissals occurring and where the following apply:

- The redundancies are in a single establishment.
- The intention is to complete the redundancies within 90 days.

When determining if an organisation's redundancy programme affects one 'establishment', the interpretation is convoluted. A single establishment could be either an entire organisation or a 'distinct entity' within an organisation such as one that:

- functions with its own organisational structure
- is reasonably permanent and stable
- can independently carry out the tasks it is assigned

- manages its own workforce
- has its own equipment and technical means.

Depending on the number of redundancy-related dismissals, the consultation periods applicable are displayed in Table 5.3.

Table 5.3 Consultation period for collective redundancies

Number of redundancies	Consultation period	Minimum consultation before first dismissal
20–99 dismissals at one establishment	90 days	30 days consultation before the first dismissal
100+ dismissals at one establishment	90 days	45 days consultation before the first dismissal

Consultation should take place with 'appropriate' representatives of the affected employees. This could include trade union representatives if relevant. If no union is present, employee representatives should be elected and appointed for the purpose of redundancy consultation. Failure to elect representatives in time, may result in having to consult with the workforce directly. Chapter 9 provides useful guidance on how to elect employee representatives and set up an employee representative committee.

During the consultation period, the employer has the responsibility to provide certain information to the employee representatives which should be in writing. The information does not all have to be available prior to the commencement of consultation nor does it have to be provided all at once. It is, however, important that the information is sufficiently detailed to allow for meaningful consultation to take place. Employers have the duty to respond to reasonable requests for further information.

Information to share with employee representatives should include the following:

- reason for the proposed dismissals
- numbers and categories of employees proposed to be dismissed
- total number of employees in each category employed by the organisation
- proposed method of selecting employees for redundancy
- proposed method of carrying out the dismissals
- proposed method of calculating the amount of any redundancy payments

- number of agency workers and their roles being used by the employer
- copy of the HR1 form.

What to include in calculating the number of redundancies for the purpose of deciding if collective consultation applies:

- count the roles being made redundant (not the people)
- include voluntary redundancies – i.e., if the proposal is to make more than 20 employees redundant, but some of the 20 opt for voluntary redundancy, collective consultation still applies
- include employees that get redeployed (thus include all employees that were at risk of redundancy, even if they remain in the organisation, based on securing suitable alternative roles).

What to exclude in calculating the number of redundancies:

- employees whose fixed-term contract ended at the agreed duration within this period of consultation
- redundancies that are part of a separate/previous redundancy programme.

Deliberately attempting to avoid collective consultation by implementing redundancies in stages over a longer period, should be avoided and is not well received by tribunal judges. Such scenarios could lead to protective awards being paid to claimants.

CASE LAW:

Rockfon A/S v Specialarbejderforbunet i Danmark, acting for Nielsen and others [1996] IRLR 168 ECJ
Usdaw and another v WW Realisation 1 Ltd (in liquidation) and others [2015] IRLR 577 ECJ

Protective awards

Insufficient consultation or sharing of information when 20 or more employees are being made redundant in a 90-day period can lead to protective awards payable to all employees made redundant. Protective awards based on inadequate consultation could include a maximum of 90 days' actual pay per employee. Protective awards would depend on the seriousness of the employer's lack of consultation or failure to inform.

The UK government requires advance notification of redundancies from employers, where it is anticipated that 20 or more employees in a single establishment will be dismissed. Failure to comply with the requirements without good cause, may result in an unlimited or summary conviction. This notice is also known as business, energy and industrial strategy (BEIS) notification.

The redundancy payments service (RPS) collects redundancy information that gets distributed to the appropriate government departments who offer training or job brokering services with the aim to help the employees facing dismissal.

To notify the government, an organisation needs to submit the 'advance notification of redundancies form' known as HR1, available from www.gov.uk/government/publications/redundancy-payments-form-hr1-advance-notification-of-redundancies.

If an organisation has redundancies at different sites, each one is treated separately for notification and consultation purposes. The definition of an establishment relates to the site where an employee is assigned to work. An HR1 form is required for each site where 20 or more redundancies are proposed.

HR1 forms must be submitted at least 30 or 45 days (as per Table 5.3) before the first dismissal and before any individual notices of dismissal are issued.

The employee representatives should also receive a copy of the HR1 form.

If an organisation has already notified the government of about one group of redundancies and additional redundancies are planned, these should be treated as separate events. There is no requirement to add the numbers in the respective groups together to calculate the minimum period for either group.

Redundancy selection

When deciding to implement redundancies, the employer needs to identify roles at risk and determine employees in the 'redundancy pool'. The employer needs to consider all roles that are affected by redundancy to limit any potential unfair dismissal claims.

Selection criteria

For redundancies to be fair, selection criteria need to be appropriately applied.

Selection criteria should be as objective and measurable as far as possible. Criteria used should be agreed following appropriate consultation and will be related to the business requirements and roles that have been identified as at risk of redundancy.

Some selection criteria are automatically unfair. Selecting employees for redundancy based on any of the following reasons are automatically unfair:

- pregnancy, including all reasons relating to maternity
- family, including parental leave, paternity leave (birth and adoption), adoption leave or time off for dependants
- acting as an employee representative
- an employee has been a whistleblower
- acting as a trade union representative
- joining or not joining a trade union
- being a part- or fixed-term employee
- age, disability, gender reassignment, marriage and civil partnership, race, religion or belief, sex and sexual orientation
- pay and working hours, including the working time regulations, annual leave and the national minimum wage.

Selection pools

When determining the selection pool, the employer has wide discretion with a reasonable amount of flexibility. The court tests whether the employer has 'genuinely applied their mind' to the selection of the pool. The employer will need to be able to justify the employees selected in the redundancy pool.

There are potentially two reasons why an employer does not require a redundancy pool:

1. When there is only one employee impacted, such as in the case of a unique role where only one employee fulfils that requirement. (A pool of one employee could be unfair if there were more than one employee doing the same job.)

2.   When the employer is closing the whole business and all roles are subject to redundancy. (If the organisation is closing just a particular site as part of a whole business, consultation may still be required.)

Employers should apply any customary arrangements to the selection pool and when there is no relevant previous history to adopt, consultation should take place in accordance with the criteria set out earlier in this chapter. Determining who should be included in the redundancy pool should include the following factors:

- Consider employees who undertake similar roles in an area that has been identified. Employers can only exclude employees who undertake similar roles, with robust justification for the decision.
- Consider all employees who undertake similar roles even if they operate in a different department of the organisation or work different shifts.
- Consider employees who undertake similar roles at other sites and whether their contracts of employment contain details pertaining to being site-specific, locations of work, distance between sites.
- Consider the likeliness of roles being interchangeable, which means that the pool does not have to be limited to employees undertaking similar work. In other words, when selecting retail cashiers for the redundancy pool, shelve packers can also be included in the pool if their roles are interchangeable.

CASE LAW:

Capita Hartshead Ltd v Byard [2012] IRLR 814 EAT
Blundell Permoglaze Ltd v O'Hagen EAT/540/84

Selection matrix

Once the pool of employees at risk has been identified, using a selection criteria matrix could be a practical and transparent method to use to ensure a fair redundancy procedure. A selection matrix is a scoring system where each employee is allocated a score against a range of criteria. The employees with the lowest scores are selected for redundancy. When choosing the section criteria, employers should ensure that selection criteria are relevant, objective, measurable and applied fairly. The criteria must reflect the requirements of the role and be supported with suitable evidence, i.e., performance reviews, attendance records or disciplinary records.

Cautionary areas

Any criteria used should avoid any bias or subjective factors, such as 'motivation' or 'attitude to work'. Caution should also be taken with any elements that could potentially fall foul of discrimination claims. The employer needs to balance criteria, if used against an employee with absences related to disability, pregnancy, paternity, family-friendly or maternity leave against the requirement not to disadvantage other employees. On this basis, attendance records can still be used, as long as the above-mentioned related absences are discounted. It is recommended that different weightings are given to short- and long-term absences. Absences related to shielding in accordance with the government's coronavirus guidance should also be discounted.

Another area to be cautious of is the inclusion of disciplinary records. If an employer decides to include disciplinary records, ensure warnings were applied consistently. Case law dictates that in certain cases, expired warnings can be used in selection criteria; however, it will depend on individual circumstances. Consider a suitable limit; for example, limit the inclusion of expired warnings to only warnings that have expired in the last 12 months.

Employers can select employees for redundancy based on their length of service, often referred to as 'last in, first out'; however, this should be used with caution and only if the employer can justify this criterion as it could be indirect discrimination if it affects a group of individuals more than another. Relying on length of service as your only selection criteria will most likely be regarded as age discrimination and should be considered as a last resort; for example, it may be practical to include it in tie-breaker scenarios.

The following criteria could be considered for a selection matrix, based on the individual requirements of the role:

- relevant skills
- employee knowledge
- relevant qualifications

- job performance
- suitable experience in the role (excluding length of service)
- timekeeping
- disciplinary record
- absence (excluding, disability, pregnancy, paternity, family-friendly or maternity-related occurrences).

Law dictates that the use of redundancy selection criteria should be part of the consultation process and that employee representatives or union members should be consulted on the criteria used. To demonstrate objectivity and a fair process, it is recommended that the scoring of all criteria used as part of the selection matrix are assessed by two managers independently. Both managers should have direct knowledge of the employee's work performance and access to supporting evidence. Decisions made as part of this process should be justifiable in the event of an appeal. The average score of both managers can then be used as a final score.

A template redundancy policy, Appendix 5.1 and a template redundancy selection matrix, Appendix 5.2 are provided for employers to adapt to their individual needs.

CASE LAW:

Eversheds Legal Services Ltd v de Belin [2011] IRLR 448 EAT
Mayor and Burgesses of the London Borough of Tower Hamlets v Wooster [2009] IRLR 980 EAT
Williams and others v Compair Maxam Ltd [1982] IRLR 83 EAT

Suitable alternative employment

Suitable alternative employment can help limit redundancies as discussed in Chapter 4. Exploring suitable alternative positions before redundancies occur is a requirement of a fair redundancy process. Failure to comply with this requirement could potentially lead to unfair dismissal. The legal framework suggests that the duty of the employer is to 'consider' alternative roles and not necessarily to make every possible effort to find an alternative position. Neither does the employer have to create suitable alternative roles.

Case law dictates a two-part test to establish the suitability of alternative employment offers:

Part 1

Objectively compare the employee's current duties with the duties within the alternative employment offered.

Part 2

What is the reason for the refusal to accept alternative employment, by the employee?

The criterion around both parts are discussed as follows:

To demonstrate a fair process for the contemplation of alternative employment, an employer must undertake a thorough search for alternative employment that must be documented. The duty of seeking suitable alternative roles should commence prior to issuing the redundancy notice and continue until the employee's last day of employment.

Employers should provide all employees at risk or redundancy with a list of current vacancies in the organisation including sufficient details of the role, salary and job responsibilities.

CASE LAW:

Vokes Limited v Bear [1976] IRLR 373
Quinton Hazell Ltd v WC Earl [1976] IRLR 296

Trial periods

Employees accepting alternative employment are entitled to a four-week trial period, subject to the alternative role being substantially different or different in part to the employee's previous role. The duration of the trial period can be extended beyond four weeks if retraining for the new role is applicable and subject to both the employer and the employee agreeing. Such an agreement must be:

- in writing and agreed prior to the commencement of suitable alternative employment
- include the date when training is complete
- be explicit in the terms of employment once training is completed.

Declining the offer of a suitable alternative role

The test to ascertain the reasonableness of refusal of an offer of suitable alternative employment will depend on the 'suitability' of the role offered.

An employee could lose their right to a statutory redundancy payment if they unreasonably decline a role that was deemed suitable.

The following aspects will be considered to determine reasonableness of refusal and suitability of an alternative role:

- whether the employee's skills, competencies, capabilities and experience meet the criteria on the alternative role
- how the new terms offered for the alternative role compare with the previous role, including status, place of work, duties and responsibility, salary and hours of work
- all differences unless insignificant
- consideration for each employment term, respectively
- new terms being more favourable is irrelevant
- ensure a sufficient time period for the employee to consider the alternative role.

Redundancy bumping

Bumping is a legal practice subject to a fair redundancy process. When implementing redundancies, employers may have to consider if bumping is appropriate as part of the process of exploring suitable alternative employment. Employers are, however, not obliged to bump employees.

Bumping occurs where an employee potentially at risk of redundancy is moved into another role, which was occupied by another employee. The employee originally at risk of redundancy thus stayed in the organisation with the employee who was 'bumped' being made redundant. The role of the employee being bumped is usually that of a similar or lower level. Employers should be careful to not make assumptions on behalf of an employee that an alternative role may be too junior or unsuitable.

Bumping has been considered to have a negative impact on employee relations and should receive careful consideration, including:

- whether or not there is a vacancy
- the differences between the two roles
- the difference in remuneration between the two roles
- the length of service of each employee (be cautious of age discrimination)
- the qualification of the employee at risk of redundancy.

Redundancy and maternity leave

All statutory rights during redundancy applies to an employee on maternity leave, including the right to a notice period, fair and meaningful consultation.

Regulation 10 of the Maternity and Parental Leaver regulations dictates that those employees on maternity leave have an automatic right to be offered any suitable alternative roles. The new position must be suitable and appropriate, taking into consideration place of work and other terms and conditions that should not be substantially less favourable that the previous role. The alternative job offer should be in place prior to the employee's existing contract ending and the new contract must commence immediately afterwards. Irrespective of the fact that the employee may not be ready to return to work yet, employers should continue to offer any suitable alternative positions.

If all the above criteria are met, employees on maternity can still be subject to redundancy. Subject to the employee qualifying for statutory maternity pay (SMP) and already in receipt of SMP at the time of being made redundant, SMP should continue to be paid for the 39-week qualifying period. To qualify for SMP, employees must be employed for a minimum of 26 weeks as at the end of the 15th week before the week the baby is due.

CASE LAW:

Mirab v Mentor Graphics (UK) Ltd UKEAT / 0172/17/DA
Lionel Leventhal Ltd v North [2004] UKEAT/0265/04/MAA
Samels v The University of Creative Arts UKEATPA / 0573/10/RN

Redundancy and TUPE transfers

Redundancies can occur as a result of a sale of an organisation (or part of an organisation) to another or due to the loss of a major contract that provided a particular service that your organisation's employees were working on. Related job losses may be classed as redundancies under the Transfer of Undertaking (Protection of Employment) Regulations 2006 (TUPE). If TUPE applies, employees get transferred over to the purchasing organisation or new contractor, retaining their existing terms and conditions or their employment contract with preserved continuity of employment.

Redundancies often occur before and after a TUPE transfer and can be problematic as TUPE regulations dictate that if the principal reason for an employee's dismissal is as a result of a TUPE transfer, the dismissal will automatically be regarded as unfair. The employer's defence for the dismissal is often that of economical, technical or organisational reasons. If dismissal occurs prior to a TUPE transfer and is found to be unfair, the liability transfers to the new businessowner and therefore due diligence should be carefully undertaken by the purchasing employer. TUPE may not be applicable if the businessowner implements redundancies prior to the sale of the organisation and a new buyer is not yet identified. The reason for redundancy-related dismissals in this scenario is that it is not connected to a subsequent TUPE transfer as no new buyer was identified. Although redundancies implemented due to TUPE as the principal reason will automatically be unfair, a valid defence may be offered that the organisation made redundancies not because of a TUPE situation, but because of economic necessity. Previous and new employers can have obligations after a TUPE transfer is completed and redundancies are implemented and thus due to the complications, many organisations prefer to enter into settlement agreements with employees instead, as employment rights are waivered.

It may be the case that employees choose not to transfer over to the new employer, which removes their entitlement to claim for an unfair dismissal or redundancy payment. If, however, redundancies are implemented as a result of a TUPE situation, employees are entitled to the same regulations of a fair redundancy process as detailed throughout this chapter. If an employer is faced with a TUPE transfer situation, a thorough due diligence exercise needs to be undertaken and as a new employer, ensure that there is clarity on the liabilities that are passed on to you. A due diligence exercise consists of a comprehensive investigation into the business that is being acquired and include specific details pertaining to each employee such as:

- profile (gender and age)
- commencement of service date for each employee
- notice periods of each employee
- pension details
- benefits and bonuses
- details of dismissed employees for the past 12 months and reason.

CASE LAW:

Beckmann v Dynamco Whicheloe Macfarlane Ltd [2002] IRLR 578 ECJ
Martin and others v South Bank University [2004] IRLR 74 ECJ

This chapter discusses various legal aspects of implementing redundancies, including cautionary areas for employers to avoid. Employers want to avoid employment tribunal claims where possible by ensuring they comply with legislation. For further advice, please visit www.madeleinestevens.com. This chapter concludes Part I of the book. The next section, Part II, guides employers through the strategy and practical implementation of redundancies.

APPENDIX 5.1
REDUNDANCY POLICY

Table of Contents

1 Policy scope

This policy applies to all circumstances pertaining to redundancies.

2 Introduction

The company is committed to provide a stable working environment and long-term job security for our employees. We therefore endeavour to manage the business with their best interests at heart to ensure long-term sustainability to preserve employment.

However, due to unfortunate circumstances, situations may arise that requires the company to take measures that could result in the reduction of roles in the company, despite our best intentions.

Various factors could impact the financial stability of an organisation: **External factors** such as market crashes, government deregulation, loss of customers, increased competition, lack of orders, etc.; **internal factors** such as organisational redesign, location mergers, outsourcing or relocation, harmonisation after a merger or acquisition, etc.

Redundancy, as demarcated in the UK's legalistic interpretation Employment Rights Act, 1996, section 139:1 is defined as a reason for dismissal of an employee attributable wholly or mainly to:

- Business closure:
  Ceasing or intending to cease to carry on the business for the purposes of which the employee was employed for.
- Workplace closure:
  Ceasing or intending to cease to carry on that business in the place where the employee was so employed (or)
- Reduced requirement for employees:

Having a reduced requirement for employees to carry out work of a particular kind or to do so at the place where the employee was employed to work.

In such circumstances, this redundancy policy will apply, which stipulates the approach, process and support for employees, which may potentially be made redundant. This policy does not form part of your terms and conditions of employment and may be subject to change at the discretion of management. The policy will be applied fairly and equally to all employees without any form of discrimination.

3 Avoiding and/or limiting redundancies

In the event of potential redundancies, the company will explore various measures to limit or avoid redundancies where possible. Possible factors that may be considered, include:

- recruitment freezes
- salary increase freezes
- reducing or limiting agency workers
- reducing or limiting bonus/incentives
- reducing or limiting overtime
- reducing or limiting company benefits.

The company may also actively promote various schemes such as:

- redeployment
- voluntary redundancy
- early retirement
- self-employment
- sabbaticals
- unpaid annual leave
- flexible working
- job sharing
- reduced hours
- temporary lay-offs
- furlough.

4 Redundancy selection

In some situations, such as a company closure or relocation, the whole company or specific location's employees may be impacted. Where the requirement for work is reduced in a specific area or role, a selection pool may be applicable.

Selection pool

If the need arises to reduce roles of a particular kind, there will be a requirement to select employees within this pool for redundancy. This process involves the objective selection of affected employees, which will be given notice of redundancy. The redundancy pool thus consists of employees who carry out work of a similar or the same nature and employees that have roles that may be deemed as interchangeable.

Selection criteria

Once the pool of employees at risk of redundancy have been identified, a selection criteria matrix or interviews may be used to promote a transparent method to ensure a fair redundancy procedure. A selection matrix is a scoring system where each employee is allocated a score against a range of criteria. The employees with the lowest scores are selected for redundancy. When choosing the section criteria, the company will ensure that selection criteria is relevant, objective, measurable and applied fairly. The criteria must reflect the requirements of the role and be supported with suitable evidence, i.e. performance reviews, absence reports or disciplinary records. In cases where selection is used, the following selection criteria may be used:

- job performance
- knowledge
- skills
- qualifications
- work experience
- disciplinary records
- absences
- timekeeping
- length of service.

Criteria used will be agreed following appropriate consultation and will be related to the business requirements and roles that have been identified as at risk of redundancy.

Scoring of all criteria used as part of the selection matrix will be completed by two managers independently. Both managers will have direct knowledge of the employee's work performance and access to supporting evidence. Decisions made as part of this process should be justifiable in the event of an appeal. The average score of both managers will be used as a final score.

Length of service will only be used in a tie break situation when two or more employees achieve the same score.

5 Consultation

The company is committed to meaningful consultation and will therefore ensure that consultation takes place individually with each employee at risk of redundancy. Consultation can take place in person or virtually through online platforms.

Consultation will include the following topics for discussion:

- why the organisation needs to make the proposed changes
- how the organisation intends to make the proposed changes
- what the proposed changes are
- methods of avoiding or limiting redundancies
- what the organisation's future skills and experience requirements are
- details of the selection criteria used for selecting employees for redundancy
- employee concerns
- support measures in place for employees at risk of redundancy.

Individual consultation

Individual consultation will apply in all cases and in addition to collective consultation if this applies.

The company will provide a minimum of three individual consultation meetings with employees at risk of redundancy. The consultations will cover the topics proposed above. The final meeting may result in the decision to dismiss.

Collective consultation

Collective consultation will apply where there are 20 or more proposed dismissals by reason of redundancy at a single establishment within a 90-day period. Consultation periods will apply as follows:

Number of redundancies	Consultation period	Minimum consultation before the first dismissal
20–99 dismissals at one establishment	90 days	30 days consultation before the first dismissal
100+ dismissals at one establishment	90 days	45 days consultation before the first dismissal

6 Representation and consultation

Individual consultation

All employees have the right to be accompanied by a fellow worker, employee representative or trade union official. The company will also consult with you individually in respect of your own particular circumstances, if collective consultation applies.

Collective consultation

The company will consult with nominated/elected employee representatives or recognised trade unions with the aim of reaching an agreement on the topic areas disclosed in Section 5 of this policy.

When there are no employee representatives or union representation present and the company proposes 20 or more redundancies at a single establishment over a 90-day period, the company will instigate a fair process for the election of employee representatives. Representation will be sufficient to ensure all impacted employees are represented.

The company will provide representatives with the following information in writing:

- reason for the proposed dismissals
- numbers and categories of employees proposed to be dismissed

- total number of employees in each category employed by the organisation
- proposed method of selecting employees for redundancy
- proposed method of carrying out the dismissals
- proposed method of calculating the amount of any redundancy payments
- number of agency workers and their roles being used by the employer
- copy of the HR1 form.

Where employees at risk of redundancy fail to elect representatives for the purpose of collective consultation, the company shall provide this information directly to the impacted employees.

7 Alternative employment

Employees at risk of redundancy will be considered for suitable alternative employment within the company as part of the consultation process. The company will provide employees at risk with a list of vacancies. Employees on maternity leave have an automatic right to be offered any suitable alternative roles.

The company will identify and offer suitable alternative position(s) where it exits. Any new positions offered by the company must be suitable and appropriate, taking into consideration the place of work and other terms and conditions that should not be substantially less favourable than the previous role. If the company offers employees at risk of redundancy suitable alternative employment and those who unreasonably refuse to accept it will lose their right to a statutory redundancy payment.

Where it is not possible to identify roles that are deemed as suitable alternative employment, the company may offer positions with less favourable terms to employees at risk of redundancy; however, employees do not have to accept such roles.

Trial periods

Employees accepting alternative employment are entitled to a four-week trial period, subject to the alternative role being substantially different or different in part to the employee's previous role. The duration of the trial period can be extended beyond four weeks if retraining for the new role is applicable and subject to both the employer and the employee agreeing.

The agreement must be:

- in writing and agreed before the suitable alternative employment commences
- include the date when training will be completed
- be explicit in the terms of employment once training is completed.

8 Time off work

The company recognises the pressure of finding a new job or source of income associated with redundancy situations. Employees at risk of redundancy will therefore be granted with a reasonable amount of paid time off work, which will amount to a maximum of [5] working days to attend interviews or apply for alternative work. Any such arrangements must be made in agreement with the employee's line manager.

9 Notice of redundancy

If an employee's selection for redundancy is confirmed, they will be given written notice of the termination of employment in accordance with the notice period set out in their contract of employment or the statutory minimum notice period, whichever is greater.

10 Pay in Lieu of Notice

The company may choose to pay an employee for their notice, when a decision is made to dismiss for the reason of redundancy. This is called 'Pay in Lieu of Notice' (PILON). When paying PILON, the company will pay the equivalent value of the notice period in lieu or the minimum statutory notice, whichever is greater. A PILON payment is not pensionable.

11 Redundancy payment

Employees who are facing dismissal by reason of redundancy, will be eligible to receive a redundancy payment, subject to having had at least two years of continuous service with the company. The redundancy payment will be calculated in accordance with the relevant statutory redundancy pay regulations. Redundancy calculations based on age are calculated as follows:

Age	Redundancy pay entitlement
Under 22	Half a week's pay for each full year worked
Between 22 and 41	A week's pay for each full year worked
Over 41	One and a half week's pay for each full year worked
	A maximum of 20 years' employment can be taken into account

Employees will receive a written statement showing how their redundancy pay has been calculated.

or

[We offer an enhanced redundancy payment, which includes any entitlement to statutory redundancy pay. Details include the following aspects:]

Redundancy payment under £30,000 is not taxable. Tax and National Insurance contributions will be deducted from wages or any other benefits such as holiday pay applicable.

12 Redundancy support

The company understand that redundancy situations can be very distressing for employees. As such, the company [offers to support employees by finding alternative employment outside the organisation] and or [the company is willing to provide the following elements of support: List the details:]

Any concerns about well-being can be raised to [name/line manager/ HR contact]. Alternative internal help is available through [the employee counselling scheme/employee helplines/intranet material].

13 Voluntary redundancy

Depending on the suitability of the redundancy programme, the company may choose to offer invitations for voluntary redundancy applications with the aim of reducing the requirement for compulsory redundancies. In such circumstances, the voluntary redundancy process will apply, which will be communicated alongside this policy. The use of voluntary redundancies are subject to management discretion.

14 Employees absent from work

Employees may be selected for redundancy if they are not currently in work, subject to their contract of employment being active. The redundancy policy will continue to apply to them. Possible reasons for absence may be:

- sick leave
- annual leave
- unpaid leave
- delegations
- military or public service leave
- maternity
- suspension
- sabbaticals.

15 Right of appeal

Employees that are dismissed by reason of redundancy have the right to appeal the company's decision.

The notice of redundancy letter will contain details on how to appeal any decisions. The outcome of the appeal will be final and there will be no further rights to appeal.

16 Policy status

This policy does not form part of employees' contracts of employment and may be amended at any time.

17 Data protection

The company processes personal data, including special categories of employee data, in accordance with the company's data protection policy at all stages of the redundancy process.

APPENDIX 5.2
REDUNDANCY SELECTION
MATRIX

Name of employee

Job role

Department

1st Assessment manager

Assessment date

2nd Assessment manager

Assessment date

Time frame of assessment

HR

Date of HR sign off

How to use this matrix:

This redundancy matrix should be completed by two managers independently. Both managers should have direct knowledge of the employee's work performance and access to supporting evidence. Decisions made as part of this process should be justifiable in the event of an appeal. Any differences should be captured in the final notes with a rationale of score changes if relevant. The average score of both managers will be used as a final score. HR should support managers to provide clarity of how to use matrix and to sign off final score.

1 Job performance

Use job performance as a criterion subject to all employees in the redundancy pool being assessed equally. Supporting evidence of previous performance reviews are required. If an employee has been absent for a substantial period of time, it may be necessary to extend the time frame to consider job performance before and after the period of absence.

Definition	Score 1	Score 2
Meets and exceeds performance targets	5	5
Meets performance targets most of the time	4	4
Meets performance targets for more than half of the time	3	3
Fails to meet performance targets for more than half of the time	2	2
Fails to meet performance targets	0	0

1st Assessor's comments

2nd Assessor's comments

2 Knowledge

Assessment of knowledge should be based on the specific requirements of the role as specified in the job description.

Definition	Score 1	Score 2
Displays the full range of knowledge required for the role	5	5
Displays the core knowledge required for the role	4	4
Displays some of the required knowledge with knowledge gaps identified	3	3
Displays limited knowledge specific to the role	2	2
Has insufficient knowledge to meet the requirements of the role	0	0

1st Assessor's comments

2nd Assessor's comments

3 Skills

Assessment of skills should be based on the specific requirements of the role as specified in the job description.

Definition	Score 1	Score 2
Displays the full range of skills required for the role	5	5
Displays the core skills required for the role	4	4
Displays some of the required skills, with skill gaps identified	3	3
Displays limited skills specific to the role	2	2
Has insufficient skills to meet the requirements of the role	0	0

1st Assessor's comments

2nd Assessor's comments

4 Qualifications

Assessment of qualifications should be based on the specific requirements of the role as specified in the job description. Qualifications or equivalent should be used to complete this assessment.

Definition	Score 1	Score 2
Fully qualified or equivalent as per the requirements for the role	5	5
Part qualified and actively working towards full qualification	4	4
Part qualified and not actively working towards completion of full qualification	3	3
Not qualified or part qualified and working towards qualification	2	2
Unqualified	0	0

1st Assessor's comments

2nd Assessor's comments

5 Experience

Assessment of experience should reflect the depth and breadth of experience that is directly related to the requirements of the role. Caution should be exercised to avoid any time frames that may be subject to age discrimination.

Definition	Score 1	Score 2
Has broad and varied experience specific to the requirements for the role	5	5
Has a good range of experience specific to the requirements of the role	4	4
Has some good experience with identifiable gaps for the requirements of the role	3	3
Has limited experience in relation to the role	2	2
Has no previous experience of the job role	0	0

1st Assessor's comments

2nd Assessor's comments

6 Disciplinary records

Assessment of disciplinary records should include active warnings that are no older than 12 months. The scoring of this criterion is different from that of previous methods as the scores are totalled.

Definition	Score 1	Score 2
Current final written warning	−5	−5
Current written warning	−4	−4
Current verbal warning	−3	−3
No previous warnings	0	0

1st Assessor's comments

2nd Assessor's comments

7 Absences

Assessment of absences should only relate to the previous 12 months. Any absences related to disability, pregnancy, maternity, paternity, adoption leave, parental leave, paternity leave, bereavement leave or shielding in accordance with COVID-19 guidance should be discounted. The scoring of this criterion is different from that of previous methods as the scores of a long- and short-term absence can be totalled. Short absences can only be counted once.

Definition	Score 1	Score 2
More than 3 absences totalling 15 days or more in the past 12 months	−5	−5
1–3 absences totalling less than 10 days in the past 12 months	−4	−4
1 absence of more than 4 weeks or more in the past 12 months	−4	−4
1–3 absences totalling less than 5 days in the past 12 months	−2	−2
No absences	0	0

1st Assessor's comments

2nd Assessor's comments

8 Timekeeping

Assessment of timekeeping should only relate to the previous 12 months. Timekeeping can include being on time for meetings, customer appointments, training sessions, etc. and is not limited to the start of the working day. In addition, the same principles apply for leaving appointments, meetings or the working day before the scheduled end time. Any incidents related to disability, pregnancy, maternity, paternity, adoption leave, parental leave, paternity leave, bereavement leave or shielding in accordance with COVID-19 guidance should be discounted.

Definition	Score 1	Score 2
Persistently late within the previous 12 months	−5	−5
Frequently late (more than 12 occasions) within the previous 12 months	−4	−4
Occasionally late (fewer than 12 occasions) within the previous 12 months	−3	−3
Rarely late (fewer than six occasions) within the previous 12 months	−2	−2
Never late within the previous 12 months	0	0

1st Assessor's comments

2nd Assessor's comments

Redundancy selection matrix summary scores

Criterion	Weighting	Assessor 1	Assessor 2	Calibrated score	Weighted score
1. Job performance					
2. Knowledge					
3. Skills					
4. Qualifications					
5. Experience					
6. Disciplinary records					
7. Absences					
8. Timekeeping					
9. Length of service[a]					
Total score					

a   Length of service should only be used in a tie break situation when two or more employees achieve the same score.

HR moderation date

HR professional

Date communicated

Communication manager

Comments from employee

Further action identified

Part II

RE-ORGANISE

Redundancy implementation: Planning and strategy

6

A REVIEW OF REDUNDANCY-INCORPORATING STRATEGIES

This chapter provides a review of existing strategies that incorporate redundancies including:

- asset reduction strategy
- convergence strategy
- reorientation strategy
- workforce reduction strategy
- work redesign strategy
- downscaling
- systematic strategy
- reallocation strategy.

Despite the various pitfalls identified in Part I of this book, the implementation of redundancy programmes is still a popular strategy to help organisations through recessions and to boost economic survival. Continuous recessions, such as the most recent global recession caused by COVID-19

DOI: 10.4324/9781003030416-8

restrictions, negatively impact business activities that necessitate the need for strategic intervention. When an organisation gets to the point where they believe implementing redundancies are the only option to ensure a sustainable future business, there are various factors to be considered when choosing the right and the best strategy for the future, consisting of three key elements of the organisation's status such as resource, investment and activity (de los Monteros and Bravo, 2012). There are various strategies that can be deployed as part of a redundancy strategy; some include values and organisational objectives, whereas others are tactical in nature. It is thus not surprising that many organisations combine strategies to get the best outcomes based on the organisation's needs. Strategies discussed here are mutually exclusive.

Asset reduction strategy

Asset reduction is a combination of a reduction in workforce combined with the change in the scale of assets (Morris et al., 1999, Cascio, 2002). The classification of asset reduction entails various other reductions such as financial, physical, organisational resources and the workforce (Morrow, 2003). The overall objective of an asset reduction strategy is to limit organisational growth to a level that is lower than the organisation's property, plant and equipment depreciation rate by shrinking the inventory (Pearce II and Robbins, 1993). The reduction in workforce is thus carefully aligned with the change in the assets. Some organisations only deploy the element of reducing assets, whilst maintaining employee numbers whereas others prefer a reduction in workforce instead and an increase in assets. Careful assessment of the relationship balance between asset management and workforce requirements is thus necessary before this strategy is deployed. Where the implementation of automation drives the requirement for less personnel, asset turnover may be reduced (De Meuse et al., 1994). Asset reduction strategy is most likely to achieve economic organisational improvement combined with enhanced overall organisational effectiveness, when the right combination of a reduction in physical and personnel assets are implemented with a focus on strengths (Sheaffer et al., 2009).

Convergence strategy

Convergence strategy (Tushman and Romanelli, 1985) draws from models of organisational change, which maintains that organisations go through various changes in stability (Freeman and Cameron, 1993). Convergence is the refinement of the organisation's vision, mission, structure and strategy (Freeman and Cameron, 1993, Appelbaum et al., 1999). A convergence strategy aims to harmonise the organisation's strategy with its activities through a radical change process (Tushman and Romanelli, 1985). This strategy typically denotes a longer period of change and the responsibility to implement, typically rests with middle management (Freeman and Cameron, 1993). Convergence is often more associated with incremental workforce reductions of a less severe nature, aimed at reinforcement of the organisation's existing mission, strategy and structure through a process of continuous organisational improvement. This approach is seen in large organisations such as General Electric where work processes are reviewed and streamlined continuously, which may result in work elimination and cost-cutting by requiring less employees.

Reorientation strategy

Reorientation strategy (Tushman and Romanelli, 1985) is similar to convergence strategy in the sense that it aims to redefine an organisation's vision, strategy, structure and processes (Appelbaum et al., 1999); however, it differs from convergence strategy as the period of change is short-lived and discontinuous (Freeman and Cameron, 1993). An organisation's mission is also likely to be revisited based on environmental changes. Reorientation strategy is typically associated with corrective action, brought on by poor past performance (Appelbaum et al., 1999).

A further distinction to convergence strategy is that the responsibility of implementing change rests with senior management with a rapid change in structure, strategy and control systems (Freeman and Cameron, 1993).

Workforce reduction strategy

This strategy focuses specifically on reducing the number of employees and includes various sub-strategies for workforce reduction such as the use of early retirements, dismissals, transfers and settlement agreements (Cameron, 1994). The drivers of the workforce reductions may directly influence how the strategy is deployed by the organisation. Typically, a workforce reduction strategy is reactive in nature, used in response to the declining market, recession or a crisis (Dewitt, 1998).

The main objective is to reduce headcount quickly with the intention to reap cost-saving rewards on a short-term basis. Implementing workforce reductions as a knee-jerk reaction without careful planning will inhibit the long-term adaptability of the organisation (Cameron, 1994) and should thus be avoided where possible. Reducing the workforce alone without addressing other organisational elements, such as management behaviour, products and operations, is unlikely to be successful in isolation.

Work redesign strategy

This strategy also known as 'downscoping' or 're-focusing' places emphasis on reducing the overall scope of the organisation's activity through a combination of vertical and horizontal differentiation (Johnson, 1996). Work redesign strategy depicts that instead of just reducing the workforce, the work demand is reduced accordingly by eliminating functions, products, groups and hierarchical levels (Cameron, 1994). These objectives are achieved over a longer period of time as more comprehensive planning and analysis are required to implement strategic changes, including the redesigning of tasks, merging of functions and reduction in working hours. This strategy is effective in reducing the negative impact on employees as the careful planning required allows that the changes implemented consider work processes and organisational arrangements, protecting employees from work overload or burnout (Cameron, 1994). 'Downscoping' may be an effective strategy when an organisation has a wide field with limited recent investment in capacity (de los Monteros and Bravo, 2012).

Downscaling

Downscaling is a strategy that proposes that the activities in the organisation maintain, however, that the output is reduced to suit demand. Subsequently, human and physical resources are reduced to adapt to demand cycles (Kotler, 1965). Downscaling typically involves the removal of large factories when there is a fall in demand (de los Monteros and Bravo, 2012). This strategy may therefore incorporate other strategies such as workforce reduction and work redesign strategies.

Systematic strategy

This strategy focuses on the bigger picture of organisational success by combining a reduction of the work and the workforce whilst also focusing on addressing the organisation's culture, values and attitudes (Cameron, 1994). The driver is continuous improvement as an ongoing process, rather than a specific programme that takes place as a long-term strategy that is normally proactive in nature. As the name suggests, this strategy addresses the whole organisation as a 'system' including elements such as suppliers, portfolios, production methods, design processes, sales and marketing and customer relationships (Cameron, 1994). During an organisational change situation, it may be necessary for the organisation to restructure itself more around its core purpose, which may lead to the rationalisation, divestment or closure of operations, functions, product line or assets that are no longer appropriate for the business (O'Neill, 1986). Schoenberg et al. (2013) support the systems theory by arguing that when implementing turnaround strategies, it is important to note that changing systems and structures is not enough to succeed; the behaviour and attitudes of the employees also need to change. This strategy focuses on enhancing operational efficiency and productivity by simplification. Typical areas targeted for reduction are:

- response times
- number of suppliers
- rules and regulations
- invisible costs

- reworks/repairs
- incompatibility of systems (Cameron, 1994).

The culture of the 'systematic strategy' is thus to harness the organisation's employees to help generate and implement ideas for cost savings. Based on Part I of this book, where the negative impact of workforce reductions was explored along with the unlikely success of redundancy programmes, a systematic strategy is well placed to keep employees engaged during a change programme.

Cost-containment strategy

This strategy is also referred to as 'retrenchment', 'cost reduction' or 'cost efficiencies'. The objective of this strategy is to improve organisational productivity through the process of product concentration, reengineering of processes and eliminating redundant work (Freeman and Cameron, 1993). For most organisations facing financial crisis, the reduction of costs on a short-term basis is tempting to improve cash flow as quickly as possible (Sudarsanam and Lai, 2001). Often labelled 'quick wins', 'belt-tightening' or 'firefighting', these strategies of cost efficiency are frequently the first step organisations adopt during a time of economic instability (Schoenberg et al., 2013). The key to success is a balance of reduction between human and physical resources. In a study where 300 redundancy programmes were reviewed, the findings indicated that typically where the focus was on cost-cutting alone, there was no sustained improvement, whilst the companies that had a managerial focus on increasing productivity and/ or restructuring showed an improvement in the organisation's financial performance (Kabanoff et al., 2000). Cameron et al. (1991) state that redundancy programmes are more likely to be successful if the organisation looks at reducing other elements as well, such as unnecessary products, rather than just the people. Literature supports this by demonstrating that implementing a combination of strategies such as a focus on the firm's core activities (Boyne and Meier, 2009) and cost efficiencies, typically referred to as 'belt-tightening' with the aim to gain 'quick wins' to stabilise the business in the short term (Sudarsanam and Lai, 2001) has proven to result in a positive change. Some literature explores alternative strategies employed by businesses to achieve cost savings such as the one found by Schoenberg et al. (2013) who reviewed 22 empirical studies investigating business turnaround situations and found the most prolific strategy deployed is that of cost orientation with the aim to obtain a quick impact to stabilise finances. Other popular cost-reduction strategies in literature include reducing research and development, optimising accounts receivable, reducing inventory, stretching accounts payable, reducing marketing activity and pay freezes (Hofer, 1980, Hambrick and Schecter, 1983, Stopford and Baden-Fuller, 1990, Sudarsanam and Lai, 2001). In addition, a cost-saving strategy should include reducing productions costs and overheads as well as streamlining processes (Grinyer et al., 1990).

Whilst cost-saving may be achieved by reducing the wage bill and associated overheads, processes should be put in place to contain expenditure, which could include a review of the employee expenses policy and policies for authorising large purchases with a signature approvals process. Transaction processing and information systems are also reviewed to align with the overall savings targets (Cameron et al., 1991).

This strategy may be best suited when an organisation has not invested in the product or capacity and attempts to take advantage of operating at maximum capacity (de los Monteros and Bravo, 2012).

Reallocation strategy

To limit the negative impact of redundancies on future organisational performance, a reallocation strategy can be very effective if used in conjunction with some of the above-mentioned strategies. A reallocation strategy proposes the use of implementation approaches that focus on reducing the 'least valuable' employees (Nixon et al., 2004). This involves making selection decisions specific to which departments and areas to reduce staff in (Ludwig, 1993) and that management should focus on retaining high performers (Mone, 1994). The argument that headcount reductions can be successful if the exercise encourages the least valuable employees to leave, which can be achieved by management using existing knowledge, such as knowledge of employee commitment, satisfaction, absenteeism and turnover intention to guide their redundancy programmes towards a more productive outcome is supported in the literature (Cross and Travaglione, 2004).

There are two levels of reallocation: low and high. Low reallocation proposes a shallow, across-the-board reduction, reducing personnel in equal percentages whereas high reallocation suggests focused, selective and deep reductions in specific areas of the organisation (Nixon et al., 2004). Low reallocation strategies are shown to be largely ineffective due to indiscriminate reductions of where it is needed and not needed (Flint, 2003). Further evidence indicates that across-the-board reduction strategies are prone to organisation's losing their best talent (Cascio, 1993). Implementing across-the-board strategies may have a benefit in 'sharing the pain' mindset; however, it causes damage to the future sustainability of specific functions, which is likely to lead to replacement of employees due to a lack of skills and thus overall counterproductive (Hitt et al., 1994).

This chapter explored various strategies that involves or supports redundancy implementation. Some strategies incorporate multiple dimensions, whilst others can be combined to achieve the ideal outcome for the organisation. Ultimately, the right strategy for an organisation will depend on their individual circumstances. The next chapter will focus on the practical aspects of strategic redundancy implementation.

References

Appelbaum, S. H., Close, T. G. & Klasa, S. 1999. Downsizing: An examination of some successes and more failures. *Management Decision*, 37(5), 424–37.

Boyne, G. A. & Meier, K. J. 2009. Environmental change, human resources and organizational turnaround. *Journal of Management Studies*, 46, 835–863.

Cameron, K. S. 1994. Strategies for successful organizational downsizing. *Human Resource Management*, 33, 189–211.

Cameron, K. S., Freeman, S. J. & Mishra, A. K. 1991. Best practices in white-collar downsizing: Managing contradictions. *Academy of Management Perspectives*, 5, 57–73.

Cascio, W. F. 1993. Downsizing: What do we know? What have we learned? *Academy of Management Perspectives*, 7, 95–104.

Cascio, W. F. 2002. Strategies for responsible restructuring. *Academy of Management Perspectives*, 16, 80–91.

Cross, B. & Travaglione, A. 2004. The times they are a-changing: Who will stay and who will go in a downsizing organization? *Personnel Review*, 33(3), 275–290.

De Los Monteros, H. D. E. & Bravo, C. S. 2012. Case study: Downsizing strategy influence on the structure of the firm. *Management: Journal of Contemporary Management Issues*, 17, 75–92.

De Meuse, K. P., Vanderheiden, P. A. & Bergmann, T. J. 1994. Announced layoffs: Their effect on corporate financial performance. *Human Resource Management*, 33, 509–530.

Dewitt, R. L. 1998. Firm, industry, and strategy influences on choice of downsizing approach. *Strategic Management Journal*, 19, 59–79.

Flint, D. H. 2003. Downsizing in the public sector: Metro-Toronto's hospitals. *Journal of Health Organization and Management*, 17(6), 438–456.

Freeman, S. J. & Cameron, K. S. 1993. Organizational downsizing: A convergence and reorientation framework. *Organization Science*, 4, 10–29.

Grinyer, P. H., Mayes, D. & Mckiernan, P. 1990. The sharpbenders: Achieving a sustained improvement in performance. *Long Range Planning*, 23, 116–125.

Hambrick, D. C. & Schecter, S. M. 1983. Turaround strategies for mature industrial-product business units. *Academy of managment Journal*, 26, 231–248.

Hitt, M. A., Keats, B. W., Harback, H. F. & Nixon, R. D. 1994. Rightsizing: Building and maintaining strategic leadership and long-term competitiveness. *Organizational Dynamics*, 23, 18–33.

Hofer, C. W. 1980. Turnaround strategies. *Journal of Business Strategy*, 1(1), 19–31.

Johnson, R. A. 1996. Antecedents and outcomes of corporate refocusing. *Journal of Management*, 22, 439–483.

Kabanoff, B., Brown, S. & Palmer, I. 2000. *Financial consequences of downsizing and the role of managerial attention*. Brisbane: Queensland University of Technology.

Kotler, P. 1965. Phasing out weak products. *Harvard Business Review*, 43(2), 107–119.

Ludwig, D. C. 1993. Adapting to a declining environment: Lessons from a religious order. *Organization Science*, 4, 41–56.

Mone, M. A. 1994. Relationships between self-concepts, aspirations, emotional responses, and intent to leave a downsizing organization. *Human Resource Management*, 33, 281–298.

Morris, J. R., Cascio, W. E. & Young, C. E. 1999. Downsizing after all these years: Questions and answers about who did it, how many did it, and who benefited from it. *Organizational Dynamics*, 27, 78–87.

Morrow, I. J. 2003. Responsible restructuring: Creative and profitable alternatives to layoffs. *Personnel Psychology*, 56, 788.

Nixon, R. D., Hitt, M. A., Lee, H. U. & Jeong, E. 2004. Market reactions to announcements of corporate downsizing actions and implementation strategies. *Strategic Management Journal*, 25, 1121–1129.

O'neill, H. M. 1986. An analysis of the turnaround strategy in commercial banking. *Journal of Management Studies*, 23, 165–188.

Pearce II, J. A. & Robbins, K. 1993. Toward improved theory and research on business turnaround. *Journal of Management*, 19, 613–636.

Schoenberg, R., Collier, N. & Bowman, C. 2013. Strategies for business turnaround and recovery: A review and synthesis. *European Business Review*, 25(3), 243–262.

Sheaffer, Z., Carmeli, A., Steiner-Revivo, M. & Zionit, S. 2009. Downsizing strategies and organizational performance: A longitudinal study. *Management Decision*, 47(6), 950–974.

Stopford, J. M. & Baden-Fuller, C. 1990. Flexible strategies: The key to success in knitwear. *Long Range Planning*, 23, 56–62.

Sudarsanam, S. & Lai, J. 2001. Corporate financial distress and turnaround strategies: An empirical analysis. *British Journal of Management*, 12, 183–199.

Tushman, M. L. & Romanelli, E. 1985. Organizational evolution: A metamorphosis model of convergence and reorientation. *Research in Organizational Behavior*, 7, 171–222.

7

STRATEGIC REDUNDANCY IMPLEMENTATION

The previous chapter reviewed the existing literature with regard to redundancy implementation that may influence how an organisation wishes to approach this unpleasant task. The planning and preparation stages prior to redundancy implementation are critical to ensure the aims and objectives of the redundancy programme is met. This chapter continues to build on Re-Focus and introduces the Re-Organise element of the Re-Focus, Re-Organise and Re-Build (RRR) strategy that incorporates the key aspects of planning and analysis, fairness and justice and preparing management for redundancy implementation through management training. This chapter incorporates 20 template examples that can be tailored to the employers' specific requirements to support the redundancy process. The RRR strategy is expanded on by including best practise recommendations, defining organisational goals, cost containment, planning and analysis, management training and people impact strategy. This chapter concludes with an assessment of the use of voluntary redundancies and settlement agreements.

DOI: 10.4324/9781003030416-9

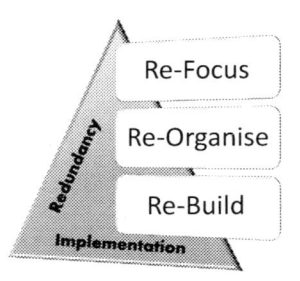

Figure 7.1 Redundancy implementation strategy: Re-Focus, Re-Organise and Re-Build.

Based on the discussions from the previous chapters and my own findings (Petzer, 2019), the recommended strategy for redundancy implementation includes three key stages: Re-Focus, Re-Organise and Re-Build (RRR) as per Figure 7.1.

Part I underpinned our understanding to 'Re-Focus' the organisation. The objectives of this strategy are to help organisations achieve their intended objectives of implementing redundancies such as cost savings and improved productivity, whilst minimising the negative impact on the workforce. The strategy incorporates eight key stages of implementation as per Figure 7.2.

RRR strategy stage 1: defining the organisational goals

One of the biggest mistakes' employers make when it comes to the implementation of redundancy programmes is that senior management decides that redundancies are needed and then 'the buck is passed' to HR and middle management to implement. A successful redundancy programme should be a marriage between the business, its operations, products and services with HR and the decision on how, where and when to reduce headcount should not be taken in isolation (Petzer, 2019).

Regardless of whether organisations need to adopt a proactive or reactive strategy for reducing headcount, the opportunity for future improvement should be carefully considered. To drive the 'Re-Focus' dimension, the organisation's mission, vision, values and culture should be revisited with a clear alignment to the organisation's strategic goals. Re-focusing on the strategic goals may also be necessary at this point.

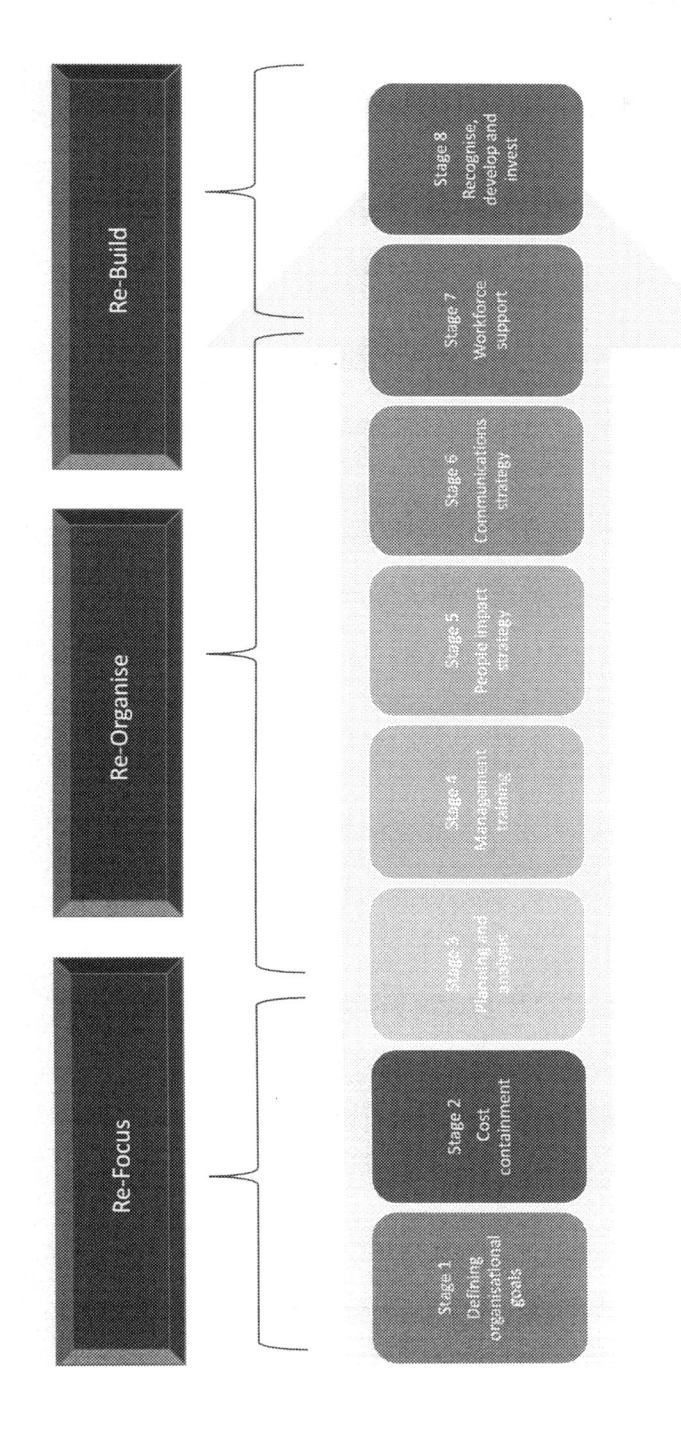

Re-Focus

Re-Organise

Re-Build

Stage 1
Defining organisational goals

Stage 2
Cost containment

Stage 3
Planning and analysis

Stage 4
Management training

Stage 5
People impact strategy

Stage 6
Communications strategy

Stage 7
Workforce support

Stage 8
Recognise, develop and invest

Figure 7.2 Eight stages of redundancy implementation.

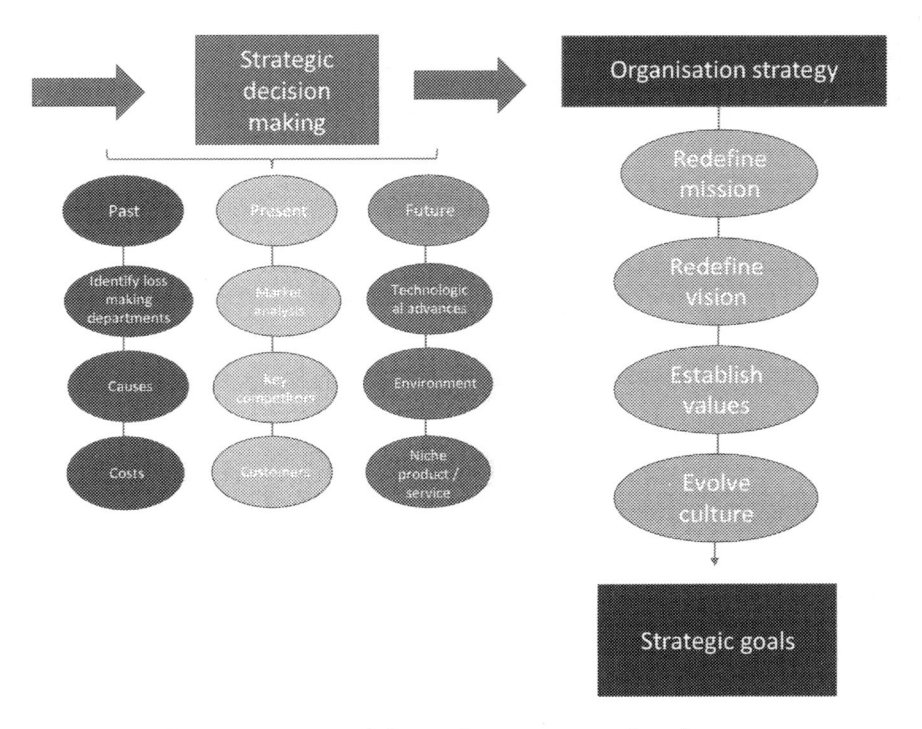

Figure 7.3 RRR strategy stage 1: defining the organisational goals.

Organisations can undertake this strategic decision-making process through a management workshop that involves the senior management team and any other strategic roles that may influence the outcome of the organisation's strategic goals. Figure 7.3 provides a visual overview of 'defining organisational goals'.

The workshop should start with an overview of the past; identifying the areas of loss, the causes and the costs associated with the losses. The next step is to move to the present, which should include up-to-date, comprehensive market analysis that provides a clear understanding of who the key competitors and the organisation's current customers are. Understanding how macro- and micro-environments, external markets and competitors can impact organisational success is critical for the organisation before they decide how they operate, where they focus their services and products within the market. Once the past and present are clearly understood, the next part of the workshop should focus on the future. Organisations should assess the current and future markets, products and customers that will reap the greatest profits for the organisation and redesign and align the workforce with the necessary skills around the findings. There are various tools available to help understand the market such as strengths, weaknesses, opportunities and threats (SWOT), political, economic, technological, legal and environmental (PESTLE) and social, technological, economic, environmental, political, legal and ethical (STEEEPLE) (Farnham and Pimlott, 1995).

In establishing organisational goals, it is important to understand the key focus of the organisation's core functions to ensure the future competitiveness and sustainability of the organisation in advance of any reductions in the workforce. If the core functions are not clearly established, organisations may not know in which areas it is best to reduce the workforce. Subsequently, poor and uninformed decision-making could lead to a loss of talented, skilled and valued employees as discussed earlier. Understanding these factors may require the organisation to undertake a combination of strategies such as a restructure of the workforce to align itself more appropriately with its core purpose and/or an asset retrenchment strategy to divest or eliminate assets that are no longer suited to the organisations' revisited strategic goals (O'Neill, 1986). Employers should also identify potential technological advances and how this may impact the organisation, including a view of the anticipated future economic market. Based on this knowledge, be clear on what the present and future niche products and services are that the organisation wants to focus on. Identification of where the biggest margins and profits are to be gained should also be established. To help plan and facilitate this management workshop, Appendix 7.1 provides an example agenda for a two-day workshop that can be tailored to the specific needs of the organisation, entitled 'Management Workshop Re-Focus Organisational Goals'.

An important benefit of the strategic decision-making workshop is that management buy-in is gained, with the key management team members obtaining a clear understanding of the financial pressures of the organisation and why redundancies are required. Chapter 3 highlighted that one of the key stressors for management during redundancy implementation is not understanding the business rationale for the decision. Involving the management team through the strategic decision-making process is thus mutually beneficial as a more informed decision is taken by the organisation about the present and future and the management team members have a clear understanding of where the organisation is heading with an opportunity to actively contribute to the future sustainability. Having this knowledge and understanding will provide management with the benefit of authenticity when they get to the stage of announcing redundancies.

RRR strategy stage 2: cost containment

The second stage, cost containment will draw on the knowledge gained from Chapter 4. It may be that some of the cost-containment strategies were already deployed before the organisation got to this stage, for example, saving costs on changing suppliers. Before announcing redundancies, the organisation has a moral and legal obligation to fully explore options to save costs with the ultimate aim to reduce or avoid redundancies. There are two main perspectives of cost containment: first, addressing operational cost savings and second, various initiatives to agree on reducing the wage bill as proposed in Figure 7.4.

Many of the proposals involving pay cuts could be part of employee's terms and conditions and will require as discussed in Chapter 5. Reducing cost through offering early retirement promotions and reducing contractors are strategies that can be considered and planned for at this stage; however, these should be clearly linked to the consultation process bearing in mind the risks identified in Chapter 4.

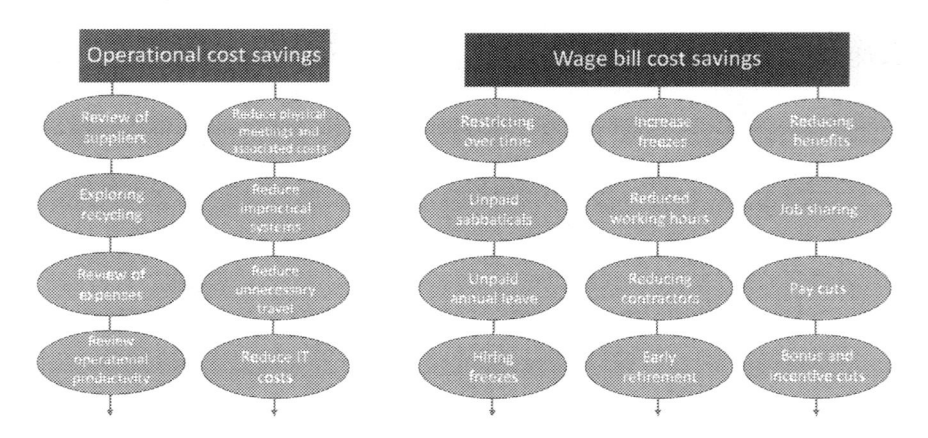

Figure 7.4 RRR strategy stage 2: cost containment.

Appendix 7.2 provides an example to populate for the analysis of contractors, which also need to be shared with employee representatives as part of the consultation process.

Appendix 7.3 provides an example for HR to populate the age demographics of an organisation's workforce, which could provide a useful overview when determining if early retirement promotions are the right decisions for the organisation. This data will also be helpful in determining the requirements of running workshops on managing pensions and early retirements at a later stage in the redundancy implementation.

RRR strategy stage 3: planning and analysis

When implementing redundancies, employers need to consider the organisational impact on a broader basis, which may include the streamlining of functions, systems redesign and fine-tuning the polices aimed at cutting costs (De Meuse et al., 1994). To achieve this, as with any significant organisational change programme, a proper plan needs to be put in place in advance of implementation that involves all the key stakeholders.

Literature highlights unequivocally the importance of effective planning and comprehensive analysis to allow for the successful implementation of redundancies (Cameron, 1994, Appelbaum et al., 1999, Freeman, 1999, Gandolfi, 2013). Literature also suggests that with proper planning, redundancies can be strategically beneficial for the future of the organisation (Clark and Koonce, 1995). Careful planning allows for a responsible approach with regards to how employees are selected for redundancy and allows for directors and managers to be involved and take ownership of the process.

A good plan should include the following aspects:

- clearly defined desired outcomes
- alignment with organisational goals
- workforce skills analysis
- robust project plan
- ensuring fairness and justice
- identification of 'redundancy pool' in line with retention of key skills
- management training

- redeployment opportunities
- severance packages
- consultation process
- communications strategy
- approach to voluntary redundancies
- employment support
- workload allocation
- re-building the organisation.

It is critical to the success of the redundancy implementation plan to ensure that the organisation has developed a long-term strategic plan that takes into account how department units and processes will be structured after a reduction in headcount (Freeman, 1999). Preparation is crucial to keeping staff onside during a redundancy programme. A key part of the planning is having a good idea of who is likely to be impacted and the potential development of the situation (Petzer, 2019). This will help to simplify the process later and help with addressing difficult questions.

Involvement during planning

Freeman (1999) contends that it is important in the planning stage to represent all the employees' interests and that all of the organisation's key stakeholders are involved at the planning stage to ensure fair representation (Cascio, 1993). Planning should involve the participation from a cross-functional team, who are agreed on the reasons for the redundancies and who identify all constituents and address their concerns effectively (Mishra et al., 1998). Involvement and participation during redundancy programmes should commence with strategic planning, where contributions should come from all levels of management (Appelbaum et al., 1999). Cascio (1993) contends that firms that involve organisational members actively from the planning stage gain better buy-in from the stakeholders and this leads employees to buy into the redundancy programme, thereby increasing the probability of success (Freeman and Cameron, 1993).

Mitigating risk during planning

Another important part of the planning process is to ensure any risks against legal action are investigated to protect the organisation against any potential claims (Labib and Appelbaum, 1993), which require a detailed strategy including how and why these redundancies will take place as discussed in Chapter 5.

Planning and analysis to help identify redundancy selection

Systematic analysis prior to the implementation of redundancies has shown to be associated with successful outcomes for the organisation (Flint, 2003). Labib and Appelbaum (1993) posit that a proper analysis of all job functions will help to establish which positions can be eliminated in which departments and which employees are least valuable to the organisation (Wooten and Decker, 1996). Management can use existing knowledge, such as knowledge of employee commitment, satisfaction, absenteeism and turnover intention to guide their redundancy programmes towards a more productive outcome (Cross and Travaglione, 2004). Staff analysis is equally important to enable understanding of the employees with vital skills and knowledge to retain (Mone, 1994, Schmenner and Lackey, 1994). Labib and Appelbaum (1993) agree that there should be a strong focus on ensuring the organisation does not lose employees with special skills, abilities and expertise. Another benefit of conducting a human resource skills audit is that it can help indicate which employees need to be retrained to ensure organisational success after implementation (Wooten and Decker, 1996).

Before any redundancy programme is implemented, it is recommended to assess and remove any non-value-added tasks to manage the increased workload for survivors (Mabert and Schmenner, 1997). By completing a skills analysis, the process of identifying non-value tasks will also be more pragmatic to achieve and eliminate.

Employers should be realistic when it comes to skills analysis as this can be a very time-consuming project. Further support is available at www.madeleinestevens.com.

Project plan

Implementing a redundancy programme requires a robust project plan, incorporating key dates and milestones. Studies indicate that it is not so much the loss of employment that causes the negative impact on employees; instead, it is the structure of the project implementation plan and how it is executed that causes the biggest impact (Labib and Appelbaum, 1993).

The Project Management Institute Guide to the Body of Knowledge guide sets out key principles in project management (Kerzner, 2017) with their various activities that outlines a great baseline for implementing redundancies:

(a) Project initiation
  i.   Selection of the best project given resource limits
  ii.   Recognising the benefits of the project
  iii. Preparation of the documents to sanction the project
  iv.   Assigning the project manager
(b) Project planning
  i.   Definition of the work requirements
  ii.   Definition of the quality and quantity of the work
  iii. Definition of the resources needed
  iv.   Scheduling of the activities
  v.   Evaluation of the various risks
(c) Project execution
  i.   Negotiation for the project team members
  ii.   Directing and managing the work
  iii. Working with the team members to help them improve
(d) Project control and monitoring
  i.   Tracking progress
  ii.   Comparing actual outcome with predicted outcome
  iii. Analysing variances and impacts
  iv.   Making adjustments
(e) Project closure
  i.   Verifying that all the work has been accomplished
  ii.   Contractual closure of the contract
  iii. Financial closure of the charge numbers
  iv.   Administrative closure of the paperwork

(PMI's PMBOK guide; cited Kerzner; p. 2)

Successful project management under this definition means achieving a continuous set of objectives within time, cost and the desired performance with the effective use of resources, resulting in satisfied customers and stakeholders (Kerzner, 2017).

Perception of fairness and justice

How a redundancy programme is implemented is very important for the perception of justice by all employees and a major element in the success of the plan. Literature that recognises the importance of the perception of fairness during the redundancy stages is abundant (Greenberg, 1990, Labib and Appelbaum, 1993, Gopinath and Becker, 2000, Spreitzer and Mishra, 2002). According to Greenberg (1990), survivors are in a unique situation to assess the fairness of redundancies, and it is found that if they feel the process is fair, it impacts on their increased commitment to the organisation. Brockner (1992) develops this argument further by stating that redundancy envoys have the capacity to influence employees' perceptions of fairness and justice and thus implementing redundancies with due diligence could have a significant impact on the success of the programme.

Labib and Appelbaum (1993) found that perceived fairness, especially on how redundancy decisions are made, can lead to improved levels of productivity and job performance. Perceived fairness also leads to improved employee attitude and has a positive impact on levels of absenteeism (Murphy, 1994). Gopinath and Becker (2000) found that perceived fairness in improved processes and procedural justice during a redundancy exercise resulted in higher levels of trust and commitment towards the organisation. Greenberg (1990) summarises that the perception of organisational justice is intrinsically linked to how a decision is made, instead of what the decision actually is, and perceived fairness has a direct impact on survivor commitment to the organisation. The approach to fairness and justice is particularly relevant to employee selection for redundancy, discussed later in this chapter.

RRR strategy stage 4: management training

Before decisions are made on whom, when and how to select employees for redundancy, management training is recommended. Managers should learn how to dismiss employees with sensitivity and effectively, whilst minimising the consequence of violence (Weide and Abbott, 1994). In addition, it is especially important during a redundancy exercise to ensure the redundancy envoys are trained with the skills to redesign jobs when considering the aftermath (Jalajas and Bommer, 1999). Providing training for redundancy envoys does not only equip them with the necessary skills to make better decisions, protect the organisation against potential unfair dismissal claims, but it is also an important component of building confidence to ensure they are ethically and emotionally ready for the process. Chapter 10 provides further discussion of how training empowers redundancy envoys during the process of redundancy implementation.

Decisions taken at this stage of how to select employees for the selection pool, for example, should be clearly understood to ensure the best outcome for the organisation and the workforce. It should be recognised that although HR staff may be more knowledgeable in understanding the law regarding the implementation of redundancies, management should feel equally comfortable in their own ability to answer questions from employees regarding technical aspects of redundancy law. Managers and directors may have many years' experience in their respective careers in business and management; however, they may never have implemented redundancies before (Petzer, 2019).

Directors and managers should thus be trained on the most recent case law, how to decide on selection pools for redundancies, the legal requirements of a fair process as well as how to deal with the emotive areas of giving bad news. Providing management with the necessary level of legal knowledge can have a positive impact on how confident they feel through the unpleasant process of implementing redundancy-related dismissals (Petzer, 2019). Training can be designed specially to address the stakeholder needs, which will vary in each organisation. Appendix 7.4 provides a comprehensive set of management training slides entitled 'Management Training: Redundancy Law and Process', completed with supporting notes for the trainer. The training content will also be useful for HR practitioners who are inexperienced when it comes to redundancy implementation or who need a general refresher course. It is advisable to run this training in three sets of priorities depending on the size of the organisation and the scope of the redundancy programme:

1. Redundancy envoys (decision makers)
2. Redundancy envoys (messengers/middle management/employee representatives)
3. All employees – condensed version that is optional to attend.

The training will be beneficial for the initial decision makers/directors on how, when and how many redundancies are required to meet the organisational objectives. The second cohort of redundancy envoys to be trained includes middle management, employee representatives and supervisors who will have responsibility in the implementation of the redundancy programme. Involving employee representatives supports earlier arguments about early involvement and participation in the planning stages. Finally, a condensed version of the training including the organisations' policies and redundancy processes should be offered as an optional session for all employees. Research has indicated that educating all employees on the redundancy process helps to ease the process of redundancy implementation by creating a clearer understanding of the legal framework (Arndt and Duchemin, 1993).

The aim and objectives of the management training are as follows:

This course is designed to give line managers confidence in managing the legal aspects and processes during a redundancy programme.

Objectives

At the end of the course, participants will have an understanding of:

- *statutory definition of redundancy*
- *redundancy warning and notice*
- *entitlement to redundancy payment*
- *individual consultation*
- *collective consultation*
- *protective awards*
- *redundancy selection*
- *suitable alternative employment*
- *redundancy and maternity*
- *redundancy and TUPE transfers.*

Various additional training modules are recommended and available from www.madeleinestevens.com where organisations can choose the modules specific to their needs:

- Module 1: Drivers behind redundancies
- Module 2: Limiting redundancies

- Module 3: Impact of COVID-19
- Module 4: Choosing the right strategy for your organisation
- Module 5: Impact on the workforce
- Module 6: Legal aspects of redundancy
- Module 7: The role of emotional intelligence during consultation
- Module 8: Support for impacted groups
- Module 9: Change management
- Module 10: Employee representatives: adding value and election
- Module 11: Communication strategy for managing redundancies
- Module 12: Re-building a sustainable organisation for the future

RRR stage 5: people impact strategy

Once training is complete, we move onto the people impact strategy. Management and employee representatives now have a better understanding of how to implement redundancies and the associated risks. At this point, it is essential to start making more strategic and challenging decisions about how implementation will work in reality.

When organisations find themselves in the position of having to implement redundancies, there are two main people strategies to consider; 'push' or 'pull' (Tomasko, 1991). 'Push' strategies are the most direct and insensitive approach; essentially forcing employees to exit the organisation via compulsory redundancies. 'Pull' strategies involve less aggressive approaches such as the encouragement of voluntary resignations, discussed in Chapter 4. Under the remit of the 'people impact strategy', attention must be focused on three key streams of information: retain, reduce and policy, presented in Figure 7.5.

Retain refers to what skills, talent and critical roles the organisation needs to preserve to ensure its future sustainability. Organisations often get blinded by the need to reduce headcount that they overlook the critical factor of organisational survival and having a competitive edge after the redundancy implementations are complete. The retention strategy should identify any single points of failures, where roles are critical to the survival of the organisation or specific project delivery. Part of the planning is to explore the design for the organisation for several months prior to implementation to ensure the right skills are retained. It may be necessary

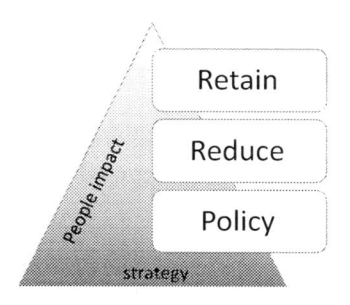

Figure 7.5 RRR strategy stage 5: people impact strategy overview.

to consider retention bonuses to ensure critical employees are retained in line with the organisation's strategic goals. As part of the retention process, organisations should identify employees with management and leadership capabilities and appoint them in leadership roles prior to the implementation of the redundancy, as it creates positive energy in the organisation (Hitt et al., 1994). Efficient, continued delivery for the organisation's customers' needs to be balanced between operational needs whilst implementing redundancies.

'Reduce' refers to where employee reductions should take place, which departments, which roles, which locations, by which dates, how many individuals and the best methods used to achieve this. Employers should focus on the correct size for the organisation rather than the number of reductions (Hitt et al., 1994). How employees are selected for redundancy, has a significant impact on the perception of fairness by both victims and survivors as they believe that unconscious stereotyping and predisposed performance criteria are used my managers (Iverson and Zatzick, 2007). It is thus critically important to have robust rationale for how decisions are made to select employees for redundancy, avoiding biases and potential discrimination claims as outlined in Chapter 5.

Research has indicated that when it comes to selection, reducing organisational layers allows for greater operational efficiency and decision-making post redundancy implementation (Hitt et al., 1994). Successful redundancy planning should facilitate a legitimate method to remove low performers and departments that do not add value to the organisational goals which are likely to limit damage to employee morale (Davis et al., 2003). Selection is one of the most challenging tasks for management and it is suggested that these decisions are made together with HR as part of a workshop.

Depending on the organisation's approach to employee relations, it may be appropriate to include employee representatives in the discussions at this stage, although this inclusion will very much be unique to each organisation. This is supported in the literature that suggests that when it comes to selection criteria, clear communication and participation helps employees to perceive the process in a fairer light (Murphy, 1994).

One of the most important factors in a redundancy programme is the perception of the selection process (Baruch and Hind, 1997). The selection methods need to demonstrate a process of clear performance- and operational-related criteria and the links to the business case and rationale needs to be transparent (Baruch and Hind, 1999). Literature also indicates that perceived fairness of selection criteria is important to keep employees engaged during the process of redundancy (Gopinath and Becker, 2000, Spreitzer and Mishra, 2002).

It is important that each department takes ownership for their own decisions, as this will impact their ability to communicate the decisions taken with authenticity and allow managers and HR to defend any potential claims with robust rationale, decision-making and evidence.

'Policy' refers to the specific policies and procedures that underpin the redundancy programme, which will include the redundancy policy (Appendix 5.1), redundancy selection matrix (Appendix 5.2) whether voluntary redundancies will be offered, and if so, in what context and what will be included in redundancy packages. Figure 7.6 provides a more detailed process map of the people impact strategy.

Due to the strategic decision-making required at this stage, it is recommended that these decisions are made at a further management workshop, entitled people impact strategy with a proposed agenda example available in Appendix 7.5.

Throughout the process of involving and consulting with redundancy envoys, it is important to remember that the whole team is experiencing a period of disruption, which is uncomfortable. The implementation of redundancy and restructuring programmes is disruptive and emotionally draining (Jacobs, 2020). It is thus recommended to build in supporting activities to help individuals deal with their emotions. A recommended activity is that of 'Hopes and Fears', which could be included at the start of the people impact workshop. At this point in time, redundancy envoys

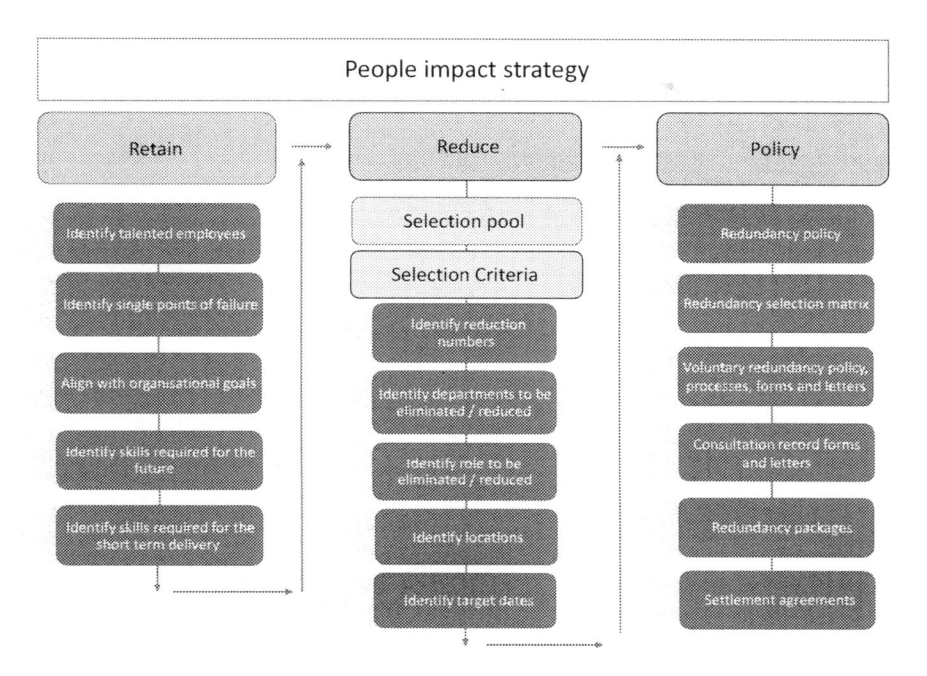

Figure 7.6 RRR strategy stage 5: people impact strategy process map.

understand the legal processes, the rationale for the workshop and the necessity for the requirement of organisational change. This exercise will help individuals understand how they feel themselves, but also provide the opportunity to understand that they are not alone. The 'fears' element of the activity will help identify problematic areas that senior management can proactively address to minimise or resolve and the 'hopes' element will help to drive motivation and aspects of success. This activity can be undertaken by using two different colours of sticky notes where each team member uses as many sticky notes as they choose to write down their fears on one colour and hopes on the other colour sticky notes. Use one topic per sticky note and post these onto a wall (or virtual wall), categorised as 'hopes' and a separate one for 'fears'. A facilitator arranges the sticky notes by theme to identify the most prominent concerns and hopes and sum-marise the group findings by sharing all the hopes first and then the fears. This is a very valuable exercise in uniting the leadership team that will be facing the tough challenge of a change management process together in the near future and critical in driving the emotional aspects of being prepared for the unpleasant task of redundancy implementation.

Voluntary redundancies

Voluntary redundancies were deliberately excluded from Chapter 4. The rationale for this is two-fold. First, technically a voluntary redundancy is still a redundancy by legal definition and second, although the strategy provides a level of 'choice' to the employee, it can still cause negative connotations such as low levels of self-esteem and self-worth, job insecurity and resentment towards the organisation. A frequent distinction between voluntary and compulsory redundancies is specific to the financial packages associated with each (Clarke, 2007). As voluntary redundancy is a 'pull' strategy, the financial package associated with voluntary redundancy quite often includes additional incentives on top of the compulsory redundancy package to entice employees to adopt this route (Turnbull and Wass, 1997).

Within the 'policy' element of the 'people impact strategy' stage, lies the important decision to make whether to offer voluntary redundancies to employees. Voluntary redundancies should be considered at the planning stage, before announcements are communicated to employees, as typically, it is a question that will be asked right from the outset and the redundancy envoys need to be prepared to answer this question.

Voluntary redundancy is separated into two main categories; classic and targeted (Lewis, 1986).

Classic voluntary redundancy is where there is a call for volunteers and an employee puts their role forward to be terminated as a redundancy.

Targeted voluntary redundancy takes place when the position is abolished and the individual occupying the role is invited (targeted) by management to accept redundancy.

Consider in advance the impact that voluntary redundancies might have on the structure of the organisation's remaining workforce and whether it could result in an imbalance of skills and experience or loss of any key members of staff. If this is the case, before voluntary redundancies can be considered, management need to be clear on the selection pools and decide if voluntary redundancies will only be accepted from the selection pools or from anywhere in the organisation. If this process is not managed properly, costs can be higher with the potential of losing key skilled workers and therefore the more targeted the better (Mabert and Schmenner, 1997).

Estimate in advance how many applications for voluntary redundancy the organisation is likely to accept and how much they would cost. Forewarned is forearmed. This exercise will help employers decide whether applications for voluntary redundancy are only accepted from agreed departments and specific roles. These measures can limit the scope for raising misleading expectations and finding the employer in the position of having to decline numerous applications, which could have a negative impact on morale.

Advantages of implementing voluntary redundancies

Research has indicated that the pull strategy of implementing voluntary redundancies instead of compulsory redundancies can reduce the negative impact on survivors (Iverson and Zatzick, 2007). Voluntary redundancy can also be regarded as an investment for the organisation as essentially payments are made to secure continued future savings (Lewis, 1986). Depending on the number of redundancies required and the relationship to the size of the workforce, implementing voluntary redundancies may help employers to avoid having to implement compulsory redundancies.

A study of a Swedish, global pharmaceutical organisation found that organisational commitment in survivors increased during a redundancy programme, as a result of offering voluntary redundancies (Bergström and Arman, 2017). Bergström and Arman (2017) posit that the rationale for the increased commitment is that the employees who stayed, made an active decision to remain whilst the employees who opted for voluntary redundancy had less commitment, resulting in the organisation retaining the employees with higher levels of commitment. The use of voluntary redundancies thus allows for a natural organisational cleansing process, where the employees that are not satisfied and who have lower levels of organisational loyalty and commitment have the opportunity to self-select to leave with a financial package (Cross and Travaglione, 2004). Implementing voluntary redundancies may also have a positive impact on reducing survivor guilt, as survivors are less likely to think 'it should have been me' when their colleagues leave through voluntary redundancies.

A further benefit of implementing voluntary redundancies is that it can be useful when consulting and negotiating with employee representatives to demonstrate that the organisation attempted to minimise compulsory redundancies (Lewis, 1986). Lewis (1986) argues that unions are committed to avoid compulsory redundancies and offering voluntary redundancies is perceived as a step in the right direction. A substantial benefit to employers often overlooked, is the reduced level of stress experienced by the redundancy envoys when employees decide to leave as a result of their own choice (Petzer, 2019). Not only is the unpleasant task of delivering the bad news of job loss reduced, the associated increased workload for managers, employee representatives and HR is also reduced as although consultations may still be required, the process is quicker, more effective with reduced negative emotional distress for all parties involved. Employees who choose to leave through the voluntary redundancy route experience a less negative impact than victims of compulsory redundancies as they perceive the redundancy as less of a breach of their psychological contract. Offering enhanced packages associated with job loss can be regarded as a welcome relief, especially if the employee is not enjoying the role (Clarke, 2005).

Whether employees apply for voluntary redundancy depends on various factors such as the financial package associated with the offering, their personal circumstances, job satisfaction or perhaps they have already secured alternative employment due to a perceived unstable working environment.

Disadvantages of implementing voluntary redundancies

Many employers offer enhanced financial and support packages when offering voluntary redundancies. This is not a necessity; however, this practice is often associated with voluntary redundancies and therefore nowadays an expectation from employees. Offering enhanced financial packages could have the undesired opposite impact, where applications for voluntary redundancies exceed the organisation's requirement, which could result in various applications being rejected. This situation could lead to survivor envy and resentment, as the employees who applied for voluntary redundancy and were rejected have already psychologically prepared to leave the organisation. If employees with key skills are excluded from applying for voluntary redundancy, it may cause resentment in survivors who are unable to apply as they perceive that their good performance is being penalised (Hitt et al., 1994).

The cost of the financial packages associated with voluntary redundancies can also be higher for the organisation than the cost of compulsory redundancies, due to volunteers often being long-serving employees who are likely to receive large redundancy payments. Mabert and Schmenner (1997) warn that if voluntary redundancy programmes are not managed properly, valued workers could leave, which can create significant costs due to replacement and retraining. In addition, employers should not be surprised if employees that are near retirement age apply for voluntary redundancy, as quite often, they are in a better position to face unemployment, due to life savings and enhanced pension pots.

The fact that employees are still left at the end without a job and an income should not be ignored, as they still experience the uncertainty through a stressful life event (Leana and Feldman, 1994). Although the process of voluntary redundancy is less stressful for all parties concerned due to the degree of employee influence, the experience from an employee perspective is still unpleasant (Thornhill and Saunders, 1998).

The process of implementing voluntary redundancies should be managed responsibly to protect the organisation from losing talented and skilled employees. If organisations decide to proceed with voluntary redundancies, a clear process for application, a voluntary redundancy policy and process should be prepared prior to the first announcement in readiness for questions. Appendices and links to various examples are available below:

- Appendix 7.6 Voluntary redundancy application form
- Appendix 7.7 Voluntary redundancy process
- Appendix 7.8 Voluntary redundancy process communication slides
- Appendix 7.9 Voluntary redundancy exit agreement example

Settlement agreements

Some organisations prefer to use settlement agreements instead of the traditional exit process of dismissal by reason of redundancy. Even if voluntary redundancy terms have been agreed, some employers still prefer to agree to the exit terms through a settlement agreement.

A settlement agreement contains legally binding terms that can be used where an agreement has been reached between the employer and employee on the basis of potential claims accounted for. A settlement agreement will stipulate the employee's termination package, which will typically agree the benefits that the employee would receive in accordance with the terms and conditions set out in their contract of employment and an as ex-gratia termination payment. These negotiations take place where agreements are reached on the final sum of money, exit date and reference details.

A benefit of settlement agreements for organisations is that it contains provisions to protect the organisation from the employee sharing confidential information or taking up employment at a competitor within a reasonable time frame and contain confidentiality clauses. Settlement agreements are only legally binding, based on the employee receiving independent legal advice. It is quite normal for organisations to pay for the legal fees up to a limited amount agreed in advance. The details of such arrangements are normally contained within the settlement agreement. Some organisations prefer to keep redundancies out of the spotlight as they fear reputation damage and thus opt for settlement agreements.

There are ambiguous views on how settlement agreements are used in the case of an alternative for redundancy exit terms. Research has indicated that HR directors have frowned on the lack of humanity by adopting this approach, which they label as 'chequebook management' (Petzer, 2019). On the contrary, when a responsible approach to dealing with people are used and the organisation has sufficient funds, using settlement agreements on a small scale could have several advantages for an employer and employee as discussed earlier.

There are some key distinctions between a redundancy exit verses a settlement agreement:

- Employees lose their right to file a subsequent complaint to an employment tribunal, subject to using the 'Without Prejudice' clause. Employers should be cautious regarding the potential admission of pre-termination negotiations to employment tribunals. Although section 111A of the Employment Rights Act 1996 states that pre-termination negotiations are not admissible in most cases of unfair dismissal claims, pre-termination discussions are not protected if an employee was dismissed for an automatically unfair reason.
- To make a settlement agreement legally binding, the employee must obtain independent advice.
- Employers do not have to report employees who leave the organisation via settlement agreements as a 'redundancy'.

- Employers do not have to go through the consultation process associated with statutory redundancy processes and essentially can therefore reduce the headcount in a shorter timescale.

Appendix 7.10 provides a settlement agreement example that can be adjusted to the individual exit terms.

Additional policy documents

Employers and specifically the HR department should not underestimate the time it takes to prepare all the individual documents and letters as part of the consultation process. These documents are key in keeping employees informed whilst also helpful in demonstrating a fair process was followed, should a claim arrive.

With the aim to help HR professionals with the necessary preparation, several examples are provided as follows:

- Appendix 7.11 Letter informing employees of potential redundancies
- Appendix 7.12 Letter informing employees of being 'at risk of redundancy'
- Appendix 7.13 Letter inviting employees to first consultation meeting
- Appendix 7.14 First individual consultation record form
- Appendix 7.15 Letter inviting employees to second individual consultation meeting
- Appendix 7.16 Second individual consultation record form
- Appendix 7.17 Letter inviting employees to the third consolation meeting
- Appendix 7.18 Third consultation record form
- Appendix 7.19 Notice of dismissal for reason of redundancy
- Appendix 7.20 Letter informing employees of redundancy deselection

This chapter provided a comprehensive overview of the planning and preparation stages prior to redundancy implementation by introducing the RRR strategy that incorporates the key aspects of planning and analysis, fairness and justice and preparing management through management training. The RRR strategy is expanded on by including best-practise recommendations. Communication strategy for redundancy implementation is discussed in the next chapter.

APPENDIX 7.1
MANAGEMENT
WORKSHOP RE-FOCUS
ORGANISATIONAL GOALS

Date:	
Time:	
Location/Web link:	
Attendees: Managing Director (MD)/CEO Finance Director (FD)/FD Head of Functions, i.e. Sales, Marketing, Products, Services, HR, Business Excellence, Health and Safety, etc.	

Agenda: Day 1

Time	Agenda item	Owner(s)
9:00–9:30	Welcome and overview	MD/CEO
9:30–10:30	Financial position	FD/CFO
	Break	
10:45–12:00	Past (3 workshop streams; identify loss-making departments, causes and costs)	
12:00–12:30	Summary conclusion of past	
12:30–13:30	Lunch break	
13:30–14:00	Present: Overview of market analysis	Marketing
14:00–14:30	Overview of key competitors	Sales
14:30–15:00	Overview of customers	Customer services
15:00–15:15	Break	
15:15–16:00	PESTLE analysis (3 workshop streams, focusing on 2 elements each)	
16:00–16:45	PESTLE feedback presentations (15 minutes each)	
16:45–17:00	Closure and agenda for the Part 2 of the workshop	

Agenda: Day 2

Time	Agenda item	Owner(s)
9:00–9:30	Welcome and summary of day 1	MD/CEO and FD/CFO
9:30–10:30	Management reflections (Post-It notes or online exercise: Fears and Hopes)	
10:30–10:45	Break	
10:45–12:00	Future (3 workshop streams; technological advances, environment, niche product/services)	
12:00–12:30	Summary conclusion of future	
12:30–13:30	Lunch break	
13:30–14:30	Mission and Vision	
14:30–15:30	Values and culture	
15:30–15:45	Break	
15:45–18:00	Strategic goals	
18:00	Close and next steps	MD/CEO

APPENDIX 7.2 CONTRACTORS TEMPLATE

Personnel No	Payroll No	Title	First Name	Known As	Last Name	Job title	Personnel Number	Department/ Business unit	Employment status	Payroll Number	Location	Work Hours	FTE	Contract start date	Contract End Date	Length of service	Contract term	Reporting Manager Name	Business Head Name

APPENDIX 7.3 AGE PROFILE TEMPLATE

Personnel No	Payroll No	Title	First Name	Known As	Last Name	Job title	Personnel Number	Department / Business unit	Employment status	Payroll Number	Location	Date of birth	Age	Start date	Length of service	Reporting Manager Name	Business Head Name

APPENDIX 7.4
MANAGEMENT TRAINING
The legal aspects of redundancy

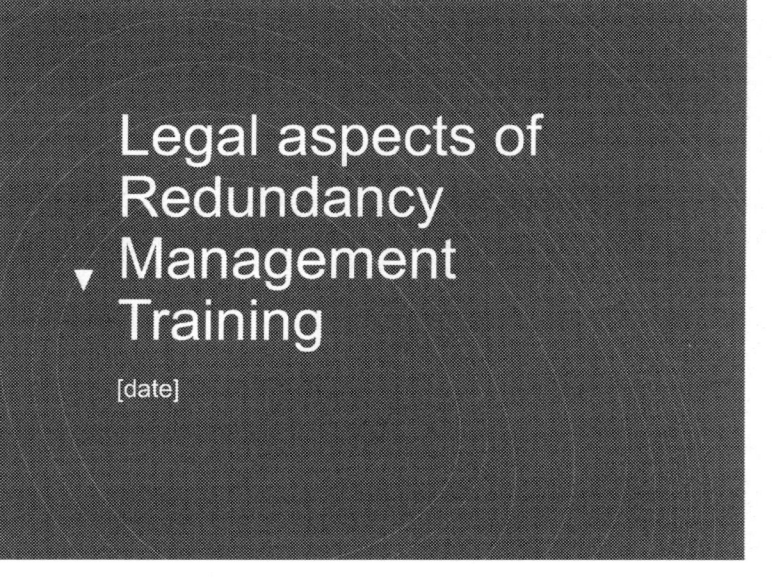

Legal aspects of
Redundancy
▼ Management
Training

[date]

Course objectives

At the end of the course, participants will have an understanding of:

- Statutory definition of redundancy
- Redundancy warning and notice
- Entitlement to redundancy payment
- Individual consultation
- Collective consultation
- Protective awards
- Redundancy selection
- Suitable alternative employment
- Redundancy and maternity
- Redundancy and TUPE transfers

Introductions

Your role in the company

Any experience of:
- Managing restructures and redundancies
- Being put at risk
- Being made redundant

What role you will play in this redundancy programme?

What you want to gain from this course?

Legal aspects of redundancies

What is a redundancy?

 Redundancy, as demarcated in legalistic interpretation Employment Rights Act, 1996, section 139 :1 is defined as a reason for dismissal of an employee attributable wholly or mainly to:

 (a) the fact that the employer has ceased, or intends to cease

 (i) to carry on the business for the purposes of which the employee was employed by for, or
(ii) to carry on that business in the place where the employee was so employed, or

 (b) the fact that the requirements of that business

 (i) for employees to carry out work of a particular kind, or
(ii) for employees to carry out work of a particular kind in the place where the employee was employed by the employer have ceased or diminished or are expected to cease or diminish.

The test to determine redundancy legitimacy

Was the employee dismissed?

If so, had the requirements of the business for employees to carry out work of a particular kind ceased or diminished (or did one of the other economic states of affairs in section 139(1) exist)?

Was the dismissal of the employee caused wholly or mainly by the state of affairs as identified above?

Did changes in an organisation lead to changes in terms or conditions due to a restructure or if it is a genuine redundancy?

A fair process for redundancy

Employers must be able to show that they have followed a fair procedure:

- Explore other alternatives before redundancy;
- Having a clear rationale of the reasons for the potential redundancy;
- Identifying the correct pool of employees at risk of redundancy;
- Warning employees of potential redundancy;
- Undertaking sufficient meaningful consultation; discussing and considering all alternatives to redundancy, including searching for alternative roles;
- Applying a robust selection process, need to ensure that any selection is fair and objective and that it is applied consistently to all those in the pool.

Redundancy warning

Redundancy warning entails the legal responsibility of the organisation to provide a 'warning' of impending redundancies as soon as possible with the intention for employees that may be impacted to start exploring alternative income sources.

Redundancy notices

YEARS OF SERVICE	NOTICE PERIOD	EXAMPLE
Employment between one month and two years	One week	1 year's service = 1 week's notice
Employment between two and 12 years	One week for each completed year served	3 years and four months' service = 3 weeks' notice
Employment of 12 years or more	12 weeks	14 years' service = 12 weeks' notice

Entitlement to redundancy payment

Redundancy payment may be applicable if

- The dismissal is subject to meeting qualifying time in employment (2 years)
- Employer terminates with / without notice
- Fixed-term contract expires and is not renewed subject to no break longer than one week, if not continuous service
- Employer's conduct entitled employee to resign with or without notice leading to constructive dismissal

Redundancy calculations

Age	Redundancy pay entitlement
Under 22	Half a week's pay for each full year worked
Between 22 and 41	A week pay for each full year worked
Over 41	One and a half week's pay for each full year worked
	A maximum of 20 years' employment can be taken into account

What should a redundancy payment include?

- Redundancy pay: if the employee has worked for the employer for at least 2 years
- Holiday pay: any unused leave the employee was entitled to take between the start of the leave year and the date of insolvency as well as any unpaid holiday taken
- Money you're owed by your employer, for example unpaid wages, overtime and commission
- Statutory notice pay: if you've worked for your employer for at least 1 month as per above calculations
- Enhanced packages may include additional payments depending on contractual clauses and the organisation's redundancy policy

Individual consultation

Consultation should include the following topics for discussion:

- Why the organisation needs to make the proposed changes
- How the organisation intend to make the proposed changes
- What are the proposed changes
- Methods of avoiding of limiting redundancies
- What are the organisation's future skills and experience requirements
- Details of the selection criteria used for selecting employees for redundancy
- Employee concerns
- Support measures in place for employees at risk of redundancy

Collective consultation

Number of redundancies	Consultation period	Minimum consultation before first dismissal
20–99 at one establishment	90 days	30 days consultation before first dismissal
100+ dismissals at one establishment	90 days	45 days consultation before first dismissal

Collective redundancies

Specified information to be shared with representatives should include the following:

- Reason for the proposed dismissals
- Numbers and categories of employees proposed to be dismissed
- Total number of employees employed in each category of the organisation
- Proposed method of selecting employees for redundancy
- Proposed method of carrying out the dismissals
- Proposed method of calculating the amount of any redundancy payments
- Number of agency workers and their roles being used by the employer
- Copy of the HR1 form

How to calculate redundancy numbers

1

Count the roles being made redundant (not the people)

2

Include voluntary redundancies

3

Include employees that get redeployed (thus include all employees that were at risk of redundancy, even if they remain in the organisation, based on securing suitable alternative roles)

What not exclude in the calculations

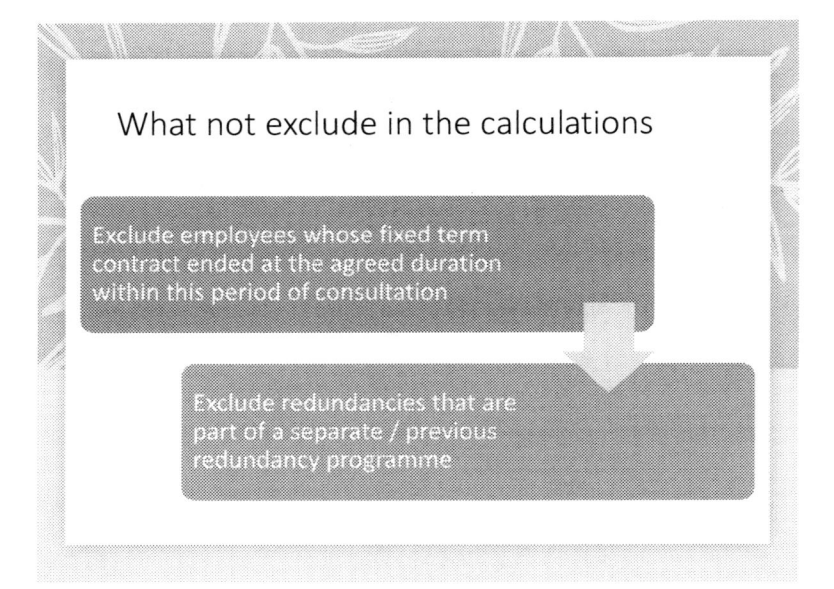

Exclude employees whose fixed term contract ended at the agreed duration within this period of consultation

Exclude redundancies that are part of a separate / previous redundancy programme

Protective awards

Insufficient consultation can lead to protective awards payable to all employees made redundant. Protective awards on the basis of inadequate consultation could include a maximum of 90 days' actual pay per employee. Protective awards would depend on the seriousness of the employer's default.

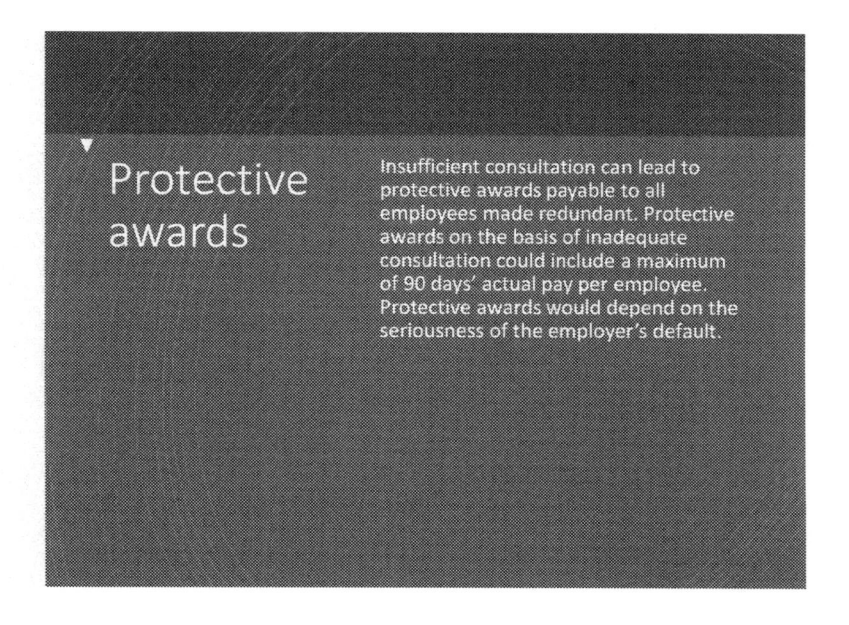

HR1 Form

HR1 form

4. Timing of redundancies	
Date of first proposed dismissal	
Date of last proposed dismissal	
If you have given less than the required 30/45 day notification period please give reason for late notification	

5. Method of selection for redundancy	
Method	

6. Staff numbers/redundancies at this establishment		
Occupational group	**Total number of employees**	**Number of possible redundancies**
Manual		
Clerical		
Professional		
Managerial		
Technical		
Apprentices/trainees		
Under 18		
Other		
Totals		

8. Closure of the business	
Do you propose to close this establishment	Yes/No

9. Reasons for redundancies		
Please tick one or more boxes to show the main reason(s) for the proposed redundancies		
A	Lower demand for products or services	
B	Completion of all or part of contract	
C	Transfer of work to another site or employer	
D	Introduction of new technology/plant/machinery	
E	Changes in work methods or organisation	
F	Other (please give brief details below)	
G	Insolvency	
Details		

10. Consultation		
a) Please provide the name(s) of:		
Recognised trade union	**Name of representative**	**Description of employee they represent**

b) If you do not recognise trade unions for any groups of employees please give the name(s) of their elected representatives below:	
Name of elected representative	**Description of employee they represent**

c) Have you given a copy of this form to all the appropriate representatives?	Yes/No
d) Have you started the consultation process with the appropriate representative?	Yes/No
e) If yes, please give the date consultation started:	
f) Have you given individual notices of dismissal to the employees?	Yes/No

11. Declaration	
I certify that the information given on this form is, so far as I know, is correct and complete.	
Name:	
Position/role	
Date:	

Selection pool

Determining who should be included in the redundancy pool, should include the following factors:

- Consider employees who undertake similar roles in an area that have been identified. Organisations can exclude employees who undertake similar roles, with robust justification for the decision.

- Consider all employees who undertake similar roles even if they operate in different departments of the organisation or work in different shifts.

- Consider employees who undertake similar roles at other sites, are subject to the consideration of contracts of employment and whether they are site-specific – actual locations of work, distance between sites and willingness of employees to work at alternative sites.

- Consider the likeliness of roles being interchangeable, which means that the pool does not have to be limited to employees undertaking similar work. In other words, when selecting retail cashiers in the redundancy pool, shelve packers can also be included in the pool if their roles are interchangeable.

Automatically unfair redundancy selection

... if the reason included any of the following:

- Pregnancy
- Maternity leave
- Parental leave
- Paternity leave
- Adoption leave
- Shared parental leave
- Bereavement leave

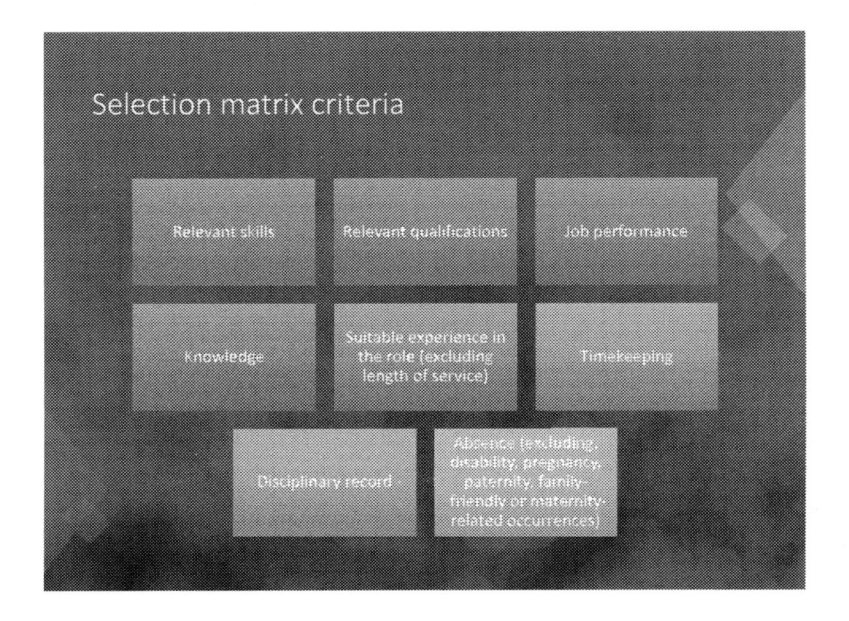

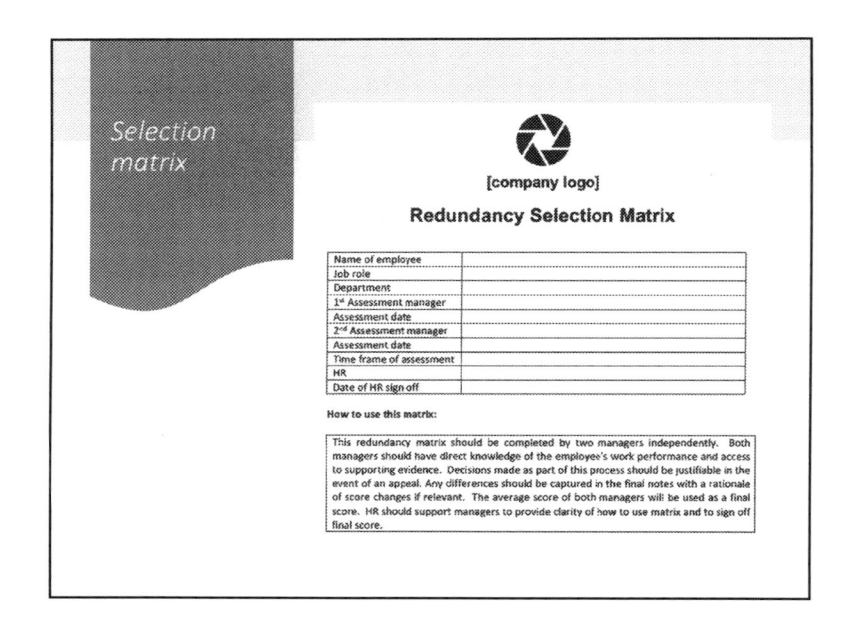

Job performance

1. Job performance

Use job performance as a criterion subject to all employees in the redundancy pool being assessed equally. Supporting evidence of previous performance reviews are required. If an employee has been absent for a substantial period of time, it may be necessary to extend the timeframe to consider job performance before and after the period of absence.

Definition	Score 1	Score 2
Meets and exceeds performance targets	5	5
Meets performance targets most of the time	4	4
Meets performance targets for more than half of the time	3	3
Fails to meet performance targets for more than half of the time	2	2
Fails to meet performance targets	0	0

Knowledge

2. Knowledge

Assessment of knowledge should be based on the specific requirements of the role as specified in the job description.

Definition	Score 1	Score 2
Displays the full range of knowledge required for the role	5	5
Displays the core knowledge required for the role	4	4
Displays some of the required knowledge with knowledge gaps identified	3	3
Displays limited knowledge specific to the role	2	2
Has insufficient knowledge to meet the requirements of the role	0	0

Skills

3. Skills

Assessment of skills should be based on the specific requirements of the role as specified in the job description.

Definition	Score 1	Score 2
Displays the full range of skills required for the role	5	5
Displays the core skills required for the role	4	4
Displays some of the required skills, with skill gaps identified	3	3
Displays limited skills specific to the role	2	2
Has insufficient skills to meet the requirements of the role	0	0

Qualifications

4. Qualifications

Assessment of qualifications should be based on the specific requirements of the role as specified in the job description. Qualifications or equivalent should be used to complete this assessment.

Definition	Score 1	Score 2
Fully qualified or equivalent as per the requirements for the role	5	5
Part qualified and actively working towards full qualification	4	4
Part qualified and not actively working towards completion of full qualification	3	3
Not qualified or part qualified and working towards qualification	2	2
Unqualified	0	0

Experience

5. Experience

Assessment of experience should reflect the depth and breadth of experience that is directly related to the requirements of the role. Caution should be exercised to avoid any timeframes that may be subject to age discrimination.

Definition	Score 1	Score 2
Has broad and varied experience specific to the requirements for the role	5	5
Has a good range of experience specific to the requirements of the role	4	4
Has some good experience with identifiable gaps for the requirements of the role	3	3
Has limited experience in relation to the role	2	2
Has no previous experience of the job role	0	0

Disciplinary records

6. Disciplinary records

Assessment of disciplinary records should include active warnings that is no older than 12 months. The scoring of this criterion is different to previous methods as the scores are totalled.

Definition	Score 1	Score 2
Current final written warning	-5	-5
Current written warning	-4	-4
Current verbal warning	-3	-3
No previous warnings	0	0

Absences

7. Absences

Assessment of absences should only relate to the previous 12 months. Any absences related to disability, pregnancy, maternity, paternity, adoption leave, parental leave, paternity leave, bereavement leave or shielding in accordance with COVID-19 guidance should be discounted. The scoring of this criterion is different to previous methods as the scores of a long- and short-term absence can be totalled. Short absences can only be counted once.

Definition	Score 1	Score 2
More that 3 absences totalling 15 days or more in the past 12 months	-5	-5
1-3 absences totalling less than 10 days in the past 12 months	-4	-4
1 absence of more than 4 weeks or more in the past 12 months	-4	-4
1-3 absences totalling less than 5 days in the past 12 months	-2	-2
No absences	0	0

Timekeeping

8. Timekeeping

Assessment of timekeeping should only relate to the previous 12 months. Timekeeping can include being on time for meetings, customer appointments, training sessions, etc. and is not limited to the start of the working day. In addition, the same principles apply for leaving appointments, meetings or the working day before the scheduled end time. Any incidents related to disability, pregnancy, maternity, paternity, adoption leave, parental leave, paternity leave, bereavement leave or shielding in accordance with COVID-19 guidance should be discounted.

Definition	Score 1	Score 2
Persistently late within the previous 12 months	-5	-5
Frequently late (more than 12 occasions) within the previous 12 months	-4	-4
Occasionally late (less than 12 occasions) within the previous 12 months	-3	-3
Rarely late (less than 6 occasions) within the previous 12 months	-2	-2
Never late within the previous 12 months	0	0

Summary scores

Redundancy selection matrix summary scores

Criterion	Weighting	Assessor 1	Assessor 2	Calibrated score	Weighted score
1. Job performance					
2. Knowledge					
3. Skills					
4. Qualifications					
5. Experience					
6. Disciplinary records					
7. Absences					
8. Timekeeping					
9. Length of service*					
Total score					

◻ Length of service should only be used in a tiebreak situation when two or more employees achieve the same score.

Suitable alternative employment

Case law dictates a two-part test to establish the suitability of alternative employment offers:

Part 1

Objectively, look at what the employee's current duties are and how does this align with the alternative employment offered.

Part 2

If the employee is offered alternative employment, what is the reasonableness of refusal to accept the role?

Trial periods

4-week trial period

Extension is possible if retraining is applicable and subject to both parties agreeing.

The agreement must:

- be in writing and agreed prior to the suitable alternative employment commences
- Include the date when training is complete
- Be explicit in the terms of employment once training is completed

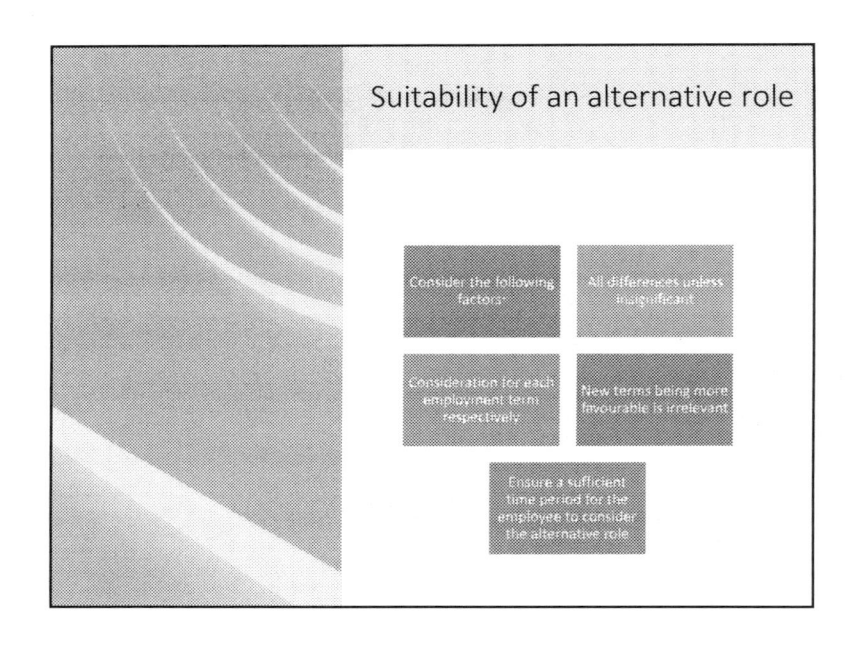

Suitability of an alternative role

Consider the following factors:

All differences unless insignificant

Consideration for each employment term respectively

New terms being more favourable is irrelevant

Ensure a sufficient time period for the employee to consider the alternative role

Redundancy bumping

- Bumping occurs where an employee potentially at risk of redundancy is moved into another role which was occupied by another employee.
- The employee originally at risk of redundancy thus stays in the organisation with the employee who was 'bumped' being made redundant.
- The role of the employee being bumped is usually that of a similar or lower level.

Maternity leave

- Regulation 10 of the Maternity and Parental Leaver regulations dictates that employees on maternity leave have an automatic right to be offered any suitable alternative roles.
- The new position must be suitable and appropriate taking into consideration place of work and other terms and conditions that should not be substantially less favourable than the previous role.

Redundancy and TUPE transfers

- Redundancies can occur as a result of a sale of an organisation (or part of an organisation) to another or due to the loss of a major contract which provided a particular service that your organisation's employees were working on.

If TUPE applies;

- employees get transferred over to the purchasing organisation or new contractor;
- retaining their existing terms and conditions or their employment contract;
- with preserved continuity of employment.

Questions

APPENDIX 7.5
PEOPLE IMPACT
WORKSHOP EXAMPLE

People Impact Workshop

Date:
Time:
Location/Web link:
Attendees: Managing Director (MD)/CEO Finance Director (FD)/FD Head of Functions, i.e. Sales, Marketing, Products, Services, HR, Business Excellence, Health and Safety, etc.

Agenda:

Time	Agenda item	Owner(s)
8:00–8:30	Welcome and overview	MD/EO
8:30–9:30	Hopes and fears activity	MD/HR
9:30–10:30	Retention:	All
	• Identify talented employees • Identify single points of failure • Alignment with organisational goals • Identify future skills requirement • Identify short-term delivery requirements	
10:30–10:45	Break	
10:45–11:15	Summary conclusion	
11:15–12:15	Reduce:	
	• Identify reduction numbers • Identify departments with reductions • Identify roles to be reduced/eliminated • Identify locations • Identify target dates	
12:15–13:00	Lunch break	
13:00–13:30	Summary conclusion	
13:30–15:00	Policy decisions:	HR
	• Redundancy packages • Settlement agreements • Voluntary redundancies	
15:00–15:15	Break	
15:15–16:00	Summary conclusion	
16:00–16:45	Further actions agreed and assigned	
16:45–17:00	Closure	

APPENDIX 7.6
VOLUNTARY REDUNDANCY
APPLICATION FORM

Personal details	
Name:	
Job title:	
Department:	
Employee number:	
Contact number:	
Email address:	

I wish to apply for voluntary redundancy.

I understand:

- that the organisation is not obliged to accept my application.
- that if I am accepted for voluntary redundancy, I will leave at a time of the organisation's choosing, which will not be less than my notice period or will be paid Payment in Lieu of Notice (PILON).

- that the decision of the organisation on my application is final and there is no right of appeal.

Signed	Date

Data protection
Personal data collected for the purposes of dealing with voluntary redundancies is treated in accordance with our data protection policy. Information about how your data is used and processed is provided within the organisation's employee privacy notice.

Please return your signed and scanned form by email to: **[email address]** Or by post to: **[postal address]** Application closing date: **[date]**

APPENDIX 7.7
VOLUNTARY REDUNDANCY
PROCESS

Introduction

The voluntary redundancy process is designed to ensure fairness and minimise disruption to organisational performance when changes mean that job losses will occur.

The purpose of offering voluntary redundancy (VR) is to limit compulsory redundancies where possible, whilst retaining our critical key skills, capabilities and knowledge pool to ensure organisational survival and future sustainability.

Objectives

The following objectives ensure organisational survival and future sustainability:

- to provide an objective, and fair approach to VR selection, which management teams will use as part of business area restructuring
- to minimise organisational disruption where possible

- to minimise the need for compulsory redundancies
- to reduce survivor guilt for our employees who remain
- to empower employees to decide to leave by their own choice.

Terms

1. There is no guarantee that VR will be granted.
2. Expressing an interest does not amount to a resignation.
3. Employees who are interested in volunteering are reassured that, if their application is not accepted, the fact that they volunteered will not be taken into account when making any compulsory redundancies or in their future employment.
4. When reviewing requests; business needs will take priority.
5. Volunteers will continue to work until the date agreed by their line manager.
6. There is no right to appeal.
7. Volunteers are invited from the following departments [explain the impacted departments, roles and locations].
8. These terms have been agreed in consultation with your [trade union/ employee representatives].

Process

During the VR process, all employees will receive a [letter/email] outlining the business plans and rationale for the proposed changes. Even though employees have volunteered for redundancy, the consultation and selection process will continue until the employee and management team have agreed which volunteers will be accepted.

VR quote

Employees wishing to request a VR confidential quote should contact [employee name and email address] up until 24 hours prior to the closing date of [time and date]. Employees will receive their quotes within [24 hours] of submitting the request. Requesting a VR quotation does not automatically imply that the employee has applied for VR and thus once the VR quote is received, employees need to still complete the VR application form.

Criteria

The Management and HR team will review each VR application, using the following criteria:

- The level of the employee's specialist knowledge, skills and experience.
- VR cannot be accepted if the loss of the role leaves an unacceptable skills or expertise gap in the department that cannot be filled satisfactorily from existing resources.
- VR will only be accepted if it prevents a compulsory redundancy.
- The total redundancy cost and if applicable, any additional costs. The costs of the redundancy exercise should not outweigh the benefit.
- The potential redundancy satisfies the overall business needs of the department.

Outcome of application

Line managers will provide suitable rationale to justify the decision reached for each VR application. Employees will be informed verbally of the outcome of their VR application on the [date] by their respective line managers. HR will follow up with the outcome of the decisions in writing to all employees who applied, confirming whether they have been accepted for VR or not by [date]. If your application is not accepted, a letter will follow, making it clear what will happen next.

Following acceptance of VR applications, employees will attend consultation meeting(s) to discuss their leaving arrangements and managers will complete the necessary forms for processing. HR will write to the employee to finalise the exit details and leaver's terms.

Should you have any queries, please feel free to contact [line manager/ HR] to discuss any concerns you may have.

Further information

Redundancy Policy
Voluntary Redundancy (VR) Application Form

APPENDIX 7.8
VOLUNTARY REDUNDANCY
PROCESS COMMUNICATION
SLIDES

Voluntary
Redundancy Process

DATE

Voluntary Redundancy Objectives:

 To provide an objective, and fair approach to (VR) selection which management teams will use as part of business area restructuring

 To minimise organisational disruption where possible

 To minimise the need for compulsory redundancies

 To reduce survivor guilt for our employees who remain

 To empower employees to decide to leave by their own choice

Terms

- There is no guarantee that VR will be granted.

- Expressing an interest does not amount to a resignation.

- Employees who are interested in volunteering are reassured that if their application is not accepted, the fact that they volunteered will not be taken into account when making any compulsory redundancies or in their future employment.

- When reviewing requests, business needs will take priority.

- Volunteers will continue to work until the date agreed by their line-manager.

- There is no right to appeal.

- Volunteers are invited from the following departments [explain the impacted departments, roles and locations].

- These terms have been agreed in consultation with your [trade union / employee representatives].

VR requests
are invited from
all employees
within the
following areas:

[insert areas, departments and roles
impacted]

Voluntary
Redundancy
Process &
Timescales

Step 1:

Obtaining a VR quotation:

Contact: [email address]

Closing date for quotes [date and time]

Employees will receive their quotes within [24 hours]

Quotations are confidential.

Voluntary Redundancy Process & Timescales

Step 2:

Applying for Voluntary Redundancy:

Employees must complete the application form

Available via the following link: [link] or [from HR office]

Returned forms to be sent to [email / postal address]

Closing day for requests [date and time]

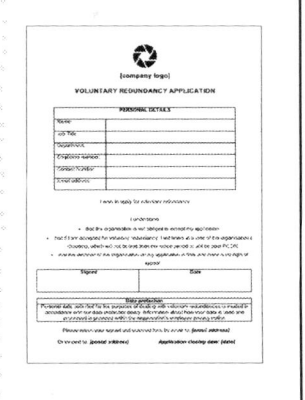

VR Selection Criteria

The Management and HR team will review each VR application, using the following criteria:

- The level of the employee's specialist knowledge, skills and experience. A VR cannot be accepted if the loss of the role leaves an unacceptable skill or expertise gap in the department which cannot be filled satisfactorily from existing resources.

- VRs will only be accepted if it prevents a compulsory redundancy.

- The total redundancy cost and, if applicable, any additional costs. The costs of the redundancy exercise should not outweigh the benefit.

- The potential redundancy satisfies the overall business needs of the department.

Outcome of Applications

Step 3:

Verbally communicated outcomes

Communicated by employee's respective line managers by [date].

Written confirmation of provisional acceptance or rejection will be communicated by email [date].

If application is accepted, follow-up invitation to a consultation meeting to discuss any outstanding issues and exit arrangements.

If application is not accepted, a letter to follow, making it clear what will happen next.

Questions

APPENDIX 7.9
VOLUNTARY REDUNDANCY
EXIT AGREEMENT EXAMPLE

Address
Date
Dear [employee]

Voluntary redundancy agreement

Further to our meeting on [date] where we discussed your application for voluntary redundancy (VR), I herewith wish to confirm the details of the agreement reached:

- Your last day of work will be on [date].
- There is no requirement for you to work any notice as agreed.
  or
- [x weeks] notice will be worked to ensure a smooth transition.
- Your payment will include the following:

- You will be paid [ ] weeks' pay in lieu of notice.
- You will be paid in lieu of [number] days' accrued and untaken holiday on termination.
- You will be entitled to [a bonus/commission] of £[ ].
- You agree that you will return all property that belongs to the organisation by [date]. Items that should be returned include [list the items, including tools if applicable].
- You will receive a redundancy payment of £[ ], which will be paid to you with your final instalment of pay. Please find attached your redundancy quotation.
- Payments in lieu of notice, untaken holiday and bonuses/commission will be paid less income tax and national insurance contributions, will be paid into the bank account into which your wages are normally paid.

To accept these terms, please sign and date this letter and return a copy to [name of individual] by [date].

Yours sincerely

[ ]

I accept the VR agreement as detailed above and attached.

Signed:

[ ]

Dated:

[ ]

APPENDIX 7.10 SETTLEMENT AGREEMENT EXAMPLE

Without prejudice/subject to contract

Settlement agreement

This Agreement is made between **[company name]** of **[address]** (the 'Company') and **[employee name]** ('You') of **[employee address]**

The company and you have agreed to settle the specific claims and other claims on the terms set out in this Agreement.

1. Your employment with the Company will terminate on **[date]** (the 'Termination Date') by reason of redundancy. The Company and you will continue to be bound by the terms and conditions of your employment until the Termination Date.

2. Provided you continue to comply with the terms and conditions of your employment, the Company will continue to provide your pay and benefits up to and including the Termination Date in the normal way. Your pay will be paid direct into your bank account each month up until the Termination Date on your normal pay day after deductions for tax and national insurance contributions.

3. The Company will pay you in lieu of any accrued but untaken holiday entitlement up to and including the Termination Date (the "Holiday Payment"). Payment will be made direct to your bank account after deductions for tax and national insurance within **[number]** days after the Termination Date.

4. The Company will pay you **[amount]** in lieu of salary to which you are entitled under your contract of employment (the 'Payment in Lieu of Notice'). Payment will be made direct to your bank account after deductions for tax and national insurance contributions within **[number]** days after the Termination Date.

5. The Company will pay you **[amount]** in payment for a discretionary **[include details]** payment **[(the xxx Benefit Payment')]**. Payment will be made direct to your bank account after deductions for tax and national insurance contributions within **[number]** days after the Termination Date and upon the Company receiving both a copy of this Agreement signed by you and a certificate from your Adviser in the form set out in the Appendix A and upon receipt of a further copy of this Agreement signed for a second time on or around the Termination Date as confirmed at Clause 8 of this Agreement.

6. The Company will pay you **[amount]** in payment for a discretionary **[include details]** payment **[(the xxx Benefit Payment')]**. Payment will be made direct to your bank account after deduction for tax and national insurance contributions within **[number]** days after the Termination Date and upon the Company receiving both a copy of this Agreement signed by you and a certificate from your Adviser in the form set out in the Appendix A and upon receipt of a further copy of this Agreement signed for a second time on or around the Termination Date as confirmed at Clause 8 of this Agreement.

7. The Company will pay you **[amount]** by way of compensation for loss of your employment (the 'Termination Payment'), which is made up of the following:

    (a) Statutory Redundancy Payment of **[amount]** (set out at Appendix B)
    (b) Contractual Redundancy Payment of **[amount]**
    (c) Ex-gratia Payment for loss of office of **[amount]**
        Payment will be made within **[number]** days of the Termination Date and upon the Company receiving both a copy of this

Agreement signed by you and a certificate from your Adviser in the form set out in the Appendix A and upon receipt of a further copy of this Agreement signed for a second time on or around the Termination Date as confirmed at Clause 8 of this Agreement. The Company will pay the first £30,000 of the Termination Payment without deduction for income tax or national insurance contributions and will deduct income tax but not national insurance contributions from the balance at the appropriate rate.

8. You agree to sign a copy of this Agreement for a second time on or around the Termination Date and to provide a copy of this Agreement to the Company upon signature.

9. You must return promptly and at the latest by the Termination Date all property belonging to the Company **[any Group Company]** or its **[their]** clients, customers or business contacts (including, but not limited to, **[include list of property]**, all documents or correspondence and copies of such documents or correspondence and all security passes, keys, credit or charge cards, mobile phones, laptops and all computer hardware and software of any description) which is in your possession or control or in the possession or control of your Adviser.

10. You must submit any unclaimed expenses together with the relevant supporting documentation no later than the Termination Date for reimbursement to be made.

11. You will be solely responsible for indemnifying the Company against and keeping the Company indemnified on a continuing basis against any liability in respect of income tax, employee's national insurance contributions and related costs and penalties arising in respect of the payment(s) made [and benefit(s) provided] and other arrangements under this Agreement, unless that liability arises directly from the Company's delay or deliberate default.

12. You warrant that (a) to (f) below are true. The Company will be under no obligation to pay the Termination Payment (excluding the Statutory Redundancy Payment), Car Benefit Payment and Payment in Lieu of Notice if they are not.

    (a) You have received independent legal advice from [*name of adviser*] (your 'Adviser') as to the terms and effect of this Agreement and

in particular, its effect on your ability to pursue your rights before an employment tribunal.

(b) Having given your Adviser all relevant facts and having received
advice from your Adviser, you are aware of no other claim that
you may have in connection with your employment, which is not
referred to as a Specific Claim below.

(c) You have not [and will not] already issued proceedings in respect
of any of the Specific Claims or Other Claims, referred to below.

(d) There are no circumstances of which you are aware or of which
you ought to be aware, which would have entitled the Company
to terminate your employment without notice.

(e) You have irretrievably deleted or will irretrievably delete before
the Termination Date any information relating to the business or
business contacts of the Company **[or any Group Company]** that
you have stored on any personal computer or electronic device of
any description.

(f) You have received neither an offer of employment nor an offer of
other work and nor are you in discussions likely to lead to such
offers being made.

13. The terms of this Agreement are in full and final settlement of specific
claims and other claims, all of which you are waiving when you sign
this Agreement. You cannot and will not bring proceedings in respect
of any of these claims.

14. The 'Specific Claims' are the following specific claims which you may
have against the Company, **[any Group Company]** or any of **[its/
their]** officers or employees, whether such claims may have already
arisen or arise in the future and whether or not you could reasonably
have knowledge of them:

(a) unfair dismissal under section 94 of the Employment Rights Act
1996 ('ERA');

(b) unfair dismissal on grounds related to health and safety matters
under s100 ERA;

(c) failure to provide a statement of employment particulars or
changes contrary to section 1 or 4 ERA;

d) failure to pay a Statutory Redundancy Payment contrary to s135
ERA;

(e) less favourable treatment on grounds of/because of sex, indirect sex discrimination, victimisation or harassment including sexual harassment under the Equality Act 2010;

(f) less favourable treatment, indirect discrimination, victimisation or harassment related to sexual orientation under the Employment Equality (Sexual Orientation) Regulations 2003 and/or the Equality Act 2010;

(g) less favourable treatment on grounds of/because of race, indirect race discrimination, victimisation or racial harassment under the Equality Act 2010;

(h) less favourable treatment on grounds of/because of disability, less favourable treatment because of something arising in consequence of disability, indirect disability discrimination, failure to make reasonable adjustments, victimisation or harassment under the Equality Act 2010;

(i) less favourable treatment on grounds of age, indirect age discrimination, victimisation or harassment under the Equality Act 2010;

(j) detrimental treatment on grounds related to health and safety matters under s44 ERA;

(k) claims relating to equal pay under the Equality Act 2010;

(l) unlawful deduction from wages contrary to section 13 ERA;

(m) breach of contract;

(n) failure to pay holiday pay due under the Working Time Regulations 1998;

(o) breach of any rights in respect of minimum statutory notice under sections 80–91 ERA;

(p) detrimental treatment and/or unfair dismissal on grounds of having made a protected disclosure under s47B ERA and/or s103A ERA;

(q) any claim that the Company, [or any Group Company], or any of its/their officers or employees have caused or contributed to an injury [including but not limited to, a psychiatric injury caused or contributed to by harassment/less favourable treatment/victimisation] contrary to the Equality Act 2010. Furthermore, including but not limited to any injury that you have or may incur when you slipped and fell **[need to particularise this – date – location].**

15. The 'Other Claims' are all other claims in connection with your employment or its termination, which you may have against the Company, **[any Group Company]** or any of **[its/their]** officers or employees whether under the law of England and Wales, the law of another country, European Union law or otherwise, whether such claims may have already arisen or arise in the future and whether or not you could reasonably have knowledge of them.

16. The terms of this Agreement are not in settlement of, and therefore do not stop you bringing proceedings in respect of the following claims:

    (a) any claim relating to your accrued pension entitlements.

    (b) any claim of personal injury, expressly excluding Clause 14(o) above, relating to an injury, which you do not know about and could not reasonably have known about when you signed this Agreement, unless your claim is that the injury was caused or contributed to by a Discriminatory Act. A 'Discriminatory Act' is something that you believe the Company [any Group Company] or any of [its/their] officers or employees did or did not do in connection with your employment, which might cause you to have a claim of unlawful discrimination contrary to one of the Acts/Regulations listed below at paragraph 17. All claims in respect of Discriminatory Acts are settled by this Agreement.

17. It is a fundamental condition of this Agreement that the conditions regulating settlement agreements contained in the following sections, provisions and regulations are intended to be and have been satisfied:

    (a) Section 288(2B) of the Trade Union and Labour Relations (Consolidation) Act 1992;

    (b) Section 203(3) of the Employment Rights Act 1996;

    (c) Regulation 35(3) of the Working Time Regulations 1998;

    (d) Section 49(4) of the National Minimum Wage Act 1998;

    (e) Regulation 41(4) of the Transnational Information and Consultation of Employee Regulations 1999;

    (f) Regulation 9 of the Part-Time Workers (Prevention of Less Favourable Treatment) Regulations 2000;

    (g) Regulation 10 of the Fixed-Term Employees (Prevention of Less Favourable Treatment) Regulations 2002;

(h) Regulation 40(4) of the Information and Consultation of Employees Regulations 2004;

(i) Paragraph 13 of the schedule to the Occupational and Personal Pension Schemes (Consultation by Employers and Miscellaneous Amendment) Regulations 2006 and paragraph 2(2) of schedule 5 of the Employment Equality (Age) Regulations 2006;

(j) Section 147(3) of the Equality Act 2010;

(k) Section 58 of the Pensions Act 2008;

(l) The Employment Relations Act 1999;

(m) Section 77(4A) of the Sex Discrimination Act 1975 (with regard to claims under that Act and the Equal Pay Act 1970);

(n) Section 72 (4A) of the Race Relations Act 1976;

(o) Paragraph 2 of the schedule 3A of the Disability Discrimination Act 1995;

(p) Paragraph 2(2) of schedule 4 to the Employment Equality (Sexual Orientation) Regulations 2003;

(q) Paragraph 2(2) of schedule 4 to the Employment Equality (Religion or Belief) Regulations 2003;

(r) Regulation 15 of the Agency Workers Regulation 2010;

18. If you seek to present a claim in respect of any of the Specific Claims or Other Claims, then the Termination Payment, Payment in Lieu of Notice less any portion of the Termination Payment representing your statutory redundancy entitlement, **[or xx Benefit Payment and xxx Payment]** will become immediately repayable in full. Repayment will be recoverable as a debt. Any sums otherwise due to you under this Agreement will not be paid. This clause will operate Without Prejudice to any other remedy that may be available to the Company.

19. You undertake to keep the existence and terms of this Agreement and the circumstances leading up to the termination of your employment confidential and will not disclose them unless you:

(a) have the prior written consent of the Company;

(b) are doing so in confidence to legal or financial advisers, relevant tax authorities or as otherwise required by law;

(c) are doing so in strict confidence to your spouse, partner or members of your immediate family and they agree to keep the information confidential.

In consideration for you giving such an undertaking, the Company will also agree to keep the existence and terms of this Agreement and the circumstances leading up to the termination of your employment confidential and will not disclose them unless it is doing so in confidence to legal or financial advisers, relevant tax authorities, appropriate levels of management or as otherwise required by law.

20. Clause 24 ("Confidentiality"), Clause 26 ("Publications and Broadcasts"), Clause 36 ("Trade Connections"), Clause 37 ("Non-Solicitation") of your Contract of Employment dated **[date]** are intended to, and You agree to, survive termination of your employment and You will abide by them.

21. On receipt of a written request from a potential employer, the Company will provide a standard company reference subject always to the Company's obligation to third parties relating to the giving of references and provided always that such requests are directed to **[address/email address/phone number]**.

22. You undertake not to make any adverse or derogatory comments about the Company or any Group Company or any director or officer of the Company or any Group Company.

23. The Company will contribute up to **[amount]** plus VAT, towards the legal fees that you incur with your Adviser in taking legal advice on the termination of your employment. Payment will be made directly to your Adviser (or their organisation) within 30 days of the Company's receipt of an appropriate invoice addressed to you but marked payable by the Company.

24. This Agreement sets out the entire agreement and understanding between the parties and supersedes any previous agreement between us concerning your employment and its termination except any restrictions on your post-employment activities or disclosure of confidential information. You have not relied on any representations when entering into this Agreement. The Company accepts no liability for any misrepresentations.

25. Notwithstanding that this Agreement is marked "Without Prejudice"/"covered by s111A of the Employment Rights Act 1996"

and "Subject to Contract", it will become open and binding when signed by both parties.

26. In accordance with the Contracts (Rights of Third Parties) Act 1999, any employee or officer of the Company [and any Group Company] will have the right to rely on paragraphs 12–17 of this Agreement.

27. In this Agreement, "Group Company" means the Company, its subsidiaries or holding companies from time to time and any subsidiary of any holding company from time to time (subsidiary and holding company to be attributed the meaning within section 1159 of the Companies Act 2006) or associated company as attributed to the meaning within section 256 of the Companies Act 2006.

Signed on behalf of **[company]**

Date:

Signed by you: **[employee name]**

Date:

APPENDIX A

Certificate from your adviser

I certify that:

1. I am a relevant independent adviser within the meaning of section 203 of the Employment Rights Act 1996 and the other sections, provisions and regulations referred to in paragraph 17 of the attached settlement agreement, being a **[Solicitor of the Senior Courts of England and Wales holding a current practising certificate/barrister] [job title and name of trade union/advice centre etc]**. I am duly authorised by **[trade union/advice centre]** to give such advice and confirmation of such authorisation is attached to this statement].
2. I have advised **[name of employee]** as to the terms and effect of the settlement agreement to which this certificate is attached and in particular as to its effect on his/her ability to pursue her/his rights before an employment tribunal.

3. There was in force at the time the advice referred to above was given, a contract of insurance or an indemnity covering the risk of a claim by **[name of employee]** in respect of loss arising in consequence of the advice.

Signed by
  Name of firm/advice centre
  Address
  Date

APPENDIX B

Calculation of the Statutory Redundancy Payment
start date: [date]
Termination date: [date]
Period of continuous employment: [amount years and months]
Age at termination of employment: [age]
Gross weekly basic salary: [amount]
Statutory cap on weekly salary: [amount]
Statutory redundancy pay calculator equates to [number x £xxx based on length of service]
Total: [£]

APPENDIX 7.11
LETTER INFORMING
EMPLOYEES OF POTENTIAL
REDUNDANCIES

Dear [ ]
[date]

Proposed redundancies

I refer to the [Director's name] announcement on [date] where we explained that the organisation needs to implement redundancies to save costs due to

[**External factors** such as market crashes, government deregulation, loss of customers, increased competition, lack of orders;

Internal factors such as organisational redesign, location mergers, outsourcing or relocation, harmonisation after a merger or acquisition.]

These factors have led to us proposing to implement redundancies in [department and location] as we are facing:

[Business closure:

Ceasing or intending to cease to carry on the business for the purposes of which the employee was employed by it.

Workplace closure

Ceasing or intending to cease to carry on that business in the place where the employee was so employed (or)

Reduced requirement for employees

Having a reduced requirement for employees to carry out work of a particular kind or to do so at the place where the employee was employed to work.]

We understand that this is a disturbing and unsettling period for all of us involved and this is not a decision that we have taken lightly.

Consultation process

Consultation will last for a period of [30/45/90] days. During this time employees who were provisionally selected for redundancy will have the opportunity to put forward any representations or alternative suggestions that they feel may affect the company's initial proposal regarding their position being at risk. This includes any suggestions on:

- how redundancies can be limited or avoided
- feedback on the selection pool
- feedback on the selection criteria and matrix
- any suitable alternative roles they may be interested in, which are available via the following link [insert link/attached document].

Please provide any feedback or suggestions to [contact name] via [email/letter] by the [date] latest for due consideration. We will continue to consider your proposals throughout the consultation period. Please also be aware that we will make no final decisions on whether your role is redundant until the consultation period is complete.

To assist us in a fair and transparent process for redundancy selection, we propose the use of the following selection criteria and matrix, which will determine which employees will be provisionally selected for redundancy:

- job performance
- knowledge
- skills
- qualifications
- work experience
- disciplinary records
- absences
- timekeeping
- length of service.*

*Length of service will only be used in a tie-break situation when two or more employees achieve the same score.

Next steps

If your role is provisionally selected for redundancy, we will inform you in writing via [email/letter]. The letter will advise you of a date for our first individual consultation meeting to discuss how your role may be impacted and what the proposed changes are.

We sincerely regret having to write to you under these circumstances.

We understand that this can be a distressing time and as such would like to remind you of the [EAP services/help line]. The company is committed to support our employees in finding alternative employment and will be providing various sources of support such as [include details] for all employees at risk of redundancy.

If you have any queries, please do not hesitate to contact [name].

Yours sincerely

[name]

[position]

APPENDIX 7.12
LETTER INFORMING
EMPLOYEE OF BEING 'AT RISK
OF REDUNDANCY'

Dear [ ]

[date]

Confirmation of being 'at risk of redundancy'

I refer to the [Director's name] announcement on [date] where we explained that the organisation needs to implement redundancies to save costs due to

[**External factors** such as market crashes, government deregulation, loss of customers, increased competition, lack of orders;

Internal factors such as organisational redesign, location mergers, outsourcing or relocation, harmonisation after a merger or acquisition.]

These factors have led to us proposing to implement redundancies in [department and location] as we are facing

[**Business closure**:

Ceasing or intending to cease to carry on the business for the purposes of which the employee was employed by it.

Workplace closure:

Ceasing or intending to cease to carry on that business in the place where the employee was so employed (or)

Reduced requirement for employees

Having a reduced requirement for employees to carry out work of a particular kind or to do so at the place where the employee was employed to work.]

We understand that this is a disturbing and unsettling period for all of us involved and this is not a decision that we have taken lightly.

Regrettably, we are informing you that your role is at risk of redundancy, as of the [date] of your meeting with [HR representative] and [name]. This does not mean that a decision has been taken with respect to your role until the consultation period is completed.

[**Voluntary redundancies**

With the aim of reducing the amount of compulsory redundancies, the company has been inviting applications from employees in the following departments and roles to apply. Please consider that not all applications will be accepted and applications are subject to management discretion as set out in the attached voluntary redundancy process.]

Consultation process

Your individual consultation period that commences on [date] will last for a period of 30 days. During this time, you will have the opportunity to put forward any representations or alternative suggestions that you feel, may affect the company's initial proposal regarding your position being at risk. This includes any suggestions on:

- how redundancies can be limited or avoided
- feedback on the selection pool
- feedback on the selection criteria and matrix
- any suitable alternative roles you may be interested in, which are available via the following link [insert link/attached document]

- an opportunity to raise any questions or concerns.

Please provide any feedback or suggestions to [contact name] via [email/letter] by the [date] latest for due consideration. We will continue to consider your proposals throughout the consultation period. Please also be aware that we will make no final decisions on whether your role is redundant until the consultation period is complete.

To assist us in a fair and transparent process for redundancy selection, we propose the use of the following selection criteria and matrix, which will determine which employees will be provisionally selected for redundancy:

- job performance
- knowledge
- skills
- qualifications
- work experience
- disciplinary records
- absences
- timekeeping
- length of service.*

*Length of service will only be used in a tie-break situation when two or more employees achieve the same score.

Next steps

We will shortly write to you to invite you to attend a consultation meeting. The consultation letter will contain the specifics of the meeting location and purpose.

We sincerely regret having to write to you under these circumstances.

We understand that this can be a distressing time and as such would like to remind you of the [EAP services/help line]. The company is committed to support our employees in finding alternative employment and will be providing various sources of support such as [include details].

If you have any queries, please do not hesitate to contact [name].

Yours sincerely
[name]
Included: [Redundancy policy
Proposed selection matrix
Voluntary redundancy process
Voluntary redundancy application form
Redundancy FAQ
Vacancy list
EAP booklet
Contact details of employee/trade union representatives].

APPENDIX 7.13
LETTER INVITING EMPLOYEE TO FIRST CONSULTATION MEETING

Dear [ ]
  [date]

First consultation meeting

Further to the meeting on the [date] where we informed you that your role is at risk of redundancy with [HR representative], we are writing to invite you to attend your first individual consultation meeting.

The purpose of this meeting is to discuss how your role may be impacted and what the proposed changes are.

The meeting will take place on
[date]
[time]
[location/online platform].

Representation

The meeting will be held by [line manager] with [HR representative] present. You may bring with you a colleague or [employee/trade union representative]. Please let me know at least 24 hours in advance if you will be joined by a representative. If your chosen companion is unable to attend this meeting, please contact [name and role] on [email/phone number] as soon as possible so that an alternative date or time can be arranged.

Consultation process

Your individual consultation period that commences on [date] will last for a period of 30 days. During this time, you will have the opportunity to put forward any representations or alternative suggestions that you feel, may affect the company's initial proposal regarding your position being at risk. This includes any suggestions on:

- how redundancies can be limited or avoided
- feedback on the selection pool
- feedback on the selection criteria and matrix
- any suitable alternative roles you may be interested in, which are available via the following link [insert link/attached document]
- an opportunity to raise any questions or concerns.

Please provide any feedback or suggestions to [contact name] via [email/letter] by the [date] latest for due consideration. We will continue to consider your proposals throughout the consultation period. Please also be aware that we will make no final decisions on whether your role is redundant until the consultation period is complete.

To assist us in a fair and transparent process for redundancy selection, we propose the use of the following selection criteria and matrix, which will determine which employees will be provisionally selected for redundancy:

- job performance
- knowledge
- skills

- qualifications
- work experience
- disciplinary records
- absences
- timekeeping
- length of service.*

*Length of service will only be used in a tie-break situation when two or more employees achieve the same score.

We sincerely regret having to write to you under these circumstances.

Time off to look for alternative work

The company recognises the pressure of finding a new source of income associated with redundancy situations. You are therefore granted with a reasonable amount of paid time off work to attend interviews, apply for alternative work or explore alternative sources of income such as starting your own business. Any such arrangements must be made in agreement with your line manager.

Support

We understand that this can be a distressing time and as such would like to remind you of the [EAP services/help line]. The company is committed to support our employees in finding alternative employment and will be providing various sources of support such as [include details].

If you have any queries, please do not hesitate to contact [name].

Yours sincerely

[name]

Attached: Vacancy list

Support workshops details

APPENDIX 7.14
FIRST INDIVIDUAL
CONSULTATION RECORD FORM

First individual redundancy consultation record

Employee name:		Date:	
Job title:		HR:	
Department:		Line manager:	

Topics to discuss:	Notes
Business rationale and overview	
Check understanding of the proposals	
Explain 'at risk' meaning and process	
Confirm 'at risk' notice letter was received	
Reason for redundancy selection and selection pool	

How the employee is affected by the selection; i.e. current role is being removed, change in reporting line, job title, department, etc.

Proposed change(s) if applicable

Discuss and explore ways of avoiding redundancies

Consider suitable alternative employment within the organisation

Discuss the opportunities available and how to apply

Discuss selection criteria and selection matrix scoring

Explain redundancy process

Explain redundancy timescales

Explain who the nominated employee/ union representatives are

Explain the role of the representatives

Explain and explore support for employee

Explain redundancy 'quotation'

Explain next steps

Document check list:

Redundancy policy

Vacancy list

Employee support

Frequently asked questions

Details of employee/union representation

Redundancy calculation

Employee questions	Feedback/comments for manager to explore/actions

I am signing to agree that this is an accurate reflection of the conversation held.

Employee Signature   Manager Signature

APPENDIX 7.15
LETTER INVITING EMPLOYEE TO SECOND INDIVIDUAL CONSULTATION MEETING

Dear [ ]
[date]

Second consultation meeting

Further to your first consultation meeting on [date] when we discussed the business rationale for the redundancies in your [department] and how the proposed changes will impact your role, we are writing to invite you to attend your second, individual consultation meeting.

The purpose of this meeting is to discuss the outcome of your selection matrix and the implications for your role.

The meeting will take place on
[date]
[time]
[location/online platform].

Representation

The meeting will be held by [line manager] with [HR representative] present. You may bring with you a colleague or [employee/trade union representative]. Please let me know at least 24 hours in advance if you will be joined by a representative. If your chosen companion is unable to attend this meeting, please contact [name and role] on [email/phone number] as soon as possible so that an alternative date or time can be arranged.

Consultation process

Your individual consultation period commences on [date] will last for a period of 30 days. During this time, you will have the opportunity to put forward any representations or alternative suggestions that you feel, may affect the company's initial proposal regarding your position being at risk. This includes any suggestions on:

* how redundancies can be limited or avoided
* feedback on the selection pool
* feedback on the selection criteria and matrix
* any suitable alternative roles you may be interested in, which are available via the following link [insert link/attached document]
* an opportunity to raise any questions or concerns.

Please provide any feedback or suggestions to [contact name] via [email/letter] by the [date] latest for due consideration. We will continue to consider your proposals throughout the consultation period. Please also be aware that we will make no final decisions on whether your role is redundant until the consultation period is complete.

Time off to look for alternative work

The company recognises the pressure of finding a new source of income associated with redundancy situations. You are therefore granted a reasonable amount of paid time off work to attend interviews, apply for alternative work or explore alternative sources of income, such as starting your own business. Any such arrangements must be made in agreement with the employee's line manager.

Support

We understand that this can be a distressing time and as such would like to remind you of the [EAP services/help line]. The company is committed to support our employees in finding alternative employment and will be providing various sources of support such as [include details].

If you have any queries, please do not hesitate to contact [name].

Yours sincerely

[name]

Attached: Vacancy list

Outcome of selection matrix

APPENDIX 7.16
SECOND INDIVIDUAL
CONSULTATION RECORD FORM

Second individual redundancy consultation record

Employee name:		Date:	
Job title:		HR:	
Department:		Line manager:	

Topics to discuss	Notes
Check whether the employee has any questions regarding the redundancy process	
Advise if any feedback was received on the proposed selection criteria and whether any adjustments have been made	
Explain the employee selection scoring and identify any points of discrepancies	

Explain the outcome; i.e. employee is still at risk of redundancy or employee application has been successful for alternative role

Discuss work priorities

Discuss potential dismissal date

Remind employee of support available

Explain next steps

Employee questions	Feedback/comments for manager to explore/actions

I am signing to agree that this is an accurate reflection of the conversation held.

Employee Signature   Manager Signature

APPENDIX 7.17
LETTER INVITING
EMPLOYEE TO THIRD
CONSOLATION MEETING

Dear [ ]
  [date]

Third consultation meeting

Further to your first and second consultation meeting on the [date] and [date] where we consulted with you on the reasons for your selection for redundancy, I regret to inform you that as a result of the outcome of the previous two consultations, that your role is at risk of being terminated by reason of redundancy.

As explained at the previous consultation meeting, this outcome has arisen as a result of the outcome of the selection matrix applied to your redundancy pool. We have and continue to take onboard your representations and suggestions until a final decision is made. You are therefore invited to your third consultation meeting.

The purpose of this meeting is to discuss any new proposals from your side and clarify aspects that will impact your Termination Date if no further suggestions are feasible.

The meeting will take place on

[date]

[time]

[location/online platform].

Representation

The meeting will be held by [line manager] with [HR representative] present. You may bring with you a colleague or [employee/trade union representative]. Please let me know at least 24 hours in advance if you will be joined by a representative. If your chosen companion is unable to attend this meeting, please contact [name and role] on [email/phone number] as soon as possible so that an alternative date or time can be arranged.

Consultation process

Your individual consultation period that commences on [date] will last for a period of 30 days. During this time, you will have the opportunity to put forward any representations or alternative suggestions that you feel, may affect the company's initial proposal regarding your position being at risk. This includes any suggestions on:

- how redundancies can be limited or avoided;
- feedback on the selection pool;
- feedback on the selection criteria and matrix;
- any suitable alternative roles you may be interested in, which are available via the following link [insert link/attached document];
- an opportunity to raise any questions or concerns.

Please provide any feedback or suggestions to [contact name] via [email/letter] by the [date] latest for due consideration. We will continue to consider your proposals throughout the consultation period. Please also be aware that we will make no final decisions on whether your role is redundant until the consultation period is complete.

Time off to look for alternative work

The company recognises the pressure of finding a new source of income associated with redundancy situations. You are therefore granted with a reasonable amount of paid time off work to attend interviews, apply for alternative work or explore alternative sources of income, such as starting your own business. Any such arrangements must be made in agreement with the employee's line manager.

Support

We understand that this can be a distressing time and as such would like to remind you of the [EAP services/help line]. The company is committed to support our employees in finding alternative employment and will be providing various sources of support; such as [include details].

If you have any queries, please do not hesitate to contact [name].

Yours sincerely

[name]

Attached: Vacancy list

Redundancy quotation

APPENDIX 7.18
THIRD CONSULTATION
RECORD FORM

Third individual redundancy consultation record

Employee name:		Date:	
Job title:		HR:	
Department:		Line manager:	

Topics to discuss: **Notes**

Check whether the employee has any questions regarding the redundancy process

Advise if any feedback was received on the proposed selection criteria and whether any adjustments had been made

Discuss work priorities and handover requirements

Discuss and agree required notice period required to be worked

Clarify Payment in Lieu of Notice (PILON) if applicable

Clarify holiday entitlement, what will be taken and what will be paid

Confirm last date of working

Identify return of company property and process of return

Remind employee of support available

Clarify when redundancy payments will be made

Explain appeals process

Explain next steps

Employee questions	Feedback/comments for manager to explore/actions

I am signing to agree that this is an accurate reflection of the conversation held.

Employee Signature   Manager Signature

APPENDIX 7.19
NOTICE OF DISMISSAL FOR
REASON OF REDUNDANCY

Dear [ ]
[date]

Notice of termination of employment

Further to your third consultation meeting on [date] with myself and [name], I am writing to confirm the outcome of your provisional selection for redundancy as our consultation period has now concluded.

On [date] the [Director's name] announcement explained that the organisation needs to implement redundancies to save costs due to

[**External factors** such as market crashes, government deregulation, loss of customers, increased competition, lack of orders;

Internal factors such as organisational redesign, location mergers, outsourcing or relocation, harmonisation after a merger or acquisition.]

These factors have led to us proposing to implement redundancies in [department and location] as we are facing

[Business closure

Ceasing or intending to cease to carry on the business for the purposes of which the employee was employed by it.

Workplace closure

Ceasing or intending to cease to carry on that business in the place where the employee was so employed (or)

Reduced requirement for employees

Having a reduced requirement for employees to carry out work of a particular kind or to do so at the place where the employee was employed to work.]

During the consultation process, we held [number] individual consultation meetings over a period of [number] days:

1st consultation meeting: [date], [location], with [name and role]

2nd consultation meeting: [date], [location], with [name and role]

3rd consultation meeting: [date], [location], with [name and role]

During the consultation process, you put forward the following representations and suggestions to secure your role; [include the suggestions]

After careful consideration, we have [made the following amendments to your selection matrix] or [we have not made any amendments to your selection matrix, based on [put forward the rationale].

Unfortunately, the outcome of your selection matrix scoring was [insert details] which meant that you were selected for redundancy based on being amongst the lowest [number] of employees.

During the consultation period, we have provided you with updated vacancy lists and also explored suitable alternative work for you; however, we have not been successful in securing a suitable alternative role for you.

On this basis, it is with regret that we have to inform you that your role will be terminated, resulting in dismissal as a result of redundancy.

Redundancy payment

You are entitled to statutory redundancy pay of [amount]. [In addition, as the company offers enhanced redundancy pay, you will also be entitled to an additional [amount].] Details of your redundancy payment calculations are attached for your perusal. Please be aware that any redundancy payment in excess of £30,000 will be liable to income tax. Your final payment will be made by [date].

OR

You are entitled to statutory redundancy pay of [amount]. Your final payment will be made by [date]. Details of your redundancy payment calculations are attached for your perusal.

OR

In accordance with redundancy law, you are not eligible for a redundancy payment as you do not meet the minimum criteria of two years continuous service. [We understand that this can be a disappointing outcome and are therefore willing to make a once-off payment as a gesture of good faith of [amount].]

Notice period

As agreed in your last consultation meeting on the [date], your last day of work will be on the [date].

We agreed that you will not be required to work your full notice period and as a result you will receive a Payment in Lieu of Notice (PILON) for the notice period of [weeks and days]. Your PILON payment will be [amount] and subject to income tax and national insurance contributions, which will be paid with your redundancy payment.

OR

You are entitled to [weeks] notice as per your contract of employment. You will be paid up to that date in the normal way. During your notice period we will continue to explore suitable alternative roles.

OR

You are entitled to [weeks] notice as per your contract of employment. You will be paid up to that date in the normal way. As agreed in the consultation meeting, you will not be required to work during your notice period. During this time, your contract will continue until your last day of work and you will continue to be paid in the normal manner. All other aspects of your contract of employment continues, except for the requirement to work. We will ask that you are contactable should we need to consult with you on any handover related matters. During your notice period we will continue to explore suitable alternative roles.

Additional payments

Final salary payment

Your final salary payment will be made in the next payroll up until your termination day, subject to income tax and national insurance contributions. Your final payslip and P45 will be sent to your home address.

[Company bonus

You will be eligible to receive a bonus payment based on [include criteria]. Your bonus payment will be [amount], subject to income tax and national insurance contributions. Your bonus payment is not pensionable.]

[Variable payments

Outstanding overtime, shift or on-call payments will be paid as part of your final salary payment, subject to income tax and national insurance contributions. If we are unable to process such payments, due to payroll run dates, this will be paid to you after your final salary payment in the following month and treated as a payment after leaving.]

Holiday pay

We agreed the outstanding accrued holiday days you are entitled to are [amount] days. You will be paid in lieu of [amount] of holiday days due as part of your final instalment, subject to income tax and national insurance contributions.

[Expenses

We will reimburse you outstanding expenses in accordance with the company's expenses policy up until your Termination Date. Please submit your expenses claim, in the usual way, by no later than [date]. If it is not possible submit your expenses by this date, please submit within one week of your Termination Date. This will be paid to you after your final salary payment in the following month and treated as a payment after leaving.]

[Overpayments or outstanding loans

Any outstanding payments to the company for a loan, travel season ticket, salary advances or overpayments must be repaid in full prior to you leaving the company. As per the terms and conditions of your loan agreement and contract of employment, the company has the right to deduct any outstanding amounts from your final payment.]

Company pension scheme

[As you are a member of the company pension scheme, your PILON will automatically have your pension contribution deducted and passed to your pension provider, together with the company's contribution.]

If you need any guidance in relation to your pension, please contact the [pension provider] on [contact number or email address].

Employment references

The company will provide you with a standard reference letter, available from HR contact [name] on [email address].

Company property

Please return all company property to [name] and [contact] on your last day of employment or as agreed in your consultation meeting by [date]. At your last consultation meeting, the following items of company property were identified to be returned:

[Company car, two sets of keys, fuel card, parking access fob, office key, filing cabinet key, laptop, laptop bag, headset, keyboard, mouse, tools, health and safety clothes, etc.]

Right to appeal

You have the right to appeal against the decision to dismiss you for redundancy. If you wish to appeal, you should do so in writing within [5] days of receipt of this letter to [name] and [contact email/address], setting out your grounds for your appeal.

Ongoing support

[We would like to remind you that our outplacement services provide support up until [amount] of days after you have settled in a new role. You can contact them on: [Outplacement services/help line].

It is really with regret that we got to this position, and we do appreciate your service to the organisation during the last [amount] years. We wish you all the very best for the future.

If you have any queries, please do not hesitate to contact [name].

Yours sincerely

[ ]

Included: [Redundancy calculation]

Supporting workshop details]

APPENDIX 7.20
LETTER INFORMING
EMPLOYEE OF REDUNDANCY
DESELECTION

Dear [ ]
[date]

Redundancy deselection: role no longer at risk

I refer to our recent redundancy consultation meeting held on [date] with myself and [name] where we discussed various aspects in relation to your role being at risk of redundancy.

[Due to a sufficient number of voluntary redundancies within the [department], we are pleased to inform you that your role is no longer at risk of redundancy. We will therefore conclude the consultation period and you will continue your employment in your current role on the same terms and conditions.

OR

After careful consideration of the representations and suggestions put forward by you, we are pleased to inform you that based on [state the factors that provided the catalyst for change] your role is no longer at risk. We will therefore conclude the consultation period and you will continue your employment in your current role on the same terms and conditions.

OR

Further to your successful application for the suitable alternative role of [job role] that commences on [date], we are pleased to inform you that your current role is no longer at risk. We will therefore conclude the consultation period and you will receive a new contract of employment under separate cover.]

We understand that this is a disturbing and unsettling period for all of us involved and we thank you for your continued commitment and dedication.

Despite your role no longer being at risk of redundancy, we would like to continue to remind you of the [EAP services/help line]. The company is committed to support all our employees during tumultuous times.

If you have any queries, please do not hesitate to contact [name].

Yours sincerely

[name]

References

Applebaum, S. H., Everard, A. & Hung, L. T. 1999. Strategic downsizing: Critical success factors. *Management Decision*, 37(7), 535–552.

Arndt, E. M. & Duchemin, K. F. 1993. *More than "Bandaids": Emotional support and education during the downsizing process. Healthcare management forum, 1993*. Los Angeles, CA: Sage Publications, 5–10.

Baruch, Y. & Hind, P. 1999. Perpetual motion in organizations: Effective management and the Impact of the new psychological contracts on "survivor syndrome". *European Journal of Work and Organizational Psychology*, 8, 295–306. doi: 10.1080/135943299398375

Bergström, O. & Arman, R. 2017. Increasing commitment after downsizing: The role of involvement and voluntary redundancies. *Journal of Change Management*, 17, 297–320.

Brockner, J. 1992. Managing the effects of layoffs on survivors. *California Management Review*, 34(2), 9–28.

Cameron, K. S. 1994. Strategies for successful organizational downsizing. *Human Resource Management*, 33, 189–211.

Cascio, W. F. 1993. Downsizing: What do we know? What have we learned? *Academy of Management Perspectives*, 7, 95–104.

Clark, J. & Koonce, R. 1995. Engaging organizations survivors: Training and development. *An American Survey Management Journal*, 49(8), 22–31.

Clarke, M. 2005. The voluntary redundancy option: Carrot or stick? *British Journal of Management*, 16, 245–251.

Clarke, M. 2007. Choices and constraints: Individual perceptions of the voluntary redundancy experience. *Human Resource Management Journal*, 17, 76–93.

Cross, B. & Travaglione, A. 2004. The times they are a-changing: Who will stay and who will go in a downsizing organization? *Personnel Review*, 33(3), 275–290.

Davis, J. A., Savage, G., Stewart, R. T. & Chapman, R. C. 2003. Organizational downsizing: A review of literature for planning and research/practitioner application. *Journal of Healthcare Management*, 48, 181.

De Meuse, K. P., Vanderheiden, P. A. & Bergmann, T. J. 1994. Announced layoffs: Their effect on corporate financial performance. *Human Resource Management*, 33, 509–530.

Farnham, D. & Pimlott, J. 1995. *Understanding Industrial Relations*. London: Cassell.

Flint, D. H. 2003. Downsizing in the public sector: Metro-Toronto's hospitals. *Journal of Health Organization and Management*, 17(6), 438–456.

Freeman, S. J. 1999. The gestalt of organizational downsizing: Downsizing strategies as packages of change. *Human Relations*, 52, 1505–1541.

Freeman, S. J. & Cameron, K. S. 1993. Organizational downsizing: A convergence and reorientation framework. *Organization Science*, 4, 10–29.

Gandolfi, F. 2013. Workforce downsizing: Strategies, archetypes, approaches and tactics. *Journal of Management Research*, 13, 67.

Gopinath, C. & Becker, T. E. 2000. Communication, procedural justice, and employee attitudes: Relationships under conditions of divestiture. *Journal of Management*, 26, 63–83.

Greenberg, J. 1990. Organizational justice: Yesterday, today, and tomorrow. *Journal of Management*, 16, 399–432.

Hitt, M. A., Keats, B. W., Harback, H. F. & Nixon, R. D. 1994. Rightsizing: Building and maintaining strategic leadership and long-term competitiveness. *Organizational Dynamics*, 23, 18–33.

Iverson, R. D. & Zatzick, C. D. 2007. High-commitment work practices and downsizing harshness in Australian workplaces. *Industrial Relations: A Journal of Economy and Society*, 46, 456–480.

Jacobs, K. 2020. Skills HR will need in 2021: Restructuring your business with confidence. *People Management, CIPD*.

Jalajas, D. S. & Bommer, M. 1999. The influence of job motivation versus downsizing on individual behavior. *Human Resource Development Quarterly*, 10, 329–341.

Kerzner, H. 2017. *Project management: A systems approach to planning, scheduling, and controlling*. Hoboken, NJ: John Wiley & Sons.

Labib, N. & Appelbaum, S. H. 1993. Strategic downsizing: A human resources perspective. *Human Resource Planning*, 16(4), 69.

Leana, C. R. & Feldman, D. C. 1994. The psychology of job loss. *Research in Personnel and HR Management*, 12, 271–302.

Lewis, P. 1986. 6. Voluntary redundancy: A Preliminary investigation. *Employee Relations*, 8(5), 39–44.

Mabert, V. A. & Schmenner, R. W. 1997. Assessing the roller coaster of downsizing. *Business Horizons*, 40, 45–53.

Mishra, K. E., Spreitzer, G. M. & Mishra, A. K. 1998. Preserving employee morale during downsizing. *MIT Sloan Management Review*, 39, 83.

Mone, M. A. 1994. Relationships between self-concepts, aspirations, emotional responses, and intent to leave a downsizing organization. *Human Resource Management*, 33, 281–298.

Murphy, E. 1994. *Strategies for health care excellence*. Washington, DC: American Society for Work Redesign.

O'Neill, H. M. 1986. An analysis of the turnaround strategy in commercial banking. *Journal of Management Studies*, 23, 165–188.

Petzer, M. 2019. *Developing effective interventions for mitigating the pscyhological impact experienced by redundancy envoys during redundancy situations*. PhD, Solent Univeristy.

Schmenner, R. & Lackey, C. 1994. "Slash and burn" doesn't kill weeds: Other ways to downsize the manufacturing organization. *Business Horizons*, 37, 80–88.

Spreitzer, G. M. & Mishra, A. K. 2002. To stay or to go: Voluntary survivor turnover following an organizational downsizing. *Journal of Organizational Behavior: The International Journal of Industrial, Occupational and Organizational Psychology and Behavior*, 23, 707–729.

Thornhill, A. & Saunders, M. N. K. 1998. The meanings, consequences and implication of the management of downsizing and redundancy: A review. *Personnel Review*, 27, 271–295.

Tomasko, R. M. 1991. Downsizing: Layoffs and alternatives to layoffs. *Compensation & Benefits Review*, 23, 19–32.

Turnbull, P. & Wass, V. 1997. Job insecurity and labour market lemons: The (mis)management of redundancy in stell making, coal mining and port transport. *Journal of Management Studies*, 34, 27–50.

Weide, A. S. & Abbott, G. E. 1994. Management on the hot seat: In an increasingly violent workplace, how to deliver bad news. *Employment Relations Today*, 21, 23.

Wooten, K. C. & Decker, P. J. 1996. A strategic human resource management model for restructuring in healthcare organizations. *Hospital Topics*, 74, 10–15.

8

COMMUNICATION STRATEGY

A critical part of a successful redundancy programme is the communication strategy. This chapter continues with the Re-Focus, Re-Organise and Re-Build (RRR) implementation strategy, focusing on stage six: the communication strategy. This chapter discusses the various aspects of communication, including the announcement to all employees, keeping employees up to date during the redundancy programme and the best methods of communicating. Various useful examples are provided to ease the communication process for employers.

Importance of communication and information

When an organisation gets to this point where the first stages of planning are complete as discussed in Chapter 7, it is good practice to start communicating with the extended workforce, being transparent with business results and challenges to gain trust. This will allow for better

DOI: 10.4324/9781003030416-10

cooperation and understanding if communicated effectively and in a timely manner. Keeping the workforce up to date on organisational issues is a key part in the successful delivery of a redundancy programme.

Communication is pivotal during any change programme and especially so when effective communication can influence key factors of employee and organisational well-being. The recognition for the importance of communication during a redundancy is prevalent in literature (Isabella, 1989, Labib and Appelbaum, 1993, Cameron, 1994, Mishra et al., 1998). Several researchers draw attention to the importance of sufficient communication and that the absence of such communication could lead to employees feeling excluded, disillusioned and rumours spreading (Appelbaum et al., 1999, De Meuse et al., 2004). In fact, Mishra et al. (1998) actually advocate overcommunication, but highlight the importance to remain honest during communications.

Reassurance and clarity can mitigate feelings of job insecurity and help create a vision for the future of the organisation, helping to drive commitment amongst the workforce during turbulent times. Transparent communication can help retain employees with skills that are critical to organisational success (Brockner, 1992, Cameron, 1994). Some of the challenges that survivors are faced with links to poor communication and being misinformed about issues, such as their role in the newly restructured organisation and information about key people leaving or changing. These findings are supported in research that found that middle managers received less information during the redundancies than senior managers in all aspects (Tourish et al., 2004). The lack of convergence between the implementation of a redundancy programme and the communication plan is often a cause of stress for all employees (Labib and Appelbaum, 1993). This can be prevented through a carefully designed communications plan. Despite the importance of transparent and open communication, research has indicated that directors are often hesitant to share meaningful information, due to fear of losing control over the programme (Kets De Vries and Balazs, 1997), which is another challenge to circumvent when designing the communication strategy.

Managing change through proactive communication

Before an organisation even starts to consider the communication of redundancies, expectation management is critical. Unless there were unforeseen circumstances such as a sudden market crash, the financial performance of the organisation should be well communicated throughout the organisation before redundancies are announced. To reduce the negative impact of survivor syndrome, it is important for the employer to manage anticipation of change with the need for change being acknowledged and expected (Cascio, 1993, Baruch and Hind, 1999).

By implementing the news of redundancies ahead of time in a generic way so that the change is not a shock, organisations will help to protect themselves from potentially angry and shocked employees that may show behaviour of reprisals and sabotage (Vickers and Parris, 2007). Mishra et al. (1998) agree that to help reduce the impact and element of shock on the victims and survivors, employees should be notified of impending redundancies in advance where possible. This is supported in literature where the expectations of employees have been shown to also have a significant impact on the responses of survivors with regard to the announcement of redundancies (Doherty and Horsted, 1995).

Cascio (1993) contends that firms who surprise employees with unanticipated redundancy activities reap overwhelmingly negative consequences. In Vickers and Parris' (2007) study on the impact of redundancies on victims, one respondent stated that he felt betrayed as he had been promoted into a new position 11 days prior to him being made redundant, and up until the actual redundancy, had only received positive feedback on his performance. Scenarios such as this can be avoided with effective expectation management.

Communication plan

When designing the communications plan, it is important to address the needs and concerns of the survivor population to maintain motivation and productivity, which may include management–employee dialogue sessions, information sessions and publications (Isabella, 1989). The commencement of the communication plan sets the foundations for the employees to psychologically prepare themselves for the implementation of redundancies (Labib and Appelbaum, 1993). Appelbaum et al. (1999) advocate establishing a communication plan that keeps employees, suppliers, customers, and investors up to date on the affairs surrounding the redundancy situation. This strategy will also help to limit the spreading of rumours.

The importance of honesty and transparency in the communication plan is critical in building trust (Baruch and Hind, 1999, Nair, 2008).

Figure 8.1 illustrates a communications strategy that focuses on tailoring communication to each respective audience specifically. Communication to the senior team should, for example, be pitched differently to the customers and the wider workforce. The information that is included does not necessarily change; it is simply adjusted to remove language and terminology to allow the message to be better understood. Audiences also have different expectations of what is important to them and thus the message should be adjusted to address the needs of each group. For example, the extended management team typically wants a broader overview of where and how redundancies are impacting the organisation and how to sustain the delivery of operations whilst reducing headcount. The management teams are also more focused on how to grow and Re-Build the organisation and what the vision is for the future.

Employees on the other hand mostly want to know how the redundancies are impacting them directly, i.e. how is the redundancy programme impacting their level of job security. Customers are less focused on the detail of how many reductions there are and the consultation process and

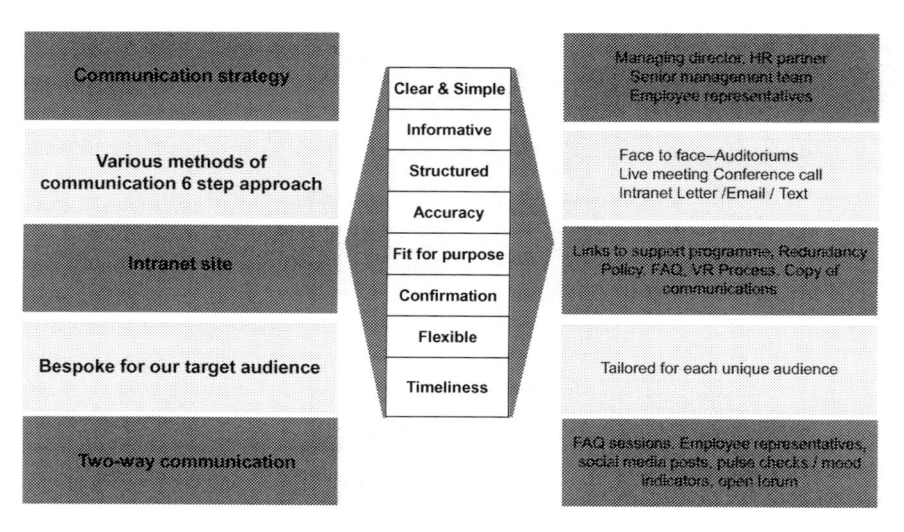

Figure 8.1 RRR strategy stage 6: communications strategy for redundancy implementation.

more interested to understand if their services, product or project delivery will be impacted.

Communications from a variety of sources, including email, staff meetings and personal interactions, help employees understand the process and increase the perception of procedural justice (Cameron et al., 1991, Gopinath and Becker, 2000). Communications also need to be frequent and timely (Mishra et al., 1998). Thus, for redundancy communication to be effective, it should be multiple, regular and diverse and include the following dimensions:

- clear and simple
- informative
- structured
- accurate
- fit for purpose
- flexible
- timely.

Consider the roles and responsibilities of employees when communicating. When communicating an update, what is the best time for optimum attendance? If employees are on leave from work, ensure they are not forgotten; include all employees who are not working due to long- and short-term absences, which respectively may include territorial army duties, long-term sick leave, sabbaticals, holiday, training, parental leave and maternity leave to name a few. To ensure no one is missed, HR should provide updated reports of personnel and absences to each department. It is recommended that for employees on leave, the employee's direct line manager should initiate contact with the news and agree regular updates and the best methods to communicate. Depending on the reason for leave, the communication approach will need to be tailored to individual circumstances.

Timing of redundancy communication

Timing of redundancies is of great importance and should be considered in the planning stages. Implementing redundancies on or near a major holiday are critiqued in literature as being unethical (Brockner, 1992).

Implementing redundancies before Christmas or summer holidays can add to the significance of the financial burden experienced by victims and are perceived as insensitive due to the timing and psychological connotations with these holidays (Petzer, 2019). Short notice of job losses is also regarded as poor practice when it comes to implementing redundancies as employees are unprepared to respond to a sudden loss of income (Pompa, 1992).

The pace of implementation attracts two schools of thought. Victims tend to prefer a gradual implementation with survivors and redundancy envoys opting for the process to be over as soon as possible. Once decisions are made and communicated, implementation of redundancies must be carried out as quickly as possible, with due consideration to the victims who prefer a gradual implementation, as it allows employees more time to adjust to the change (Labib and Appelbaum, 1993). Baruch and Hind's (1999) findings are consistent regarding the pace of communication and found that it is important to minimise survivor syndrome by implementing decisions swiftly. On the contrary, slow implementation of redundancies has been argued as successful by Flint (2003); however, it is critiqued by Ashman (2015) who found in his study that the extended period places undue stress and heightened emotions on redundancy envoys, whilst having to cope with increased workload. The notion that implementing redundancies in several steps over time has a negative impact on employee morale, resulting in decreased productivity, is supported in the literature (Hitt et al., 1994). Communication of clear time scales thus help address job insecurity and low levels of morale. There is an added risk that if redundancies are not communicated in a timely fashion, in an inappropriate manner or if the communication is perceived as inadequate, the employees are more inclined to perceive the redundancy decision as unethical (Hopkins and Hopkins, 1999).

Announcement of redundancies

Announcement of redundancies should be delivered with transparency and in a thoughtful manner. Management must announce a redundancy programme after careful consideration and in a convincing manner (Mishra et al., 1998). By sharing financial and competitive information and by showing a willingness to communicate openly, management establishes a sense of trust and honesty, which, in turn, encourages employees to cooperate and to help the company survive the temporary, unhealthy situation (Kets De Vries and Balazs, 1997, Mishra et al., 1998).

When the first announcements are made regarding redundancies, the communication methods take on prime importance. Even if the content of the message is forgotten, the way in which the message was delivered plays a role in winning the hearts and minds of employees.

Considering the importance of different channels of communication, a six-step approach is recommended as per Figure 8.2 with the aim of ensuring the message is delivered and understood, depending on the maturity of the workforce, their hours of work and the kind of work that is carried out. This process may have to be repeated, for example, if the organisation has employees who work shifts, to ensure everyone has an opportunity to hear the message, ideally directly from the senior directors. Some organisations do record the announcement, whilst others recognise the importance of a personal delivery.

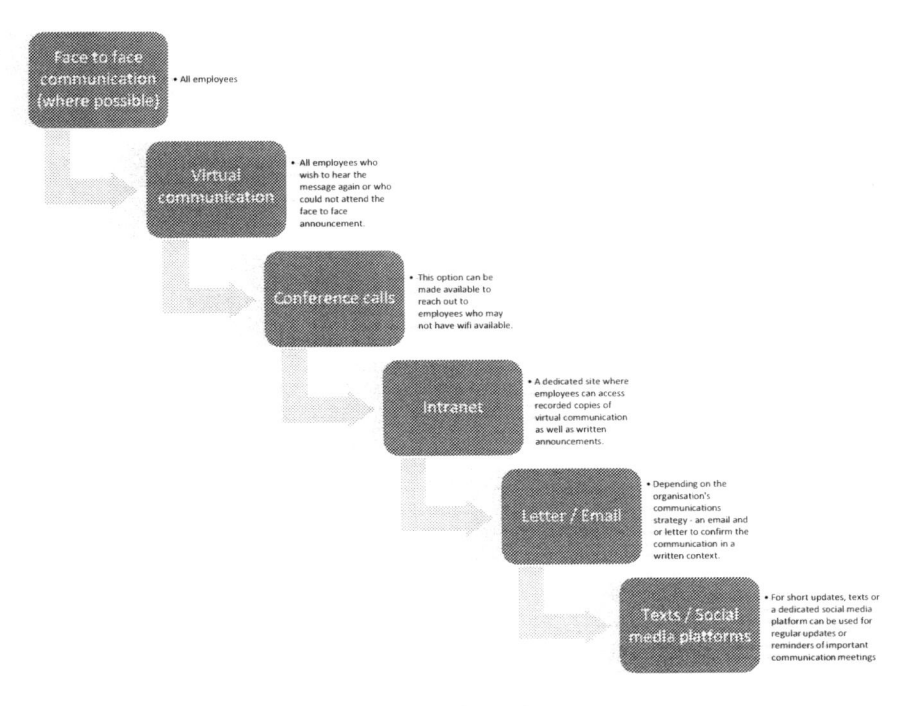

Figure 8.2 Redundancy communications channels.

It is useful to keep records of attendance for each delivery, which gives the employer the opportunity to diligently ensure that all employees are included. With the trend moving towards more home-based working during the COVID-19 pandemic, the opportunity for employees to attend the face-to-face sessions are limited. An alternative option is thus to hold virtual meetings as well as conference calls immediately afterwards, which allows employees, who may be travelling, non-office-based or simply with limited or no WIFI access, the opportunity to attend.

The use of a bespoke intranet site to store all relevant information helps points employees in the same direction, receiving a consistent message from one direct and controlled source. This method also relieves pressure on redundancy envoys, by being able to point employees to a self-help source to obtain clarity or to find answers to questions.

Virtual meetings and conference calls can be recorded for the benefit of employees who could not attend or who prefer to hear the message again. The next step is to follow up with an email (or letter) communication to all employees, summarising the key points with a link to the recordings, frequently asked questions (FAQs) document and related policies. Research has indicated that having either a social media platform or published document that contains FAQs with answers help to address specific areas of concern and limit the questions being posed to redundancy envoys, mitigating some of the workload of redundancy implementation (Petzer, 2019).

- Appendix 8.1 provides a helpful example with prepopulated questions and answers for employers to adapt.
- Appendix 8.2 provides a PowerPoint example for employers to adapt with proposed communications for the announcement of redundancies to all employees.

Communication for employees on leave of absence should be agreed and established after the first phone call/virtual meeting. Each communication channel should allow for questions to be presented with the answers published where appropriate and where questions were not of a personal nature. The FAQ document can thus be referred to and be kept updated to help streamline the process for all parties involved.

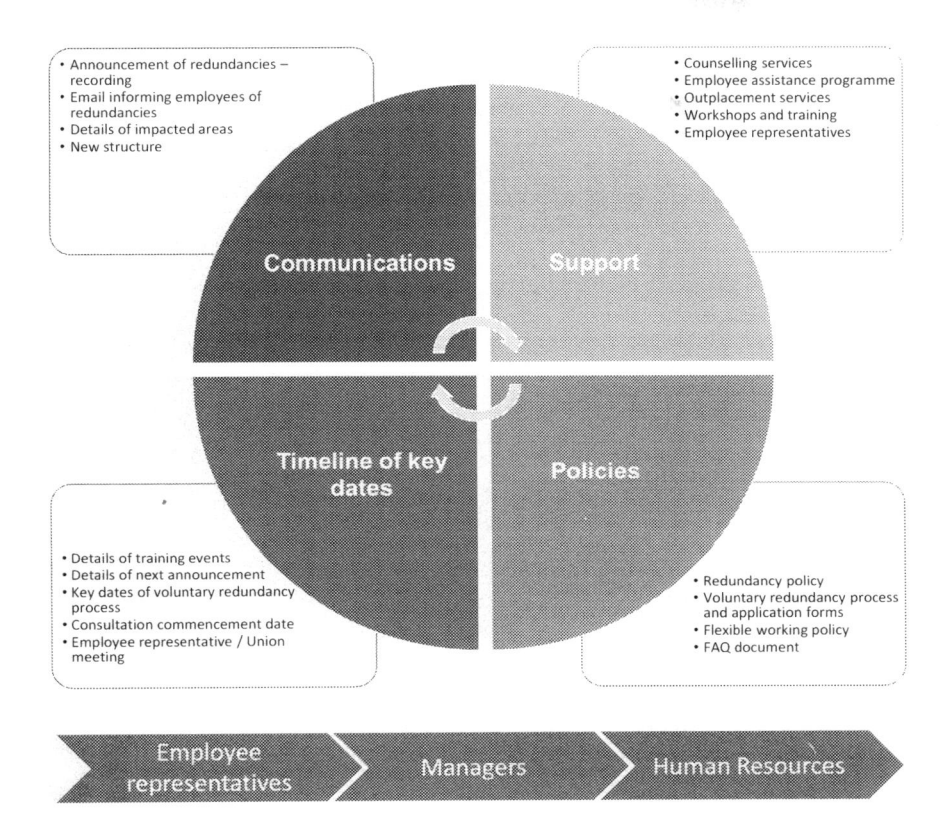

Figure 8.3 Redundancy intranet dashboard example.

An intranet dashboard can be useful to aid communications as they are released in a chronological order, with the latest and most recent communications leading. A proposed dashboard is displayed in Figure 8.3.

Helpful links and sections can be established, such as a confidential section, only accessible by managers, a confidential section accessible to employee representatives and one for HR. Similarly, an easy way to contact employee representatives or HR could be signposted.

Policy documentation can be made available such as:

- redundancy policy
- voluntary redundancy process and application forms
- flexible working policy
- FAQ document.

A dedicated dashboard for support such as:

- details of counselling services
- list of vacancies
- contact details for employee representatives
- details of employee assistance programme
- details of outplacement services.

Several researchers concur on the importance of breaking the news with confidence (Weide and Abbott, 1994, Mihaly, 1995, Gandolfi, 2009, Torres, 2011).

It is of utmost importance that redundancy envoys are in a strong and confident position to deliver the news of redundancies and support this with the ability to give succinct answers as to the typical questions of why, what, where and when. The ability to deliver the announcement and subsequent communications with confidence should be well established if the earlier steps in the RRR strategy were followed by involving redundancy envoys in the decision-making and providing training as per Chapter 7.

Gandolfi (2009) found that one of the areas that frustrated redundancy envoys was the lack of objectivity and information in the entire process and it is thus important the information is cascaded down from senior executives through to middle management, HR and employee representatives.

Weide and Abbott (1994) found several cases in their research where employees that were dismissed returned to work the next day after being made redundant, simply as they did not understand the message given to them. It is therefore recommended that managers should rehearse what message they want to get across during critical communications to avoid misplaced words and immeasurable damage. Torres (2011) argues that with the implementation of redundancies, the meeting should take place with someone who took part ownership for the decision to avoid any evasiveness. It is also recommended that managers should own the statement that redundancy is a business decision and final as it helps to deflect guilt. Weide and Abbott (1994) support this recommendation by stating that when giving bad news to employees, managers must ensure the message comes across with confidence and that the decision is communicated as irrevocable and backed by the most senior levels in the company. The communications strategy will thus only succeed if the messengers who deliver the strategy, firstly, believe in the strategy and, secondly, have the correct knowledge and skills to communicate the redundancy programme to the workforce.

During the redundancy process, it is important to communicate any news of redundancies with empathy, with the goal to make staff feel valued, despite the situation. Job loss as a result of redundancy is not the fault of the employee and it is important to remind employees that it is the role they fulfil that is no longer required, not the person. Correspondingly, management ought to communicate to employees the organisation's commitment and intent on retaining high performers to help combat feelings of job insecurity (Mone, 1994).

In a study where the impact of communication on the perception of redundancies were assessed, it was found that with greater communication and improved staff participation, the perception of the redundancy exercise improved positively (Murphy, 1994). It is pivotal to ensure the communication programme demonstrates the organisation's vision and commitment to the employees (Labib and Appelbaum, 1993), which helps to minimise the negative impact of survivor syndrome. Another study indicated that it was not necessarily the redundancies that created a sense of bitterness amongst employees, but rather the manner in which they were handled (Schweiger et al., 1987). When handling critical communications, the redundancy envoy must engage and involve themself (Weide and Abbott, 1994). It is not an academic exercise – redundancy envoys must recognise that they are dealing with people's lives and livelihood. A good manager is also a human being.

Business rationale

Literature on the importance of a solid and clear business rationale with a clear vision when communicating redundancies is plentiful (Cameron et al., 1991, Mishra and Spreitzer, 1998, Baruch and Hind, 1999), along with the importance of being able to demonstrate that the redundancies are implemented as a last resort (Mishra et al., 1998, Baruch and Hind, 1999, Sronce and McKinley, 2006).

During the implementation of a redundancy programme, clear explanations on the rationale for the headcount reduction is necessary (Mishra and Spreitzer, 1998).

Cameron et al. (1991) state that to be successful during redundancy implementation, it is important to emphasise that the programme is a means to an end and only a temporary mechanism to help the firm survive through a challenging time. Baruch and Hind (1999) refer to their best practice framework for implementing redundancies, which proposes that it should be conveyed to employees that redundancies are a necessity for business survival, with a clear business rationale and that this measure would only be implemented as a last resort.

Being able to demonstrate the use of redundancy as a last resort only, and that all other cost savings options have been considered and utilised where possible, minimises the impact on the survivors (Baruch and Hind, 1999). The organisation should be able to demonstrate that all other alternatives were considered or deployed, such as early retirement, selling off a part of the company (which is often the most preferred option by employees), reducing or stopping recruitment for a limited period, job-sharing and internal cost-cutting exercises as covered in Chapter 4. Labib and Appelbaum (1993) agree that it has an important impact on all of the workforce to see that all alternative methods have been considered and deployed prior to the implementation of redundancies.

Two-way communication, involvement and participation

The benefits of employee voice through employee involvement and participation are well established in the literature (Marchington, 2015). It is also advocated that when employees themselves are involved to identify roles and functions that are redundant and identify methods to improve efficiency, it is likely for the redundancy programme to be more successful (Flint, 2003).

Employees need sufficient opportunities for providing upward feedback, which can positively impact on engagement (Ruck and Welch, 2012). The factors that drive employee engagement are reported as:

(1)   Having opportunities to feed your views upwards
(2)   Feeling well-informed about what is happening in the organisation
(3)   Thinking that your manager is committed to the organisation.

(Truss et al., 2007: 45)

Organisational justice is often perceived as fair, when employees feel they are involved or have a voice when decisions are made during a redundancy programme (Greenberg, 1990). It is thus recommended to ensure two-way communication is openly encouraged and acted on. The communication strategy in Figure 8.1 proposes five communication streams to encourage employee voice:

- question and answer sessions at all employee communications that are published and distributed
- the active use of employee/union representatives
- social media platform for posting anonymous questions
- the use of 'pulse checks' or 'mood indicators' to understand concerns and the impact on morale
- direct, one-to-one communication through an open forum with individual members of the senior team with a small group of employees of six to eight people from different parts of the business.

A study by Petzer (2019) found that the opportunity for randomly selected employees to meet up with directors on an informal basis improved employee engagement during a period of redundancy implementation. This approach of informal support activities to exchange information is supported as being a key part of successful redundancy implementation (Arndt and Duchemin, 1993). This strategy support communicative leadership, which facilitates the willingness to listen, to answer questions and be transparent in the sharing of suitable information (Johansson et al., 2014). Labib and Appelbaum (1993) contend that sometimes frequent dialogue with a key member of the senior team may be sufficient to appease the needs of employees.

The importance of involvement and participation during redundancies is well documented with a link to perceived control for employees (Freeman and Cameron, 1993, Weide and Abbott, 1994, Appelbaum et al., 1999, Gandolfi, 2013). It is recommended that full participation should include all organisational stakeholders (Freeman and Cameron, 1993). Weide and Abbott (1994) agree that to create a better work environment, organisations must ensure that employee involvement and empowerment programmes are in place to give employees the feeling of more control and subsequent reduced stress. Mishra et al. (1998) and Freeman and Cameron

(1993) expand by suggesting that even customers and suppliers could be consulted during a redundancy programme as they may offer innovative ways for a firm to accomplish its mission.

Studies that have looked at successful redundancy implementations have found that a key element in the success is to encourage active participation from all stakeholders, including a healthy information exchange (Cameron, 1994; Appelbaum et al., 1999).

A contributing factor for the successful implementation of a redundancy programme is to ensure the implementation is top-down as well as bottom-up. Redundancy envoys should therefore be visible and share their vision with the workforce, and employees should be involved in the decision-making regarding which jobs are eliminated (Cameron et al., 1991).

Communication during consultation

At one point, I was responsible for a redundancy programme where an employee who was off work on long-term sick leave, receiving cancer treatment, had to be informed and consulted with about her role being at risk of redundancy. These situations require extreme sensitivity with how the news is communicated and delivered and suitable training is recommended for managers and HR on how to deal with these emotive situations. Redundancies impact employees at the basic physiological level, requiring food, water, warmth and rest (Maslow and Lewis, 1987) and thus requires the redundancy envoy, who breaks the news to do so with dignity and respect. It is therefore recommended to support redundancy envoys by providing them with the necessary training on how to break bad news. When delivering bad news, managers should aim to let employees feel like they are treated with fairness and with genuine concern as people, not just employees (Weide and Abbott, 1994). During one-to-one consultation, the communication method needs to be tailored to be sympathetic to each individual's circumstances. Delivering the message of bad news with dignity and respect can have an important influence on how it is received (Petzer, 2019). Consider the timing of the meetings. Offer employees the rest of the day off to clear their heads, and if they choose to do so help them to manage work priorities to facilitate this support.

This chapter discussed the importance of effective, timely and appropriate communication, which concluded with the benefits of proactive employee involvement and participation. A communications strategy was recommended with various communication channels. Key partners in the communication process are employee representatives, whether the company is unionised or not. The next chapter will explore the value of employee representatives during a redundancy programme as well as details of selecting employee representatives.

APPENDIX 8.1
REDUNDANCY – FREQUENTLY
ASKED QUESTIONS

Human Resources

Ref.	Question	Answer	Date
1.	Will the company consider voluntary redundancies?	We are and will continue to work closely with our employee representatives to consider alternative ways to minimise compulsory redundancies. Voluntary redundancies will be invited from the following departments and roles: [name departments and roles]. More details on the voluntary redundancy process and how to apply can be found [here]. Please note that applications will not automatically be accepted and are subject to management discretion as set out in the voluntary redundancy process.	

Ref.	Question	Answer	Date
2.	Will the company be reducing the contractors we use?	The company will review and work closely with the employee representatives on limiting redundancies by assessing the requirements for contractors and reduce numbers where it is feasible and in line with business continuity. Where possible, we will endeavour to bring roles 'in house' to limit redundancies.	
3.	Will all departments be subjected to redundancies?	The management team has carefully considered in which areas of the business redundancies are required. Based on these decisions, redundancies are proposed in the following departments or roles. [list departments and roles].	
4.	Will the company offer alternative roles with training?	We will carefully consider redeployment where skills and expertise may fulfil the requirements of the role. Reasonable levels of training will be offered if employees at risk of redundancy secure suitable alternative roles.	
5.	Will there be pay increases during this year?	The company has decided with the agreement of the employee representatives that any costs that can be saved will reduce the number of redundancies necessary. On that basis, we have agreed to freeze all pay increases for this financial year. Where pay increases are related to exceptional circumstances such as promotions, exceptions may apply.	
6.	Is the financial package for employees applying for voluntary redundancy enhanced?	[Unfortunately, due to financial restraints, voluntary redundancy packages are not enhanced] OR [Voluntary redundancy packages are enhanced and offer additional incentives. Please contact the HR department on [email/name] for a confidential voluntary redundancy quotation.]	
7.	When will I know if I am being made redundant?	After the company wide announcement on [date] by [director's name], we will write to all employees who are at risk of redundancy. We will then follow a period of 30 days individual consultation. No final decision will be made on any employee's role until consultation is completed. OR/AND	

(Continued)

Ref.	Question	Answer	Date
		[Due to the number of roles being impacted, we will follow a collective redundancy consultation process, which will involve [number] days before any final decisions are made.]	
8.	Is there support for employees after redundancy?	Yes. [Outplacement provider] provide support up until [number] of days after the employee is in a new role. Full details of their service are available on [include link].	
9.	I started in my role less than 3 years ago. Are we operating a 'last in, first out' policy?	We are working closely with our employee representatives on the selection criteria for the redundancy pool. We will use objective, measurable criteria as set out in the redundancy policy available from this [link].	
		Length of service will only be used in redundancy selection as a last resort, such as when two or more employees are in a tie-breaker situation.	
10.	As stated, the skill set of employees at risk will be looked at when deciding those to be made redundant. What 'Tool' will be used to assess these skills? Will it be the opinion of the Line Manager, or do we have this information documented and is this available for those affected to review?	We are conscious in ensuring we do not lose critical skills during the redundancy process. We will be working closely with our employee representatives on the selection criteria used and will also be consulting with individuals on the criteria used. The selection matrix will be provided to all employees at risk of redundancy at the start of their consultation period and all outcomes will be determined by two independent managers with prior knowledge of the employee's skills and work experience. The scoring will be made available to the individual employee after being validated by an HR representative. For more information of the proposed criteria, please refer to the redundancy policy available here [link].	
11.	Would the company consider early retirements?	Yes. The company will also be providing training to employees who are considering retirement on how to manage their finances with a private consultation made available to interested parties with the pensions department.	
		Please contact [name] for more details on [contact details].	

Business Strategy

Ref	Question	Answer	Date
1.	If we are reducing numbers in [department] how will we continue to provide good service to our customers with less employees?	We are restructuring the organisation to the optimum size, so we can focus on delivering good customer service in the right areas. We are implementing redundancies so we can deliver to our customer needs in the right departments by having the right number of staff where they are needed and reducing the numbers in the areas where the business is not as successful.	
2.	We are already understaffed in the [department] with numerous vacancies waiting to be filled. How will we deal with this whilst reducing headcount?	This is a great opportunity to offer redeployment in the area of shortage if we can fulfil the suitable alternative employment criteria for employees at risk of redundancy. We have to reduce staff in the areas where we are overstaffed and focus on getting the vacancies filled where we need people.	
3.	Why have the company decided to implement these redundancies now and not earlier?	We understand that implementing redundancies is a very distressing time for all of us involved and can be quite upsetting. For this reason, implementing redundancies was our absolute last resort. We waited as we anticipated some orders, which did not realise, and we were trying to change our go-to-market strategy to win better quality business. In the interim, we also attempted to save costs [include examples] to prevent this situation. Unfortunately, with the order worth [include figure] not materialising, we are at a point now where we have no alternative option.	
4.	We seem to be not bidding for a lot of new work. Why are we doing this when potentially we could have created more work?	We have to be sure that the work we are bidding for is right for our business and is profitable. In some areas, the work is not right for our market and expertise.	

(Continued)

Ref	Question	Answer	Date
5.	It looks like we are going to lose the [name] contract. Could we do more to retain this contract? Potentially if we keep this contract, we reduce the number of redundancies.	We really appreciate innovative ideas on income generation. We always need to ensure we are profitable when we execute a contract and delivering the right level of service to our customer. If we have had to increase our price to remain profitable, then we expose ourselves to losing the contract. We must make sure each and every contract is right for us, that we can deliver it effectively and we make money on it.	
6.	What costs have the business tried to save to prevent this situation?	[List examples; typically fuel costs, reduced expenses, we tried to renegotiate our real estate costs, renegotiate with our suppliers, generate extra income through recycling.]	
7.	We have lost so much potential work recently, in the [department] and in the long run, the service contracts that come with them. If we get this resolved, we could generate more income.	We really appreciate innovative ideas for income generation, keep them coming. We need to ensure we remain competitive in the market. We are reshaping the go-to-market so that we win the right kind of business, but the barriers to entry is high. We cannot compete in the areas where the barriers are low, and the market is aggressive. Generating good revenue and profit is essential for the future sustainability of the organisation. We are aware that we need to focus on this area to improve it. Please contact [name] to arrange a meeting to discuss opportunities for business development.	
8.	Our sales pipeline continues to look positive, opportunities with more than a 50% chance of becoming an order in the next four months, so why are they not materialising as actual orders?	Our pipeline has looked better for a number of months and there is an improving picture. However, our conversion rate has got slightly worse, and we are finding it very competitive. We need to make sure the opportunities in the pipeline are right for us. If we continue to do the right things, we will win more orders.	

Ref	Question	Answer	Date
9.	Are we in this position due to having an adverse appetite for risk and how will this change in the future?	This is less about our appetite to take on risk and more about how we deliver the project effectively and profitably with a focus on mitigating any risk. Losing our biggest customer [include detail] was not due to our appetite for risk, it was unexpected with factors beyond our control. Our customer outsourced the production to a country with cheaper labour costs – a market condition beyond our control.	
10.	Are any senior management at risk?	We are implementing redundancies in all areas where there is a requirement for reducing staff and in some areas this does include senior management.	
11.	Can you identify the specific roles and skills areas at risk within [department]?	Once we commence the consultation period, the skills and roles we need to retain and where we need to reduce will be discussed and explained to all impacted staff.	
12.	Will you be reducing people based on salary cost savings; i.e. one senior manager = two junior staff members?	We are restructuring the business based on the optimum level of project delivery. The cost savings in our business is achievable through reducing the headcount due to allocated costs per person, not just salary related.	
13.	Is the structure shown final or could this also be subject to change?	The outline structure will only have minimal change; however, we will look to change our structure to ensure we meet customer needs, which may be impacted by voluntary redundancies.	
14.	Before you gave a total number of employees of [number] in the organisation. Do you have numbers of employees in each area, i.e. service, sales, etc. against the number of reductions in that area?	[Provide a list of employees per area with the deductions in each area.]	
15.	Will there be further redundancies announced?	It is not our plan to reduce the workforce further. We hope that things will improve with the aim to build the business up again.	

(Continued)

APPENDIX 8.2 REDUNDANCY ANNOUNCEMENT ALL EMPLOYEE COMMUNICATIONS

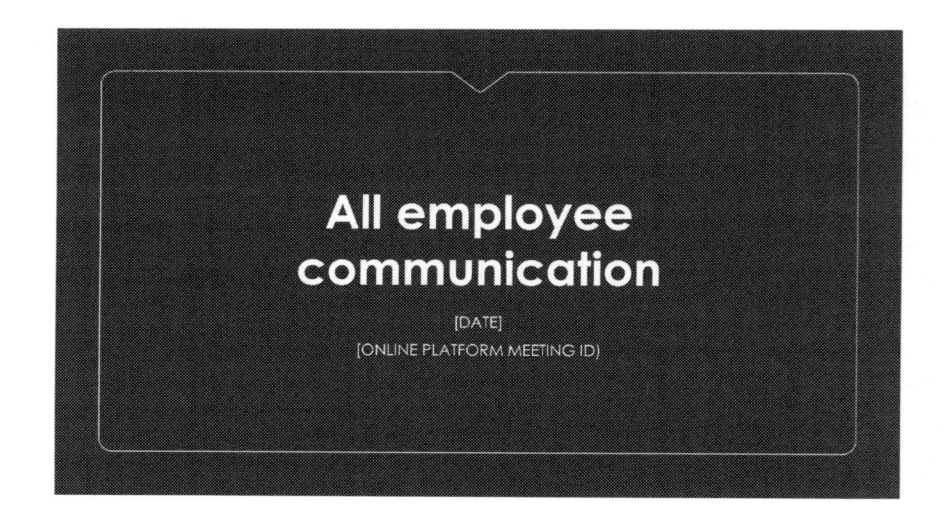

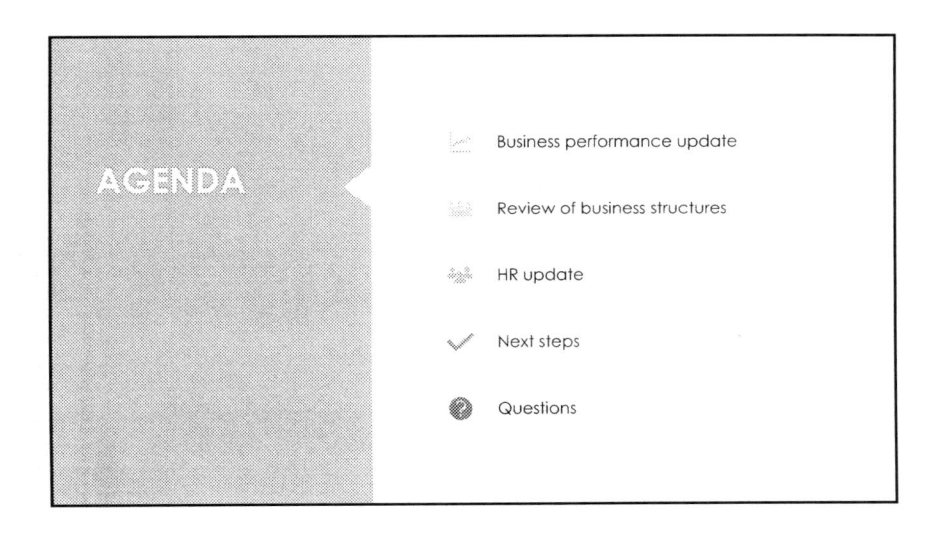

RESTRICTED INFORMATION

THIS INFORMATION IS NOT FOR ONWARD COMMUNICATION

WE WILL COMMUNICATE TO OUR CUSTOMERS DIRECTLY

WE WILL KEEP YOU UP TO DATE OF EXTERNAL COMMUNICATION AND KEY DATES

AGENDA

Business performance update

Review of business structures

HR update

Next steps

Questions

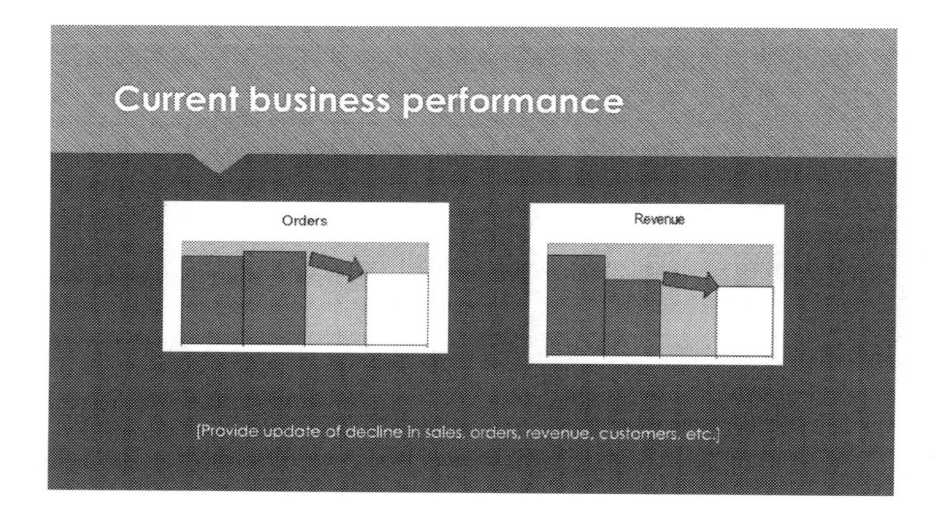

Business strategy

[include overall update – with vision and mission]

Strategy update

- Over the past few months, we have made considerable progress in creating and agreeing a sustainable structure for [company]

We have enabled cost savings of circa [xxxx] through the following:

- [list activities]

- We have improvement activity ongoing with the areas, sales, service and projects in line with our strategy and goals

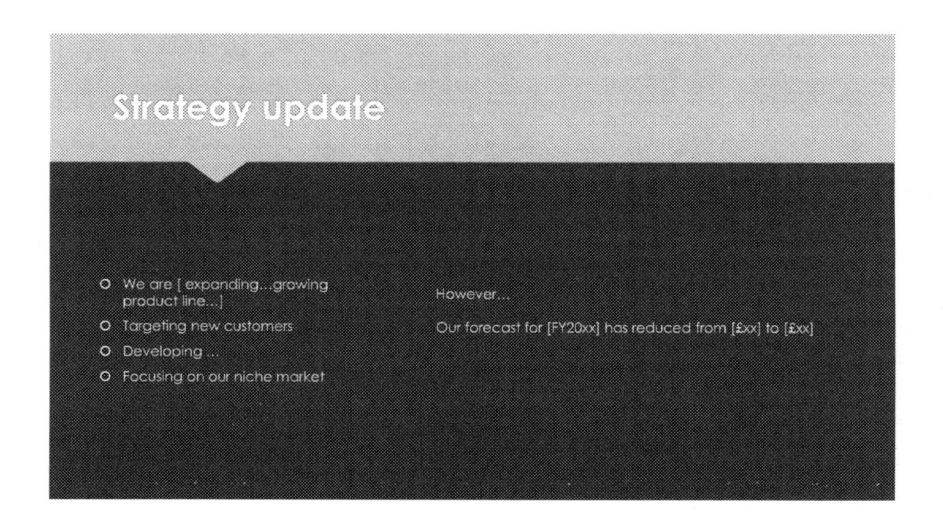

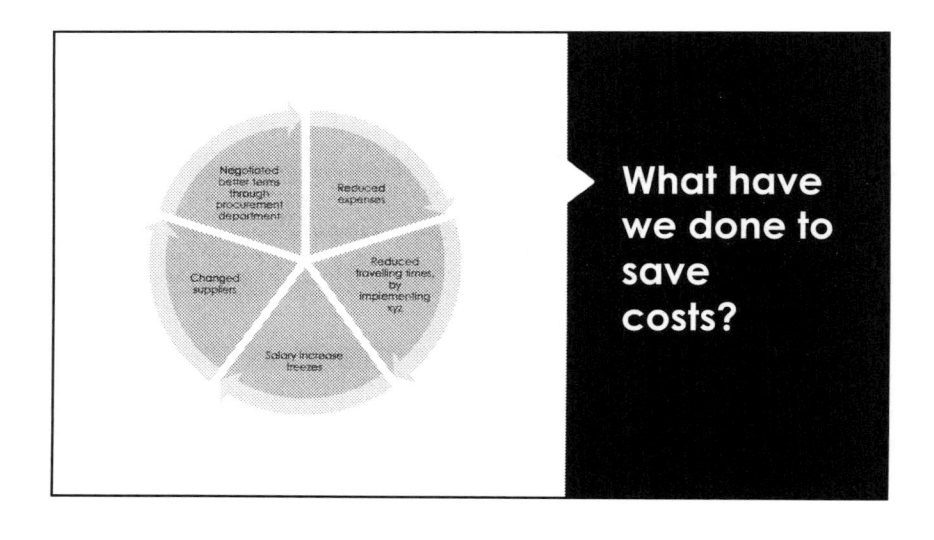

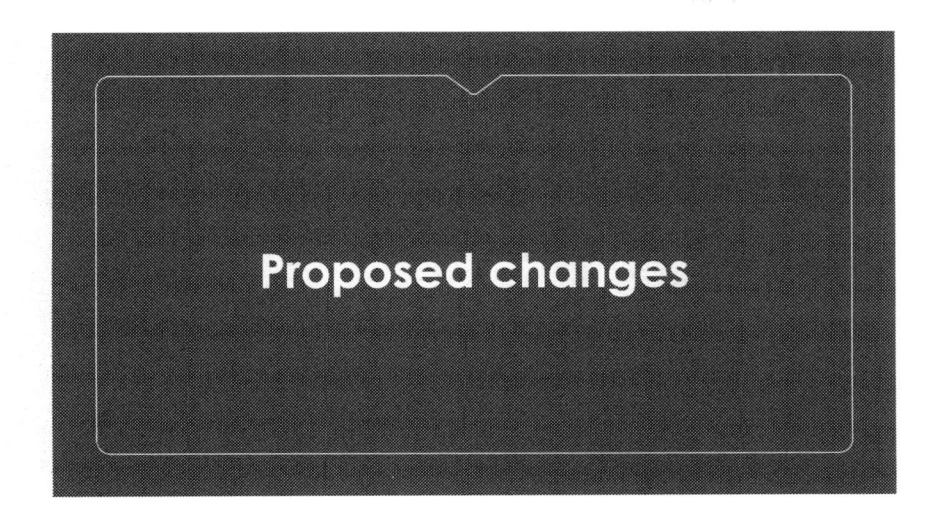

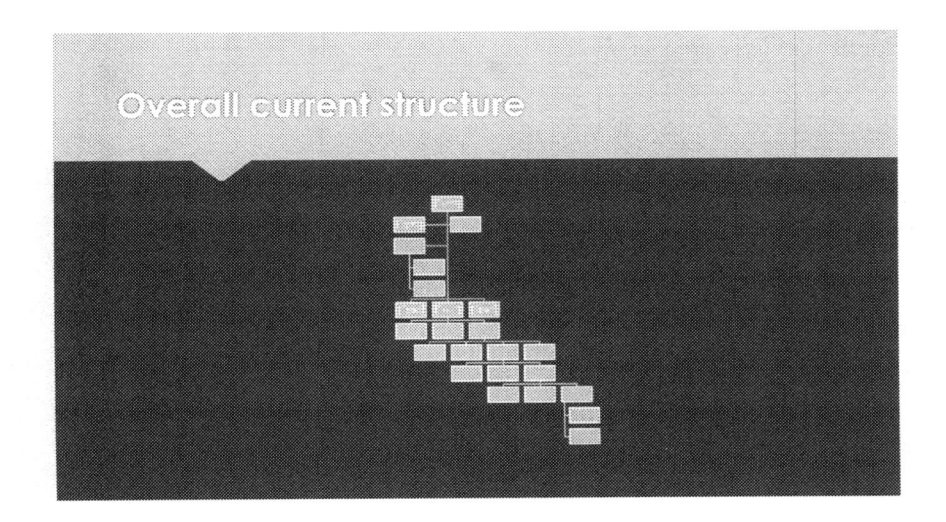

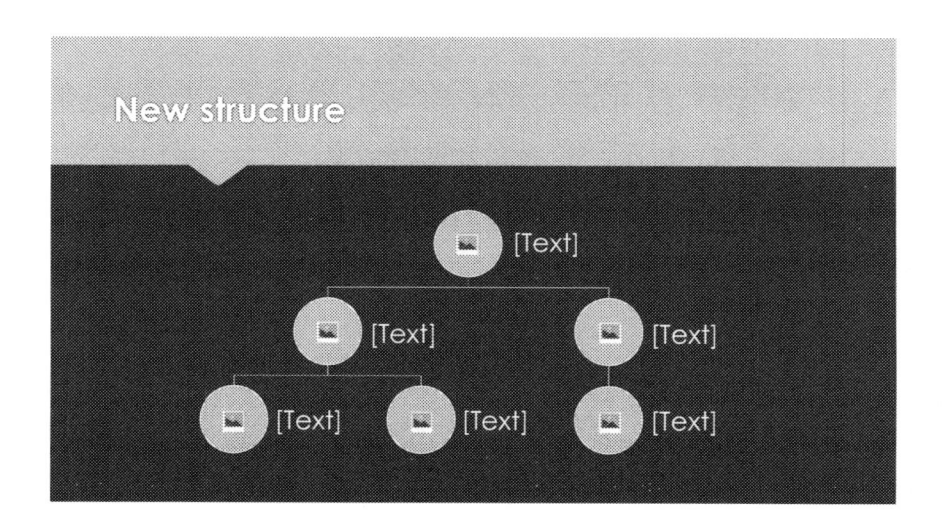

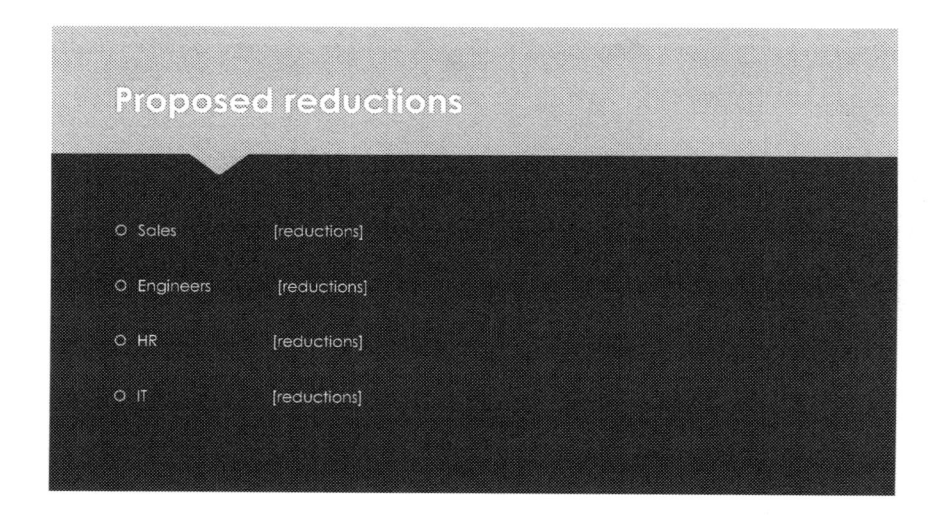

Consultation process

| Individual consultation | Collective consultation for [30/45/90] with [trade union / employee representatives] |

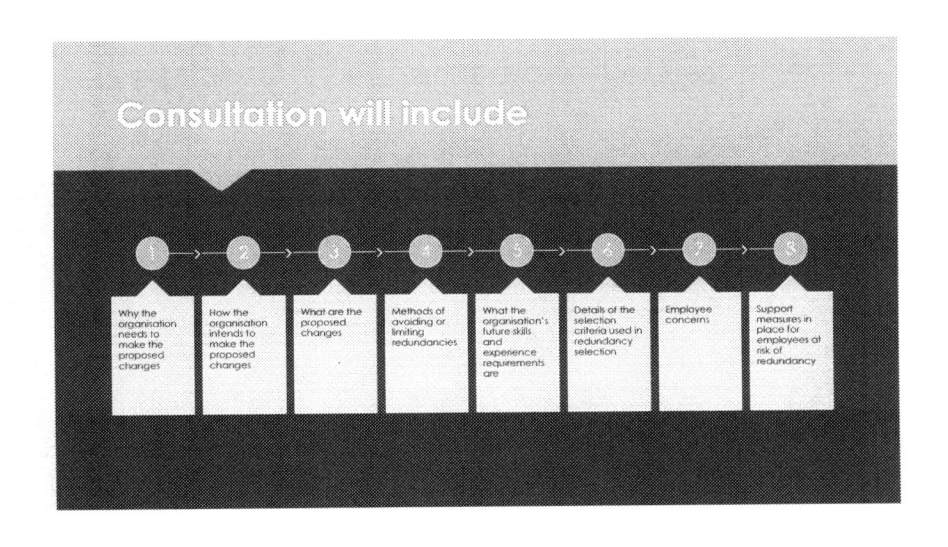

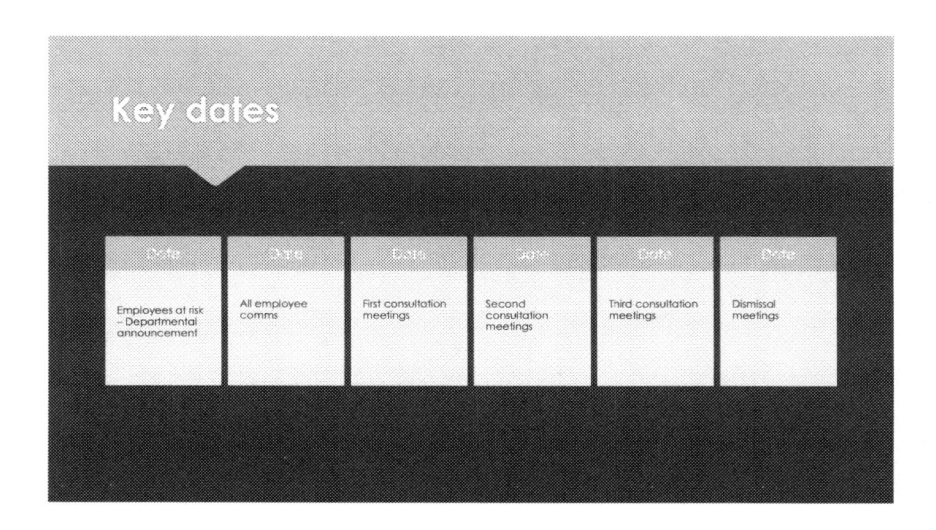

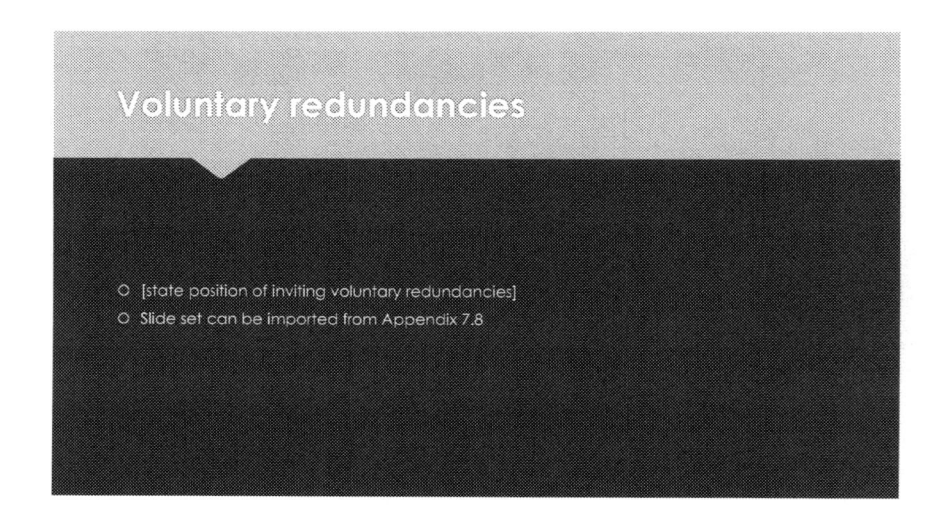

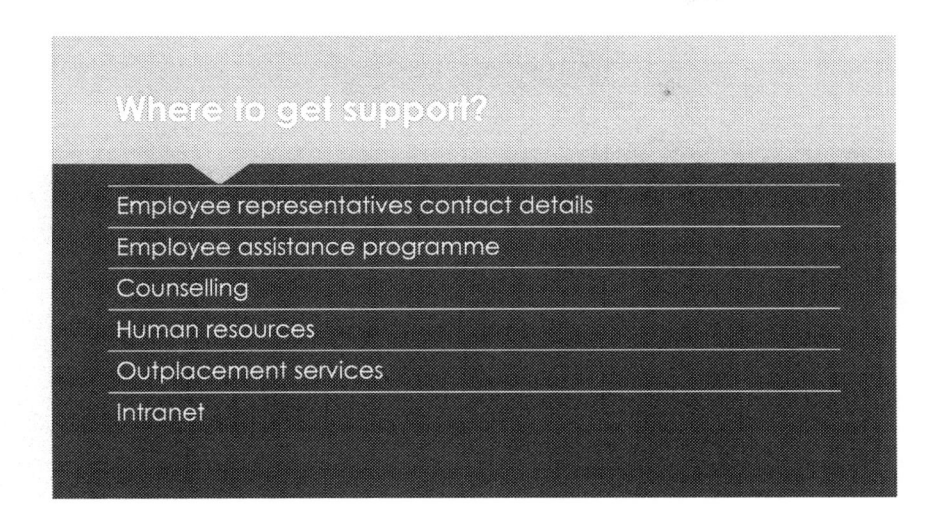

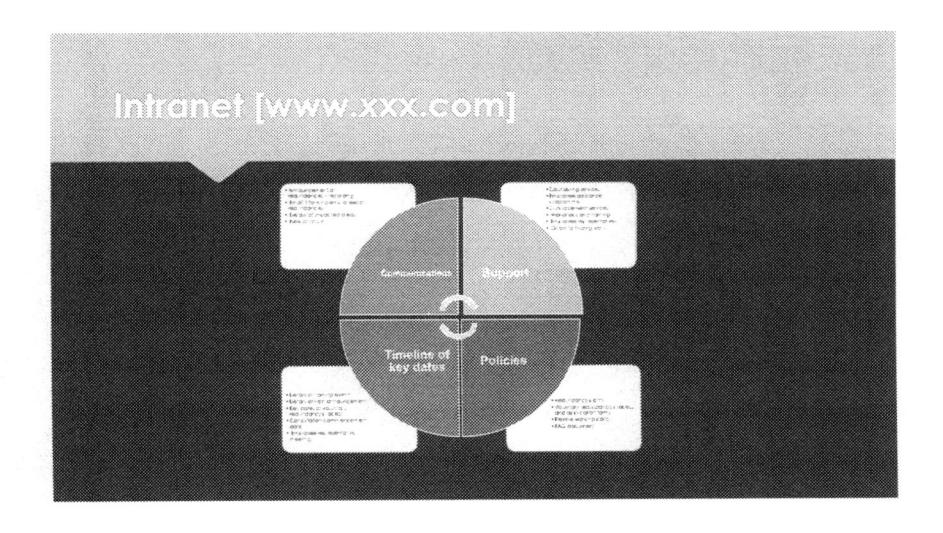

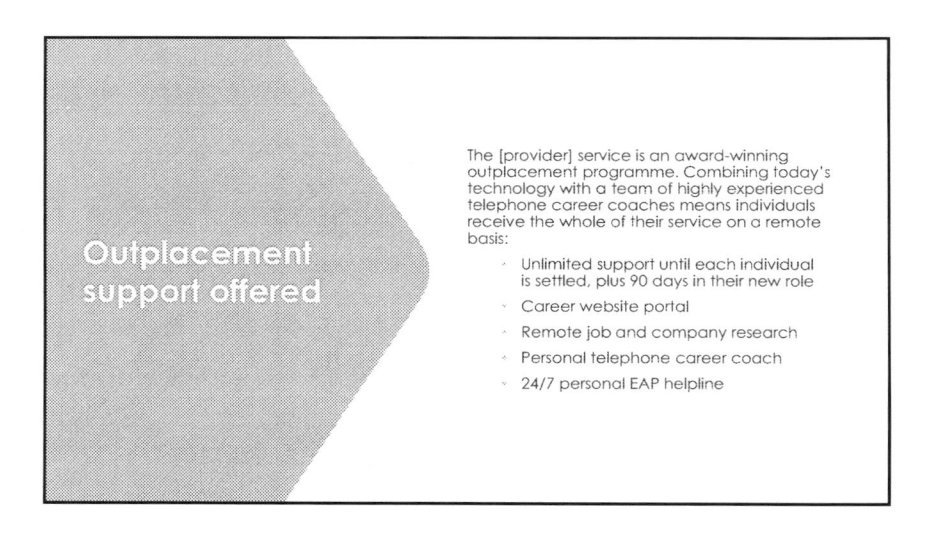

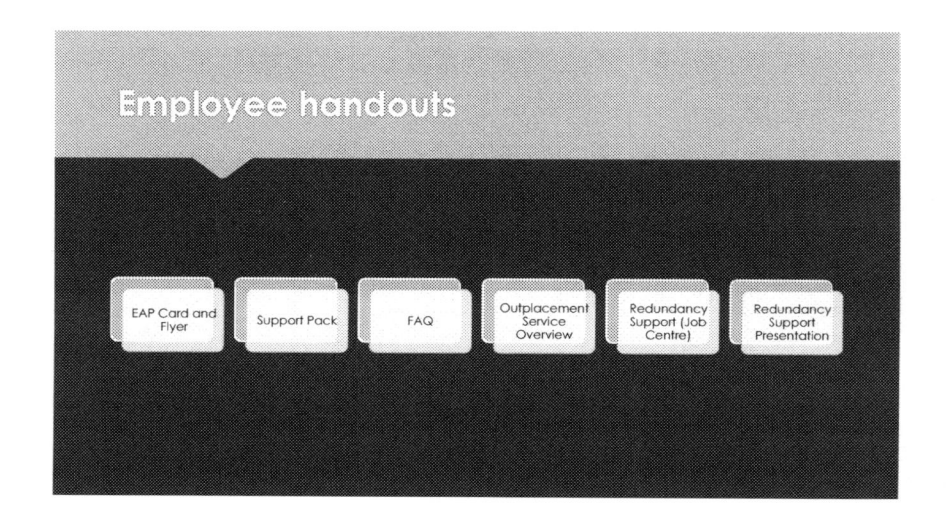

Reading guides available

Title:	Borrowing money
Title:	Getting financial advice
Title:	Making the most of your money
Title:	Problems paying your mortgage
Title:	Income withdrawal
Title:	Your retirement options

Reminder of what happens next

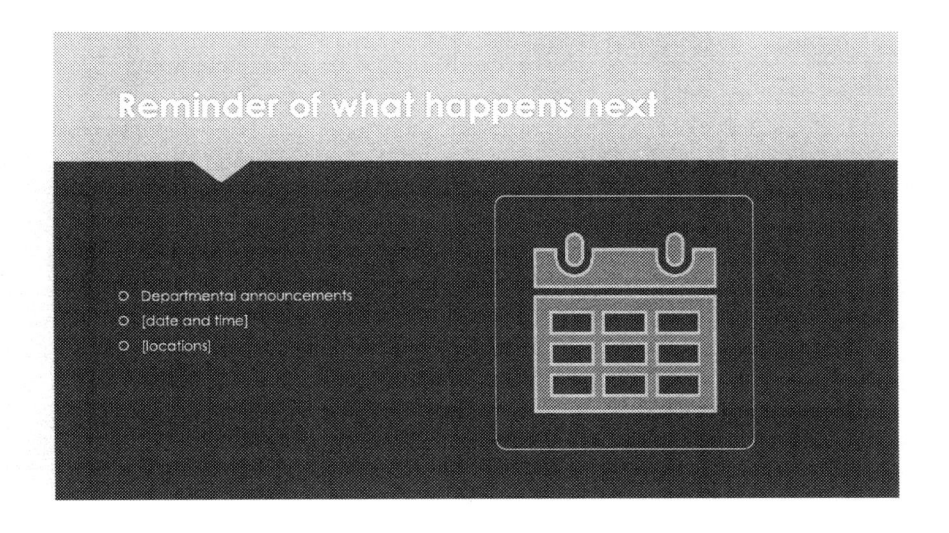

- Departmental announcements
- [date and time]
- [locations]

References

Appelbaum, S. H., Everard, A. & Hung, L. T. 1999. Strategic downsizing: Critical success factors. *Management Decision*, 37(7), 535–552.

Arndt, E. M. & Duchemin, K. F. 1993. *More than "Bandaids": Emotional support and education during the downsizing process. Healthcare management forum, 1993.* Los Angeles, CA: Sage Publications, 5–10.

Ashman, I. 2015. The face-to-face delivery of downsizing decisions in UK public sector organizations: The envoy role. *Public Management Review*, 17, 108–128.

Baruch, Y. & Hind, P. 1999. Perpetual motion in organizations: Effective management and the impact of the new psychological contracts on "survivor syndrome". *European Journal of Work and Organizational Psychology*, 8, 295–306.

Brockner, J. 1992. Managing the effects of layoffs on survivors. *California Management Review*, 34, 9–28.

Cameron, K. S. 1994. Strategies for successful organizational downsizing. *Human Resource Management*, 33, 189–211.

Cameron, K. S., Freeman, S. J. & Mishra, A. K. 1991. Best practices in white-collar downsizing: Managing contradictions. *Academy of Management Perspectives*, 5, 57–73.

Cascio, W. F. 1993. Downsizing: What do we know? What have we learned? *Academy of Management Perspectives*, 7, 95–104.

De Meuse, K. P., Bergmann, T. J., Vanderheiden, P. A. & Roraff, C. E. 2004. New evidence regarding organizational downsizing and a firm's financial performance: A long-term analysis. *Journal of Managerial Issues*, 16(2), 155–177.

Doherty, N. & Horsted, J. 1995. Helping survivors to stay on board. *People Management*, 1, 26–30.

Flint, D. H. 2003. Downsizing in the public sector: Metro-Toronto's hospitals. *Journal of Health Organization and Management*, 17(6), 438–456.

Freeman, S. J. & Cameron, K. S. 1993. Organizational downsizing: A convergence and reorientation framework. *Organization Science*, 4, 10–29.

Gandolfi, F. 2009. Unraveling downsizing: What do we know about the phenomenon? *Revista de Management Comparat Internaţional*, 10, 414–426.

Gandolfi, F. 2013. Workforce downsizing: Strategies, archetypes, approaches and tactics. *Journal of Management Research*, 13, 67.

Gopinath, C. & Becker, T. E. 2000. Communication, procedural justice, and employee attitudes: Relationships under conditions of divestiture. *Journal of Management*, 26, 63–83.

Greenberg, J. 1990. Organizational justice: Yesterday, today, and tomorrow. *Journal of Management*, 16, 399–432.

Hitt, M. A., Keats, B. W., Harback, H. F. & Nixon, R. D. 1994. Rightsizing: Building and maintaining strategic leadership and long-term competitiveness. *Organizational Dynamics*, 23, 18–33.

Hopkins, W. E. & Hopkins, S. A. 1999. The ethics of downsizing: Perceptions of rights and responsibilities. *Journal of Business Ethics*, 18, 145–155.

Isabella, L. A. 1989. Downsizing: Survivors' assessments. *Business Horizons*, 32, 35–41.

Johansson, C., Miller, V. D. & Hamrin, S. 2014. Conceptualizing communicative leadership. *Corporate Communications: An International Journal*, 19(2), 147–165.

Kets De Vries, M. F. & Balazs, K. 1997. The downside of downsizing. *Human Relations*, 50, 11–50.

Labib, N. & Appelbaum, S. H. 1993. Strategic Downsizing: A Human Resources Perspective. *Human Resource Planning*, 16(4), 69.

Marchington, M. 2015. Analysing the forces shaping employee involvement and participation (EIP) at organisation level in liberal market economies (LME s). *Human Resource Management Journal*, 25, 1–18.

Maslow, A. & Lewis, K. 1987. Maslow's hierarchy of needs. *Salenger Incorporated*, 14, 987.

Mihaly, M. 1995. Sorry, your last day is Friday. *Industry Week/IW*, 244, 31–33.

Mishra, A. K. & Spreitzer, G. M. 1998. Explaining how survivors respond to downsizing: The roles of trust, empowerment, justice, and work redesign. *The Academy of Management Review*, 23, 567–588.

Mishra, K. E., Spreitzer, G. M. & Mishra, A. K. 1998. Preserving employee morale during downsizing. *MIT Sloan Management Review*, 39, 83.

Mone, M. A. 1994. Relationships between self-concepts, aspirations, emotional responses, and intent to leave a downsizing organization. *Human Resource Management*, 33, 281–298.

Murphy, E. 1994. *Strategies for health care excellence*. Washington, DC: American Society for Work Redesign.

Nair, S. K. 2008. Organizational downsizing: A study of survivor attitudes. *ICFAI Journal of Organizational Behavior*, 7, 23–40.

Petzer, M. 2019. *Developing effective interventions for mitigating the psychological impact experienced by redundancy envoys during redundancy situations*. PhD, Solent University.

Pompa, V. 1992. Managerial secrecy: An ethical examination. *Journal of Business Ethics*, 11, 147–156.

Ruck, K. & Welch, M. 2012. Valuing internal communication; management and employee perspectives. *Public Relations Review*, 38, 294–302.

Schweiger, D. M., Ivancevich, J. M. & Power, F. R. 1987. Executive actions for managing human resources before and after acquisition. *Academy of Management Perspectives*, 1, 127–138.

Sronce, R. & Mckinley, W. 2006. Perceptions of organizational downsizing. *Journal of Leadership & Organizational Studies*, 12, 89–108.

Torres, O. 2011. The silent and shameful suffering of bosses: Layoffs in SME. *International Journal of Entrepreneurship and Small Business*, 13, 181–192.

Tourish, D., Paulsen, N., Hobman, E. & Bordia, P. 2004. The downsides of downsizing: Communication processes information needs in the aftermath of a workforce reduction strategy. *Management Communication Quarterly*, 17, 485–516.

Truss, C., Soane, E., Edwards, C., Wisdom, K., Croll, A. & Burnett, J. 2007. *Working life: Employee attitudes and engagement 2006*, Chartered Inst. of Personnel and Development.

Vickers, M. H. & Parris, M. A. 2007. "Your job no longer exists!": From experiences of alienation to expectations of resilience – a phenomenological study. *Employee Responsibilities and Rights Journal*, 19, 113–125.

Weide, A. S. & Abbott, G. E. 1994. Management on the hot seat: In an increasingly violent workplace, how to deliver bad news. *Employment Relations Today*, 21, 23.

9

EMPLOYEE REPRESENTATIVES

Adding value to redundancy implementation

This chapter addresses the various elements of employee/trade union representatives, including the selection of employee representatives, their role and responsibilities, their rights and how to establish a constitution. This chapter highlights the value employee representatives can bring to an organisation and the workforce during the implementation of a redundancy programme. For the purpose of this book, I will refer to trade union representatives and non-trade union representatives as 'employee representatives' from here on. This chapter provides helpful template examples for consulting and communicating with employee representatives.

The value of employee representative committees (ERC) are not recognised sufficiently as a key component in the successful implementation of redundancies (Petzer, 2019). Ashman (2015) supports this notion by contending that there is implied recognition that both employee representatives and redundancy envoys share the organisations' vision, which is to minimise the negative impact on employees at risk of redundancy. The insight of employee representatives into the process of implementing redundancies

DOI: 10.4324/9781003030416-11

is often done so with more wisdom than managers as employee representatives have a 360-degree view of the situation. Not only should employee representatives get exposure to the decision-making process with early communication as discussed in Chapters 7 and 8, but they should also be supported to the same extent as managers and supervisors with implementation responsibilities.

Redundancy envoys recognised that employee representatives have a significant role during the implementation of redundancies by supporting victims and by implication, the redundancy envoys (Ashman, 2015). They carry the burden of doing what is right for the future sustainability of the organisation, as well as representing the concerns of the individuals who are affected by redundancies (Petzer, 2019).

The value of employee representatives during the implementation of redundancies

Employee representatives play a key role as part of the process of sharing information and consultation and fostering two-way dialogue within organisations. Their unofficial roles extend beyond the scope of the requirements of the Information and Consultation of Employees (ICE) Regulations 2004. Employee representatives represent an important channel of communication and consultation between management and employees on matters relating to the plans and performance of each business unit and of the business as a whole. The involvement of employee representatives has proven to legitimise change and stop the spread of negative information (Bergström and Arman, 2017). Studies have also found that the involvement of employee representatives during redundancy implementations improve survivor reactions and that, as a result, no significant decline in survivor's performance has been noted (Ichniowski, 1986). Their role is intended to complement and not replace other channels of communication such as team meetings and one-to-one meetings between employee and manager. Collaborative practices where employees can voice their suggestions through joint consultation helps to develop a culture of trust (Baker et al., 2002).

In practice and with good collaboration from management, ERC offers a voice of reason to decisions being taken by both management, as well as the constituents they represent and therefore have a significant impact on reducing workplace conflict. As a result, the negative aspects on the workforce of redundancy implementation such as employee attitudes and behaviour do not suffer (Cregan et al., 2021).

The success of their role is however controlled, to some extent, by organisational approaches and the opportunities organisations allow within their employee relations strategies. There are various organisational approaches to employee relations, with the main schools of thought being unitarism, pluralism, Taylorism or Marxism. The value of employee representatives are widely debated in literature, however, the recommendations here are based on a hybrid partnership that incorporates direct employee involvement and participation combined with the benefits of management and employees working collaboratively (Guest and Peccei, 2001). An approach of a hybrid partnership is also known to promote mutual gains (Kochan and O'sterman, 1994). Another benefit to organisations is the importance of informal conversations that includes the exchange of information and advice in building and developing the relationship between representatives and management (McCarthy, 1966). This notion is supported that the value of employee representatives are focused on the organisational benefits of dialogue (Sako, 1998). Benefits of a partnership with employee representatives in general are reported to improve employee commitment, reduce absence, decrease conflict and promote valuable contributions to the organisation (Kochan and O'sterman, 1994, Becker and Gerhart, 1996) as well as improving the psychological contract (Guest, 1995).

The CIPD (2020) promotes organisational benefits of comprehensive information and consultation arrangements such as:

- improvement when dealing with change
- improved engagement and productivity
- increase in organisational trust
- sounding board for decisions
- promotion of idea sharing from the workforce
- increased job satisfaction (CIPD, 2020).

From the constituents' perspective, there are additional benefits, such as a safe platform to provide feedback via anonymous communication channels to get your view across, being kept up to date on important business topics and improved decision-making for the future sustainability of the organisation.

Naturally, there will be arguments for and against the value and the benefits of employee representation, which is not disputed. Personally, I am a strong advocate for the value and contribution of employee representation, recognising the benefits of sufficient training, support, early communication and due respect from senior management, which can foster countless benefits during the implementation of redundancies.

Role and responsibilities or employee representatives

Despite the legal requirements of consultation, having a workplace committee in place is good practice to keep employees informed of important and relevant matters that affect them. Therefore, by consulting informally with employee representatives, decisions can be made with a collaborative approach that reduces the risk of future disagreements. There are also direct benefits for employee representatives, such as:

- opportunities to learn more about the organisation and how decisions are made at a senior level
- developing new skills such as influencing, planning, communication and presentation skills
- raising their profile and presence in the organisation
- opportunities to be a key part in the future sustainability of the organisation
- making an active contribution to the well-being of their constituents.

Respectable employee representatives are often excellent communicators and active leaders within their organisations. Key competencies for a successful employee representative are proposed in Figure 9.1.

Best practice for the success of ERC includes:

- **representation that embodies the interests of the affected employees appropriately.** The question of deciding how many representatives are needed should be made based on the individual redundancy

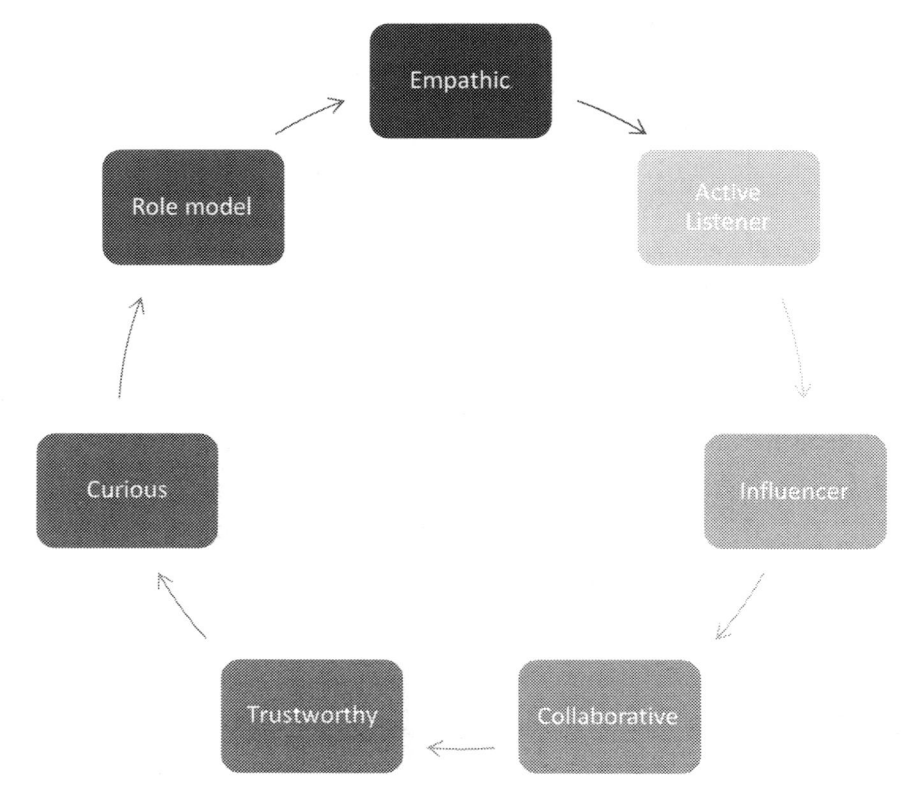

Figure 9.1 Key competencies for employee representatives.

programme, the size of the affected population, the locations and the practicalities of fair representation across the affected employees. Section 188 of the TULR(C)A defines the meaning of 'fair and sufficient' representation. Organisations need to identify the correct balance between representatives for both management and employees to represent the workforce. Be cautious not to allow the committee to be too big, as this can be counterproductive by encumbering decision-making and thus causing a delay in reaching agreement. A recommended committee size is optimum between six and eight participants. Employers should also consider sufficient representation such as when an elected employee representative is unable to attend meetings or consultations, ensuring that a suitable alternative representative is available to stand in. It is therefore recommended that there are more representatives trained than needed to attend each meeting with management.

Depending on the structure of the organisation, all parts of the business should be represented by the committee members. If the business has several branches across the country, this could be achieved by selecting representatives from different geographical locations. For example, in an organisation with a national workforce, representation could include areas where the organisation operates in, such as:

- Scotland
- Ireland
- Wales
- North West
- North East
- Yorkshire and the Humber
- West Midlands
- East Midlands
- South West
- East West
- Greater London
- East of England.

Another method for selecting representatives could be based around the practical hierarchical structure of the organisation as per Figure 9.2, which proposes the selection of a representative from each department or functional area to each constituent, for example:

- finance
- marketing
- sales
- customer services
- production
- IT
- projects
- factory.

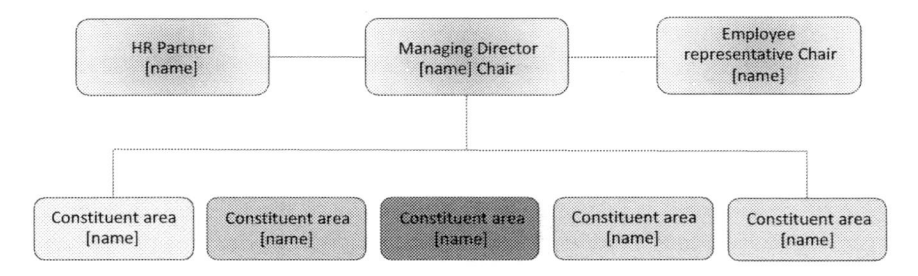

Figure 9.2 Employee representative committee structure.

- **Clear boundaries and terms of reference for the committee**, which includes details such as:
  - the term of office for an employee representative
  - the process of electing employees are inclusive
  - all affected employees are entitled to vote for their employee representatives
  - whether nominations are excepted for representatives
  - the voting process is anonymous.

Having clarity on the role as an employee representative

All employee representatives should receive adequate training to fulfil the requirements of the role. Trade unions typically provide comprehensive training to their representatives. When organisations establish their own employee representative committee, they have a responsibility to train their representatives to allow them to succeed in their roles as the 'voice' of the workforce.

Employee representatives' roles during redundancy implementation include:

- seeking views and suggestion from employees
- exploring ways in which redundancies can be avoided or reduced through proposing alternative options
- discussing the proposed method of selecting employees for the 'at-risk' population
- discussing levels of support and assistance for the affected employees
- exploring elements of the redundancy package
- addressing employee concerns and feeding back to management
- attending individual consultations

- attending collective consultations meetings
- reporting back to employees on the outcome of consultations.

Employee representative rights

Employee representatives should be supported with adequate time and 'space' to attend consultation meetings and to fulfil their duties, which includes the following rights:

- to not be subjected to detriment or dismissal as a result of their role
- reasonable access to constituent employees and use of organisational facilities (such as meeting rooms or online platforms)
- reasonable paid time off to perform their duties and receive relevant training.

Electing employee representatives

During a redundancy programme, employers may need to consult with their employee representatives due to the requirement of employment regulations; i.e. there are 20 or more employees proposed to be dismissed by reason of redundancy. If there is no ERC or trade union in place, employers need to elect employee representatives and establish an employee representative committee. Timing is critical as if collective consultation apply, consultation needs to take place prior to redundancy notices are issued. In addition, the time frame of consultation periods before the first dismissals are issued can extend the period even longer, i.e. at least 30 days consultation prior to the first dismissal where 20 or more employees are impacted and 45 days if a 100 or more employees are impacted.

Fair selection of employee representatives should ensure:

- employee representatives elected represent the interests of the affected employees appropriately
- employees affected by redundancy should be included for election
- all employees affected by the redundancy can vote
- employees who stand for election are actually affected by the redundancies when the election process occurs – this could include employees that were initially affected, but not made redundant

- voting is anonymous and employees can cast their vote in secret
- voting is accurately counted and reported
- employees are entitled to vote for as many candidates as there are representatives to represent them.

If no qualifying employees come forward for election or if the employees fail to elect representatives, the organisation has the responsibility to consult with the affected employees directly and share the necessary information with each employee at risk of redundancy. In accordance with the Consultation and Employees Regulations 2004, an independent ballot supervisor must be appointed. Due to timescales and pressures of planning a redundancy programme, many organisations choose to outsource the process of setting up an employee representative committee. More support on establishing an ERC is available from www.madeleinestevens.com.

Voting

Voting can take place through a physical process or online platform, with the key qualifying criteria being; it must be available to all affected employees, even if they are on a 'leave of absence'. Voting should also have the ability to take place in secret. Election can thus take any form such as:

- traditional voting papers
- online platform
- texting
- telephone
- email.

Irrespective of the method used, an election process needs to be robust and demonstrate due credibility in the process. Reasonable steps should be put in place to ensure integrity of a fair process, such as:

- ensure voting papers are sufficient and easily accessible
- ensure voting papers are sequentially numbered to prevent copied/ multiple votes
- ensure ballot boxes are placed in accessible locations that are secure, tamper proof and sufficiently supervised

- ensure counting takes places with supervision and cross checking
- communication of successfully appointed representatives are within good timing
- online platforms should follow necessary data protection protocols
- anonymity of voters should be protected.

The ICE Regulations 2004 requires the method of election to be publicised with election only taking place 21 days after the publication. Establishing an ERC can be time consuming and therefore it is recommended that enough time is allocated by scheduling this process early on in the redundancy planning stages.

Principles of the constitution

For an employee representative committee to be successful and effective, some guiding principles should be agreed in conjunction with management:

- regularity and logistics of meetings
- meeting agendas and minutes of meetings
- terms of office
- identifying a chairperson and establishing terms of tenure for the chair
- methods of feedback from the constituents.

Regularity and logistics of meetings

During normal operations, meetings can take place quarterly; however, during periods of disruption and change such as a redundancy programme, regularity of meetings should be adjusted to be more regular, e.g. biweekly or monthly. An optimal time for a meeting is an hour to an hour and a half, maximum. Allow for physical meetings as well as online platforms to promote meeting attendance.

Identifying a chairperson and establishing terms of tenure for the chair

Having a chairperson appointed helps drive the communication channel to be more succinct through the decision-making process. Differences between opinion amongst employee representatives can therefore be resolved prior to a final view being shared in a meeting with management.

Meeting agendas and minutes of meetings

To allow for a productive meeting, ensure feedback is obtained from both management and employee representatives on key topic areas to discuss, in advance of the meeting. During a redundancy situation, the topic areas are likely to be driven around topics of consultation such as how to reduce redundancies, voluntary redundancies, selection methods, redundancy pay calculations and employee support.

It is good practise to minute meetings for reference and having a record of assigned actions for individuals to follow up on. A record of minutes of meetings are also useful to demonstrate a fair redundancy process if needed. Recognising the careful consideration that goes into employee representative consultation, various template examples are included to stimulate ideas for ERC consultation and to ensure a fair and respectful approach is adopted:

- Appendix 9.1 Letter informing employee representatives of proposed redundancies
- Appendix 9.2 Employee representative committee first consultation minutes example
- Appendix 9.3 ERC first consultation communication slides
- Appendix 9.4 ERC follow-up consultation communication slides

Terms of office

The terms of office should be pragmatic and is determined by the employer. The term should be long enough for an employee representative to build credibility in their role, but not too long so that opportunities for 'fresh perspectives' are limited. A recommended period is between two and four years. When a term ends and voting takes place, it is possible that the same representative may be successful again in securing a role as an employee representative.

This chapter summarised the value of employee representation to the organisation, the workforce and employee representatives directly. The process or establishing a constitution, the role and responsibilities and rights of employee representatives were discussed. The next chapter address support offered to the workforce during redundancy implementation.

APPENDIX 9.1
LETTER INFORMING
TRADE UNION/EMPLOYEE
REPRESENTATIVES OF
PROPOSED REDUNDANCIES

Strictly Private and Confidential

Employee representatives	Constituency
[name]	[area/department]
[name]	[area/department]
[name]	[area/department]
[name]	[area/department]

[date]

Consultation about proposed redundancies

Dear [name of representative]

The Company is writing to you in accordance with s.188 (4) of the Trade Union and Labour Relations [Consolidation] Act 1992 [the "Act"] in connection with proposed redundancies in [the "Company"].

We write to you in your role as [trade union/employee representative] of the [union or area/location] members for the statutory consultation exercise as advised in the announcement of [date] by the Company.

The Act obliges the Company to consult with employee representatives in certain circumstances [as defined under the Act]. This includes the current situation where the Company regrettably has to consider making redundancies. The collective consultation period will last for a minimum of [include amount] days. The Company will inform and consult elected representatives of affected employees with a view to trying to reach agreement on the proposals.

Should the outcome of the consultation process be such that dismissals cannot be avoided, the Company also has an obligation to notify the Redundancy Payments Service (RPS), as well as the Department for Business, Energy and Industrial Strategy (BEIS) and to give a copy of the notification to the representatives of the employees being consulted. As such, we attach with this letter a copy of the HR1 form for your information.

We would like to know what you and the employees you represent think about our proposals. In particular, we would like your feedback about whether the redundancies could be reduced or avoided and on how we can reduce the impact on employees who are made redundant. You should know that we have considered ways in which we might avoid redundancies and some of these measures have previously been put in place, such as [restrictions on recruitment, various cost saving initiatives; zero salary increases, reduction of overtime, reducing costs e.g. size of email accounts, savings, reduction of expenses, productivity review, etc.]

We look forward to having a constructive working relationship with you and hope that it will be possible to reach agreement on key issues in a meaningful manner. We take consultation seriously and would like to emphasise that we have not made any final decisions because we want to take our employees' views into account first.

Disclosure of information

Set out below is certain information about the Company's proposals to assist you in ensuring that the consultation process will be meaningful. Please let me know if you require further information and we will endeavour to provide it to you, subject to it being available and any possible commercial sensitivities that may exist in relation to its disclosure. If such sensitivities exist or the information is not available, the Company will let you know during the course of the consultation. The information in respect of the proposals is set out below:

The reasons for the proposed redundancies

[The Company] is experiencing increasingly difficult market conditions. We are suffering the adverse effects of the economic slowdown and a sharp drop in public spending, particularly on … An example of this is …

As reported in the [Team Brief of date], we have suffered significant losses due to … The downturn in the market is more permanent and shows no signs of recovery … We are therefore, under enormous pressure to reduce our cost structure and improve both profitability and flexibility in relation to the volatile market conditions that we see in the coming years.

Regrettably, it is therefore necessary to propose the loss of up to [number] jobs within the business, from across all [areas/sites].

The numbers and descriptions of employee roles whom it is proposed to dismiss as redundant

The numbers and descriptions of those affected by the proposals are as follows.

Site

Role	Today	Proposed reduction	Future
[job role/department]			
[job role/department]			
[job role/department]			
[job role/department]			

Site

Role	Today	Proposed reduction	Future
[job role/department]			
[job role/department]			

Department totals

Role	Today	Proposed reduction	Future
[job role/department]			
[job role/department]			
[job role/department]			
[job role/department]			

The proposed method of selecting the employees who may be dismissed

To minimise the impact on our workforce and with the aim to reduce compulsory redundancies, we would like to propose volunteers for redundancy from affected areas only. We will retain absolute discretion over whether a volunteer will be accepted for redundancy. All employees will be briefed on the [date] on the Voluntary Redundancy Process which will run until [date].

If insufficient employees volunteer for redundancy, we would envisage selecting individuals for redundancy with the use of a selection matrix. This is to assist us in a fair and transparent process for redundancy selection, we propose the use of the following selection criteria and matrix, which will determine which employees will be provisionally selected for redundancy:

- job performance
- knowledge
- skills
- qualifications
- work experience

- disciplinary records
- absences
- timekeeping
- length of service.*

*Length of service will only be used in a tie-break situation when two or more employees achieve the same score.

A copy of the selection matrix is attached for consideration.

The proposed method of carrying out the dismissals, with due regard to any agreed procedure, including the period over which the dismissals are to take effect.

The company will enter a formal [amount] day collective consultation process on [date] with the [trade union/employee representative forum]. Those employees identified as being 'at risk' of redundancy will also be consulted individually.

Any redundancies and earliest leave date is anticipated as [date] subject to consultation.

The proposed method of calculating any redundancy payments

Employees with two years' continuous service at the time they are made redundant will be entitled to a Statutory Redundancy Payment (SRP) under the regulations at the time. These are currently:

[Company Redundancy Pay] (CRP) is paid in additional to SRP. CRP is payable after one year's service. The CRP available is one week's salary for each year of service. This is based on the final basic gross salary in the last payroll before termination of employment, and before any salary sacrifice. This excludes any other remuneration such as overtime, commissions, shift pay, allowance and befits of any type.

Services for the purposes of SRP and CRP must have been continuous.]

OR

Employees are entitled to statutory redundancy pay of [amount] per year worked. Final payment will be made by [date].

OR

In accordance with redundancy law, employees are not eligible for a redundancy payment as they do not meet the minimum criteria of two years continuous service. [We] understand that this can be a disappointing outcome and are therefore willing to make a once-off payment as a gesture of good faith of [amount].

If dismissals are necessary and the Company has not suitable alternative employment to offer the affected employees, those employees will be paid a redundancy payment in accordance with the appropriate policy, and/or their statutory right to receive a redundancy payment as appropriate.

Contractors

As part of our strategy to reduce redundancies we are reviewing the use of contractors accordingly.

We currently use contractors as follows:

Role	Department	Number of employees	Duties

Proposed meetings

We will hold a series of meetings with you over the coming weeks to discuss our proposals. We have provisionally booked the following dates for such meetings and will confirm the dates in writing via a letter (and/or email) to invite you to a consultation meeting:

- [date] [location/platform]
- [date] [location/platform]

If you have any questions about this process, please feel free to ask me.

Yours sincerely,

[name]

[title]

[company]

Enc Copy HR1

Redundancy policy

Voluntary Redundancy Process

Voluntary Redundancy application form

Selection matrix

APPENDIX 9.2
EMPLOYEE REPRESENTATIVE COMMITTEE FIRST CONSULTATION MINUTES EXAMPLE

Name
Department
Phone
Email
Date
Meeting place
ERC Meeting: [date]

Attendees		Apologies
[Employee representatives] [HR representation] [Chair]	[name] (taking minutes)	[insert name]

Agenda item	Action

Apologies

- [detail]

Introduction

- MD stressed confidentiality of the content of the meeting.
- Agenda confirmed:

  - business rationale
  - UK market situation
  - proposed changes
  - selection pool and criteria
  - opportunities to limit redundancies
  - contractors
  - voluntary redundancy
  - redundancy calculations

  - redundancy support
  - consultation meetings
  - any other business

Business rationale, UK market situation   **MD**

- MD explained the business rationale; i.e. [due to COVID-19 restrictions, decline in business, orders, revenue. External factors; i.e. UK market, backlog].
- MD provided update on the organisational strategy with a key list of activities.
- MD invited feedback.

Proposed changes   **MD and HR**

- HR explained the proposed changes; how long consultation will last, the old structure, the new structure, in which areas proposed redundancies will take place, the roles impacted and the anticipated numbers of roles to be reduced.
- HR explained what the consultation process will include.
- HR invited feedback. [Employee representative] expressed the difficulty in maintaining staff's positivity. HR explained organisational support and interventions to limit survivor syndrome.

Selection pool and criteria   **HR**

- HR explained process of redundancy selection and the use of selection matrix that will be agreed and adapted for each role.

(Continued)

- HR explained each criterion and how it will be applied:

  - job performance
  - knowledge
  - skills
  - qualifications
  - work experience
  - disciplinary records
  - absences
  - timekeeping
  - length of service

HR explained that length of service will only be used in a tie-break situation when two or more employees achieve the same score.

Opportunities to limit redundancies   **MD and HR**

- HR explained that the company is willing to consider the following measures to save costs and limit redundancies:

  - recruitment freezes
  - salary increase freezes

  - reducing or limiting agency workers
  - reducing or limiting bonus/incentives
  - reducing or limiting overtime
  - reducing or limiting company benefits

The company may also actively promote various schemes such as:

- redeployment
- voluntary redundancy
- early retirement
- self-employment
- sabbaticals
- unpaid annual leave
- flexible working
- job sharing
- reduced hours
- temporary lay-offs
- furlough
- MD explained what additional measures were put in place and already deployed to limit redundancies, including reducing IT costs, reduction in over time, transfer of [details], productivity review, generated savings by …
- HR invited feedback.

Contractors   HR

- HR went through the current list of contractors.
- [Employee representative] asked if contractors can be reduced in [department] based on [contract] ending imminently.
- MD confirmed that it was a great idea and already in consideration.

Voluntary redundancy (VR)   HR

- HR explained that the company are willing to consider VR; however, careful consideration will have to take place as part of the process.
- HR advised that VRs can be successful in reducing compulsory redundancies.
- HR explained pros and cons of seeking applications for VR.
- [Employee representative] raised a concern that some staff may request VR due to feeling demotivated by the current situation and the Company could lose key people as a result. HR stressed that VRs will be accepted based on selection criteria as the organisation cannot afford to lose critical skills in the business. On this basis VR's will not automatically be accepted and each applicant will be carefully considered.
- [Employee representative] asked if the ERC could provide feedback   ERC All
  on this the following day.

Redundancy calculations

- HR explained the process of how redundancy packages will be calculated.
- [Employee representative] asked if packages will be enhanced.
- HR stipulated that packages will be enhanced for VR applicants, but not for compulsory redundancies due to limited budget and that the company wanted to reserve a pot for training of 'survivors' and rebuilding the organisation.

Redundancy support   HR

- HR explained various types of support available:

  - trade union/employee representatives contact
  - Employee Assistance Programme
  - counselling
  - human resources
  - outplacement services
  - intranet

(Continued)

Consultation meetings   **HR**

- HR provided update of provisional meetings for further
  consultation.

AOB

- [Employee representative] suggested to reiterate to staff who the   HR
  ERC members are in case staff have queries.
- [Employee representative] asked how often the vacancy list will be
  updated.
- HR advised on a daily basis – available on the company recruitment
  site.
- Date of next meeting agreed [date, location/platform].

APPENDIX 9.3
ERC FIRST CONSULTATION
COMMUNICATION SLIDES

Employee Representative
Committee Consultation
Launch

[date]

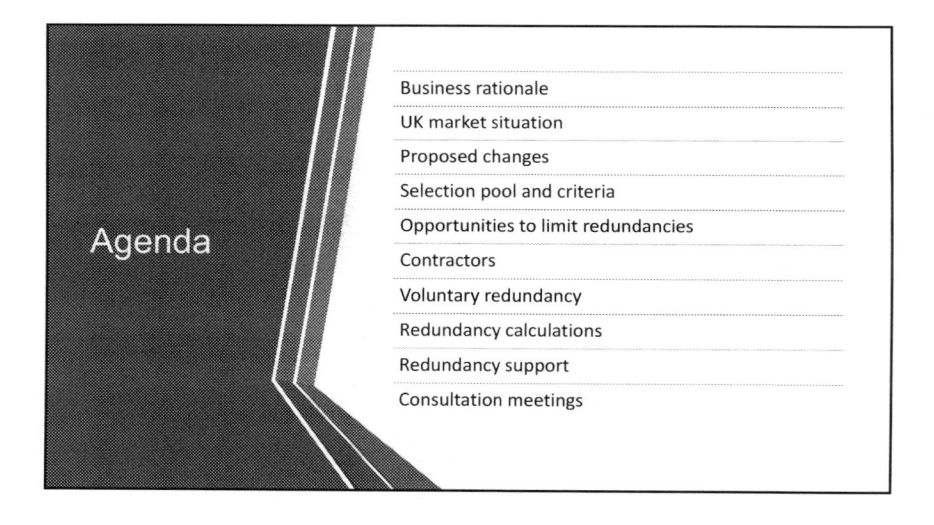

[Company] needs structural changes to overcome competitive weaknesses

In the last five years, the [company] could not reach the necessary profitability improvements compared to its competitors, despite the increasing business volume.

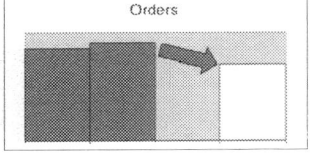

Orders

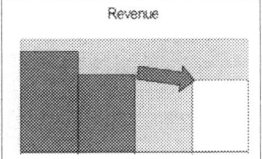

Revenue

[Provide update of decline in sales, orders, revenue, customers, etc.]

Impact of COVID-19

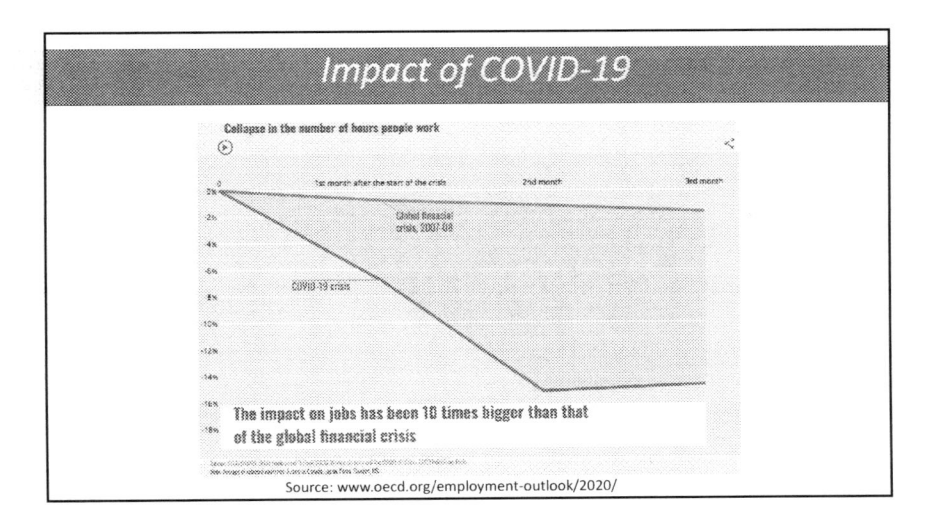

Source: www.oecd.org/employment-outlook/2020/

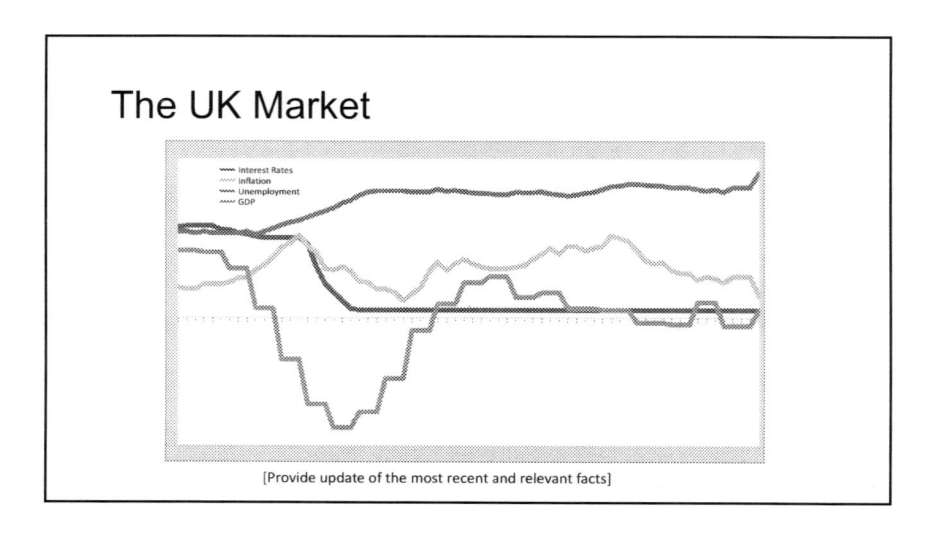

The UK Market

[Provide update of the most recent and relevant facts]

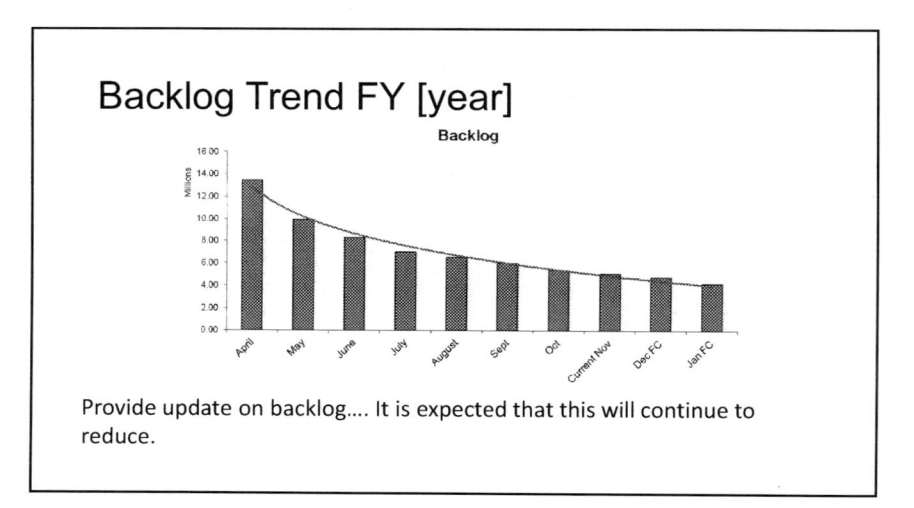

Backlog Trend FY [year]

Provide update on backlog…. It is expected that this will continue to reduce.

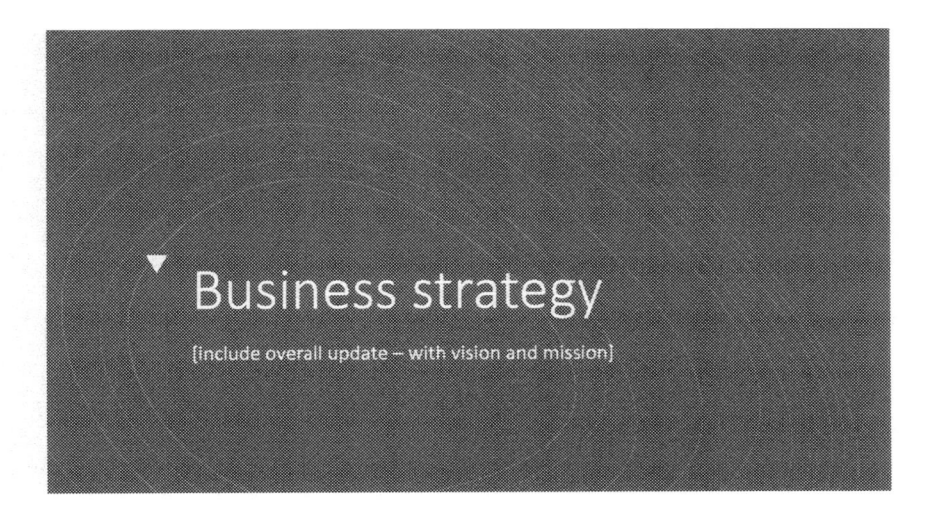

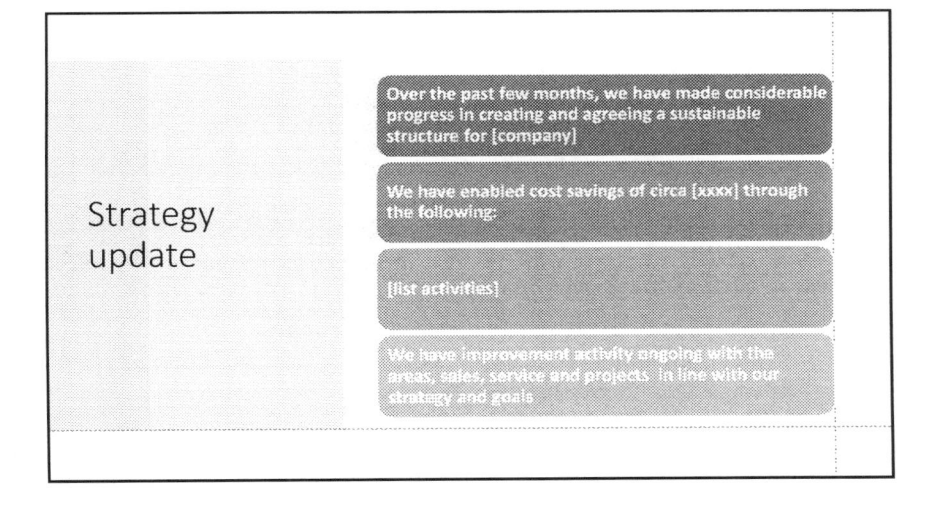

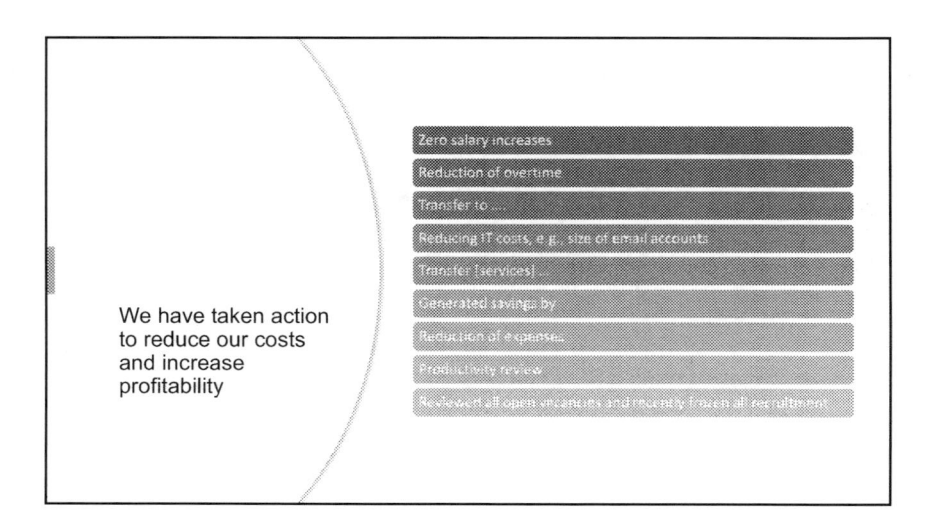

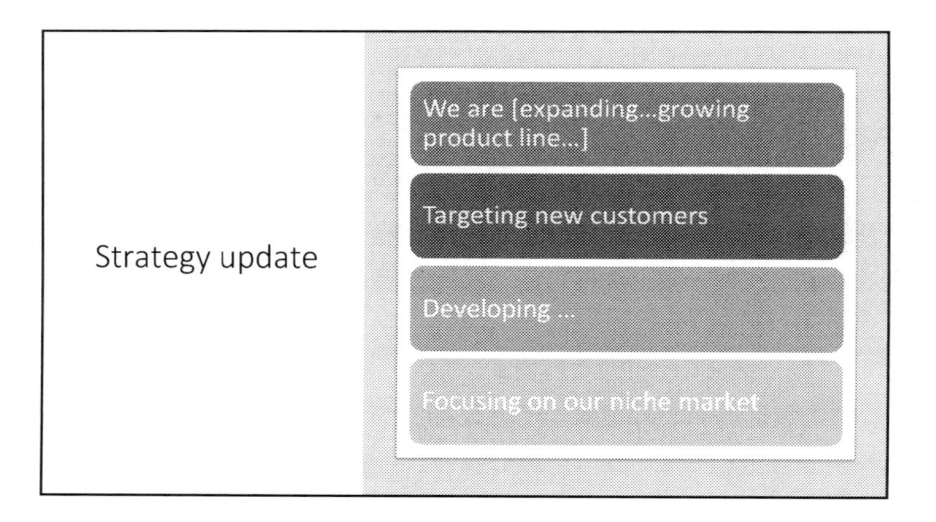

We need to address this now

- The business cannot continue to survive with our current cost base

- The business needs a stable base to move forward from, and until the company's income is greater than its costs, that stable base will not be achieved

Actions defined of recovery programme

We planned three programmes to increase its competitiveness and profitability in the long term.

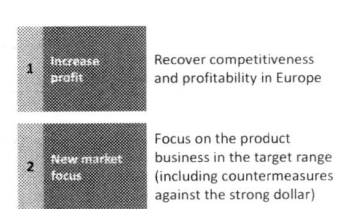

1 Increase profit — Recover competitiveness and profitability in Europe

2 New market focus — Focus on the product business in the target range (including countermeasures against the strong dollar)

3 Cost reductions — Reduction of the number of jobs and costs in headquarter and units in [details of locations / functions] whilst changing from a business unit-oriented organisation to a stronger region-oriented structure

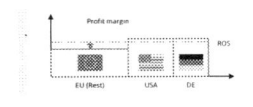

Profit margin — EU (Rest) — USA — DE — ROS

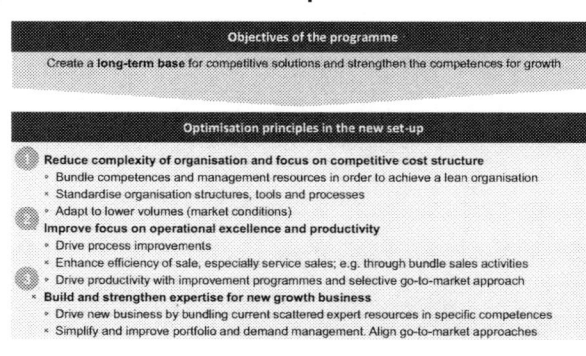

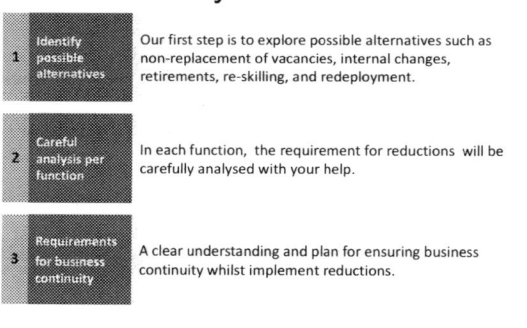

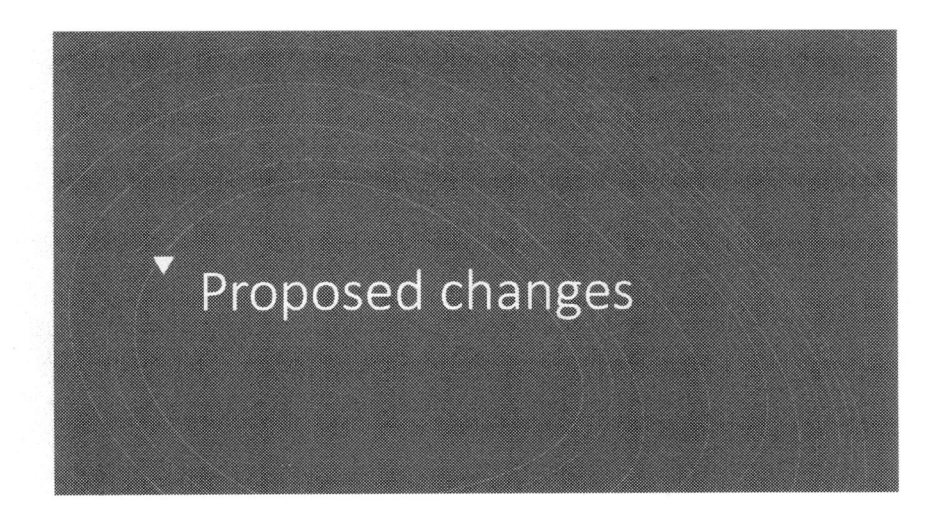

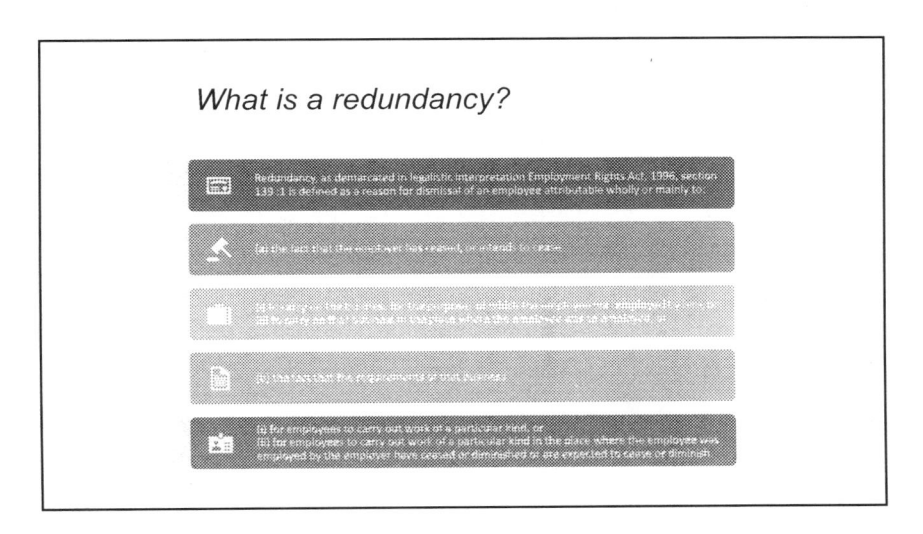

Redundancy notices

Years of service	Notice period	Example
Employment between one month and two years	One week	1 year's service = 1 week's notice
Employment between two and 12 years	One week for each completed year served	3 years and four months' service = 3 weeks' notice
Employment of 12 years or more	12 weeks	14 years' service = 12 weeks' notice

Collective consultation

Number of redundancies	Consultation period	Minimum consultation before first dismissal
20–99 at one establishment	90 days	30 days consultation before first dismissal
100+ dismissals at one establishment	90 days	45 days consultation before first dismissal

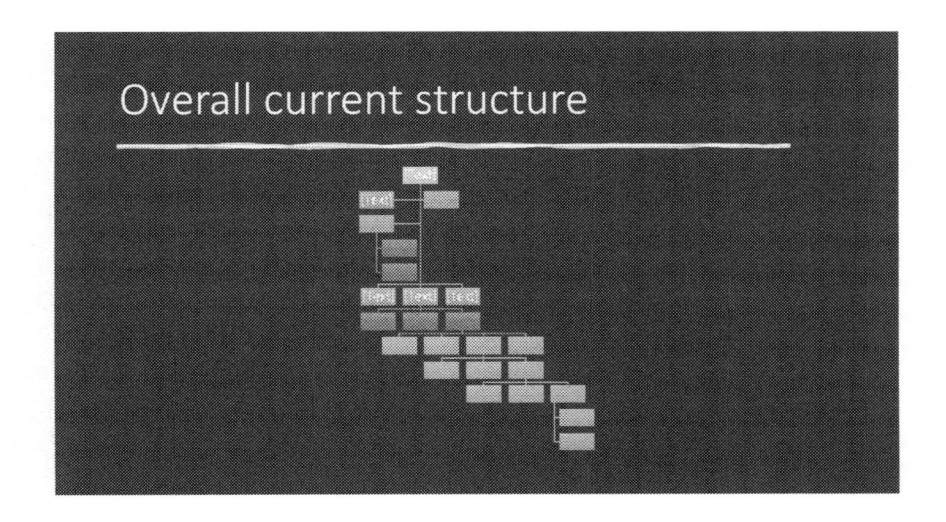

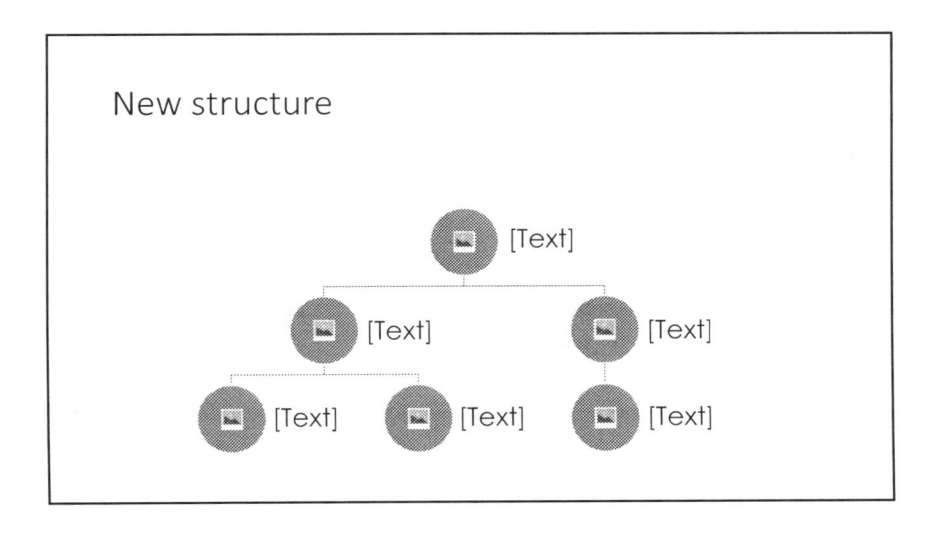

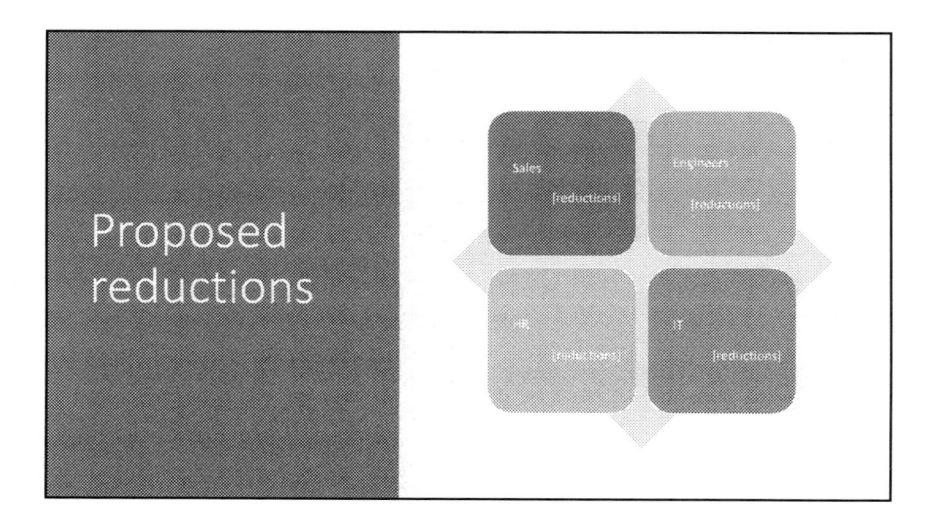

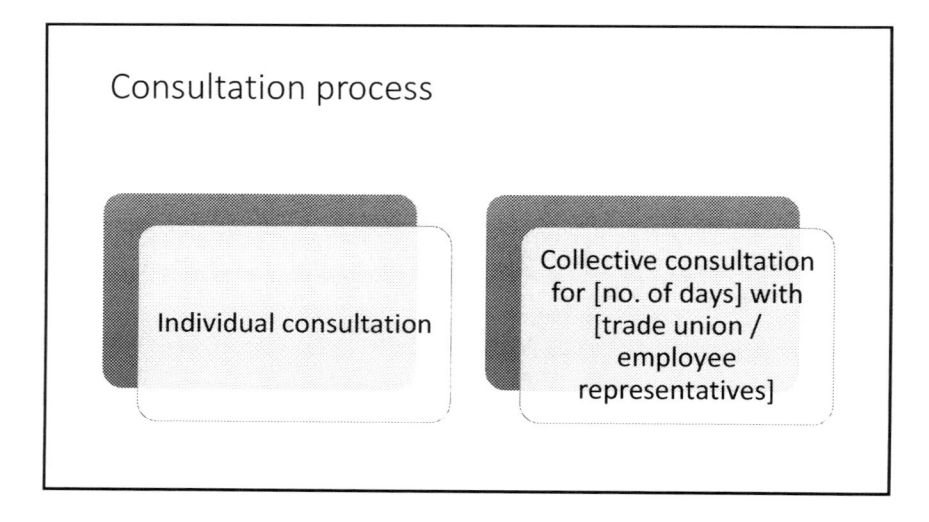

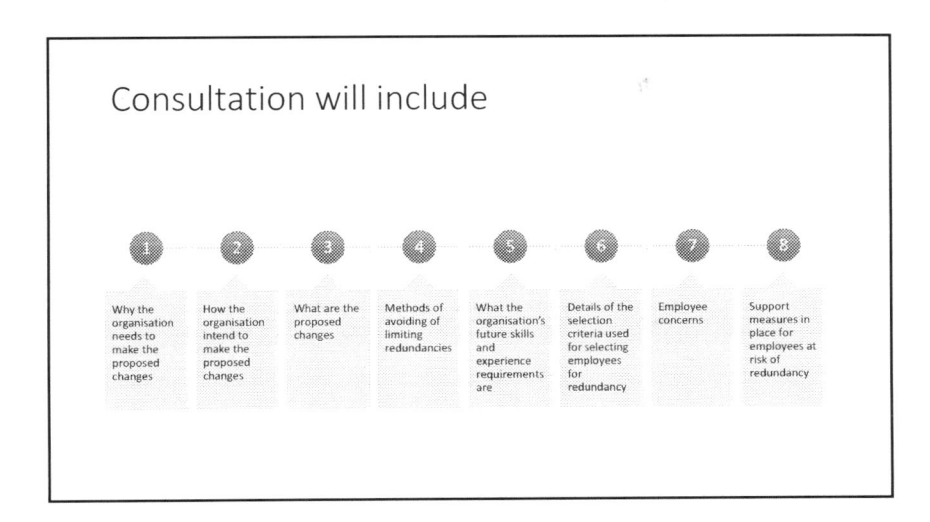

Consultation will include

1. Why the organisation needs to make the proposed changes
2. How the organisation intend to make the proposed changes
3. What are the proposed changes
4. Methods of avoiding of limiting redundancies
5. What the organisation's future skills and experience requirements are
6. Details of the selection criteria used for selecting employees for redundancy
7. Employee concerns
8. Support measures in place for employees at risk of redundancy

Selection pool and selection matrix

Selection pool

Determining who should be included in the redundancy pool, should include the following factors:

- Consider employees who undertake similar roles in an area that have been identified. Organisations can exclude employees who undertake similar roles, with robust justification for the decision.
- Consider all employees who undertake similar roles even if they operate in different departments of the organisation or work in different shifts.
- Consider employees who undertake similar roles at other sites, are subject to the consideration of contracts of employment and whether they are site-specific – actual locations of work, distance between sites and willingness of employees to work at alternative sites.
- Consider the likeliness of roles being interchangeable, which means that the pool does not have to be limited to employees undertaking similar work. In other words, when selecting retail cashiers in the redundancy pool, shelve packers can also be included in the pool if their roles are interchangeable.

Selection matrix criteria:

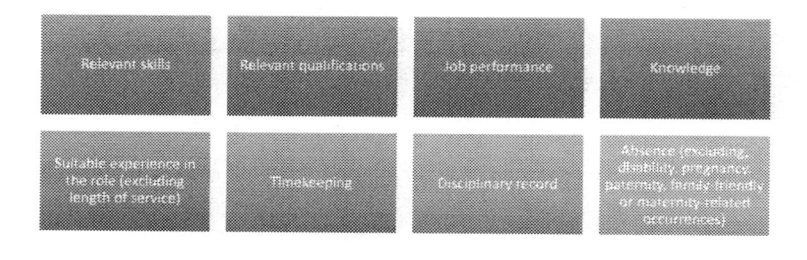

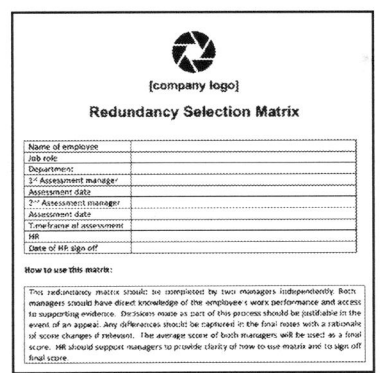

[company logo]

Redundancy Selection Matrix

Name of employee	
Job role	
Department	
3rd Assessment manager	
Assessment date	
2nd Assessment manager	
Assessment date	
Timeframe of assessment	
HR	
Date of HR sign off	

How to use this matrix:

This redundancy matrix should be completed by two managers independently. Both managers should have direct knowledge of the employee's work performance and access to supporting evidence. Decisions made as part of this process should be justifiable in the event of an appeal. Any differences should be captured in the final notes with a rationale of score changes if relevant. The average score of both managers will be used as a final score. HR should support managers to provide clarity of how to use matrix and to sign off final score.

Job performance

1. Job performance

Use job performance as a criterion subject to all employees in the redundancy pool being assessed equally. Supporting evidence of previous performance reviews are required. If an employee has been absent for a substantial period of time, it may be necessary to extend the timeframe to consider job performance before and after the period of absence.

Definition	Score 1	Score 2
Meets and exceeds performance targets	5	5
Meets performance targets most of the time	4	4
Meets performance targets for more than half of the time	3	3
Fails to meet performance targets for more than half of the time	2	2
Fails to meet performance targets	0	0

Knowledge

2. Knowledge

Assessment of knowledge should be based on the specific requirements of the role as specified in the job description.

Definition	Score 1	Score 2
Displays the full range of knowledge required for the role	5	5
Displays the core knowledge required for the role	4	4
Displays some of the required knowledge with knowledge gaps identified	3	3
Displays limited knowledge specific to the role	2	2
Has insufficient knowledge to meet the requirements of the role	0	0

Skills

3. Skills

Assessment of skills should be based on the specific requirements of the role as specified in the job description.

Definition	Score 1	Score 2
Displays the full range of skills required for the role	5	5
Displays the core skills required for the role	4	4
Displays some of the required skills, with skills gaps identified	3	3
Displays limited skills specific to the role	2	2
Has insufficient skills to meet the requirements of the role	0	0

Qualifications

4. Qualifications

Assessment of qualifications should be based on the specific requirements of the role as specified in the job description. Qualifications or equivalent should be used to complete this assessment.

Definition	Score 1	Score 2
Fully qualified or equivalent as per the requirements for the role	5	5
Part qualified and actively working towards full qualification	4	4
Part qualified and not actively working towards completion of full qualification	3	3
Not qualified or part qualified and working towards qualification	2	2
Unqualified	0	0

Experience

5. Experience

Assessment of experience should reflect the depth and breadth of experience that is directly related to the requirements of the role. Caution should be exercised to avoid any timeframes that may be subject to age discrimination.

Definition	Score 1	Score 2
Has broad and varied experience specific to the requirements for the role	5	5
Has a good range of experience specific to the requirements of the role	4	4
Has some good experience with identifiable gaps for the requirements of the role	3	3
Has limited experience in relation to the role	2	2
Has no previous experience of the job role	0	0

Disciplinary records

6. Disciplinary records

Assessment of disciplinary records should include active warnings that is no older than 12 months. The scoring of this criterion is different to previous methods as the scores are totalled.

Definition	Score 1	Score 2
Current final written warning	-5	-5
Current written warning	-4	-4
Current verbal warning	-3	-3
No previous warnings	0	0

Absences

7. Absences

Assessment of absences should only relate to the previous 12 months. Any absences related to disability, pregnancy, maternity, paternity, adoption leave, parental leave, paternity leave, bereavement leave or shielding in accordance with COVID-19 guidance should be discounted. The scoring of this criterion is different to previous methods as the scores of a long- and short-term absence can be totalled. Short absences can only be counted once.

Definition	Score 1	Score 2
More that 3 absences totalling 15 days or more in the past 12 months	-5	-5
1-3 absences totalling less than 10 days in the past 12 months	-4	-4
1 absence of more than 4 weeks or more in the past 12 months	-4	-4
1-3 absences totalling less than 5 days in the past 12 months	-2	-2
No absences	0	0

Timekeeping

8. Timekeeping

Assessment of timekeeping should only relate to the previous 12 months. Timekeeping can include being on time for meetings, customer appointments, training sessions, etc. and is not limited to the start of the working day. In addition, the same principles apply for leaving appointments, meetings or the working day before the scheduled end time. Any incidents related to disability, pregnancy, maternity, paternity, adoption leave, parental leave, paternity leave, bereavement leave or shielding in accordance with COVID-19 guidance should be discounted.

Definition	Score 1	Score 2
Persistently late within the previous 12 months	-5	-5
Frequently late (more than 12 occasions) within the previous 12 months	-4	-4
Occasionally late (less than 12 occasions) within the previous 12 months	-3	-3
Rarely late (less than 6 occasions) within the previous 12 months	-2	-2
Never late within the previous 12 months	0	0

Summary scores

Redundancy selection matrix summary scores

Criterion	Weighting	Assessor 1	Assessor 2	Calibrated score	Weighted score
1. Job performance					
2. Knowledge					
3. Skills					
4. Qualifications					
5. Experience					
6. Disciplinary records					
7. Absences					
8. Timekeeping					
9. Length of service*					
Total score					

☐ Length of service should only be used in a tiebreak situation when two or more employees achieve the same score.

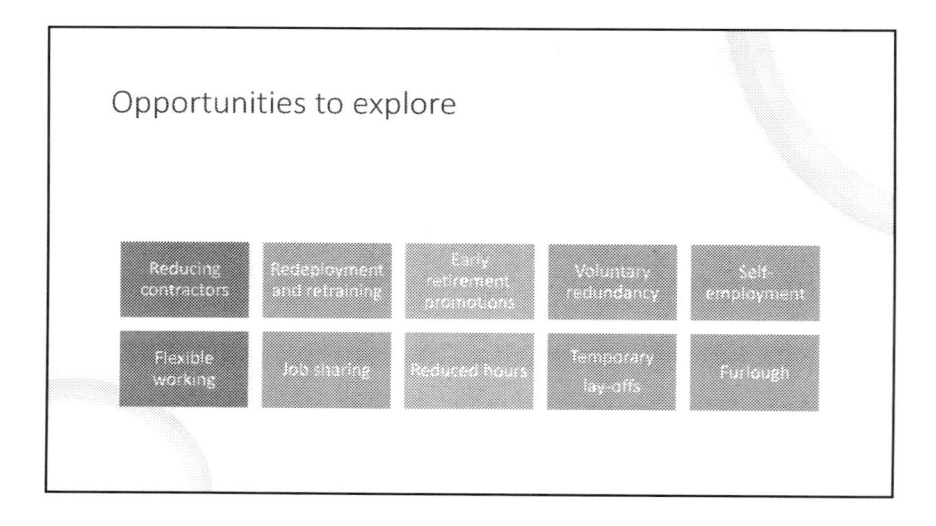

Additional cost savings

- Recruitment freezes
- Salary increase freezes
- Reducing or limiting bonus / incentives
- Reducing or limiting overtime
- Reducing or limiting company benefits

▼ Contractors

Contractors list and duties [date]

Role	Department	Number of employees	Duties

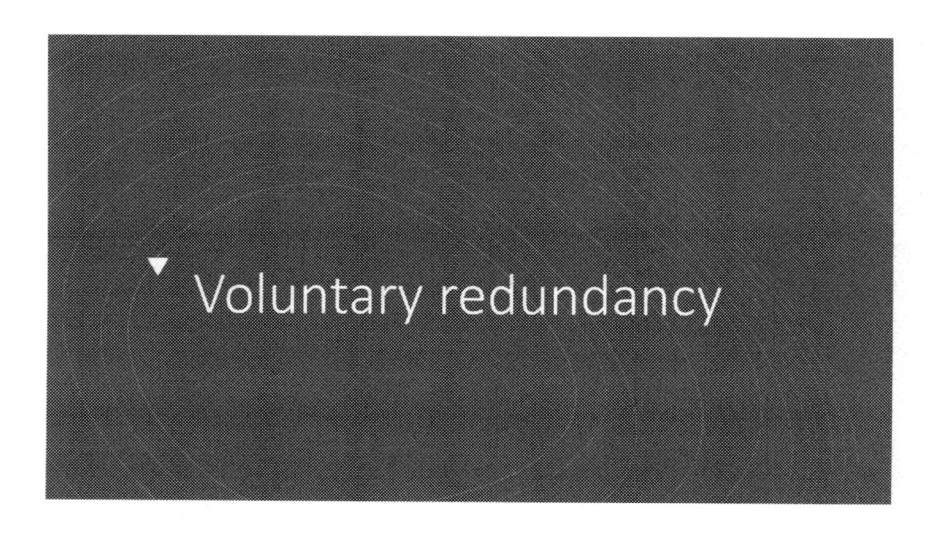

Voluntary redundancy

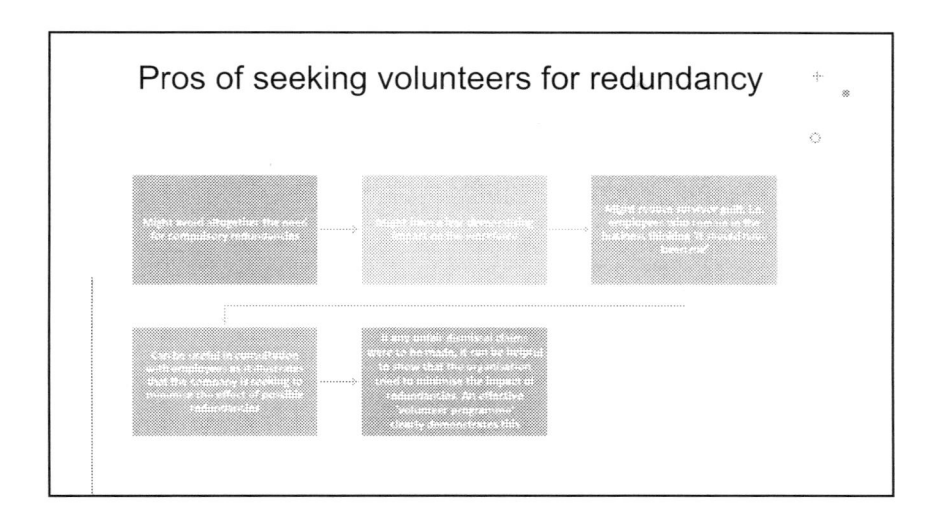

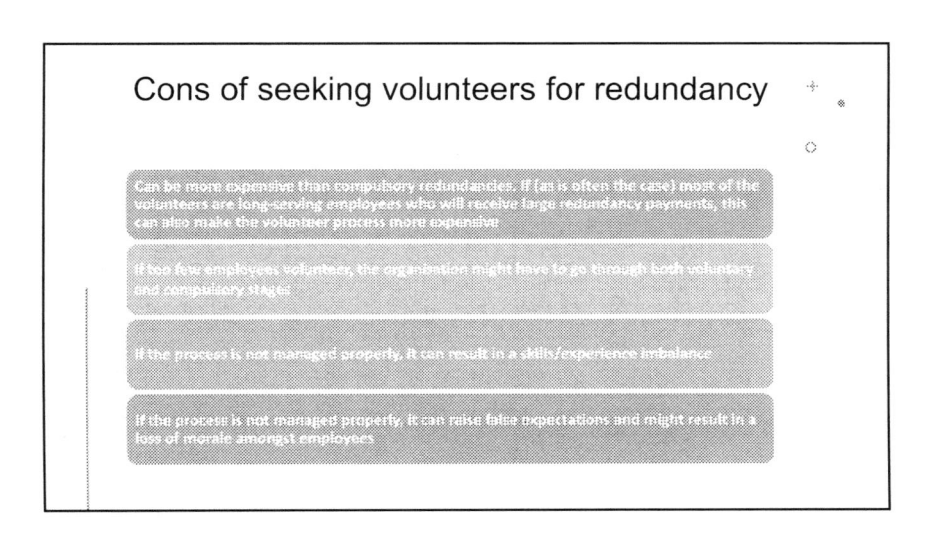

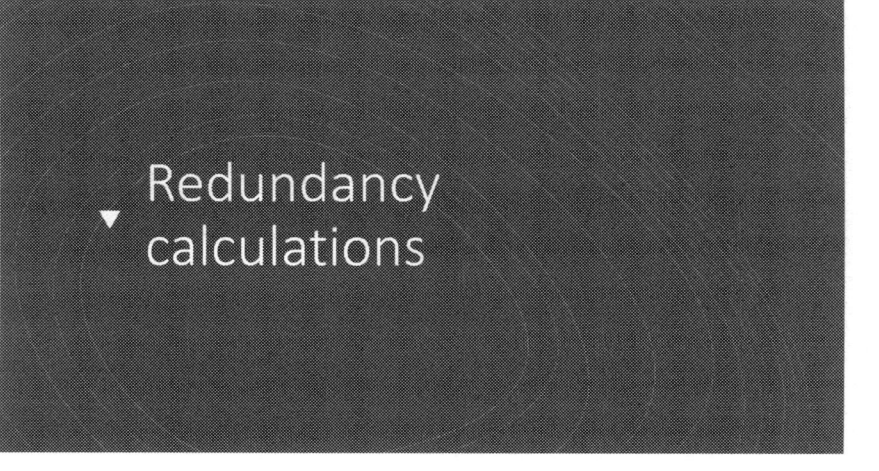

Issues to consider before going down the volunteer route

Consider in advance the impact that voluntary redundancies might have on the structure of the workforce and whether there is a risk of an imbalance of skills and experience or loss of any key members of staff

Estimate in advance, how many applications for voluntary redundancy we would be likely to receive, who would be likely to apply, and whether we would want to accept those applications

These measures can limit the scope for raising false expectations and finding ourselves in the position of having to decline numerous applications

▼ Redundancy calculations

Redundancy calculations

You are entitled to statutory redundancy pay of [amount]. In addition, as the company offers enhanced redundancy pay, you will also be entitled to an additional [amount]. Details of your redundancy payment calculations are attached for your perusal. Please be aware that any redundancy payment in excess of £30,000 will be liable to income tax. Your final payment will be made by [date].

OR

You are entitled to statutory redundancy pay of [amount]. Your final payment will be made by [date]. Details of your redundancy payment calculations are attached for your perusal.

OR

In accordance with redundancy law, you are not eligible for a redundancy payment as you do not meet the minimum criteria of two years continuous service. [We understand that this can be a disappointing outcome and are therefore willing to make a once-off payment as a gesture of good faith of [amount]].

Where to get support?

Trade union / employee representatives contact

Employee assistance programme

Counselling

Human resources

Outplacement services

Intranet

Outplacement support offered

The [provider] service is an award-winning outplacement program me. Combining today's technology with a team of highly experienced telephone career coaches means individuals receive the whole of their service on a remote basis:

- Unlimited support until each individual is settled, plus 90 days in their new role

- Career website portal

- Remote job & company research

- Personal telephone career coach

- 24/7 personal EAP help line

Employee handouts

| EAP Card and Flyer | Support Pack | FAQ | Outplacement Service Overview | Redundancy Support (Job Centre) | Redundancy Support Presentation |

Reading guides available

Title: **Borrowing money**

Title: **Getting financial advice**

Title: **Making the most of your money**

Title: **Problems paying your mortgage**

Title: **Income withdrawal**

Title: **Your retirement options**

Proposed consultation dates

- [date and time]
- [locations]

Questions

APPENDIX 9.4
ERC FOLLOW-UP
CONSULTATION
COMMUNICATION SLIDES

Employee Representative
Committee Consultation
Follow-Up
[date]

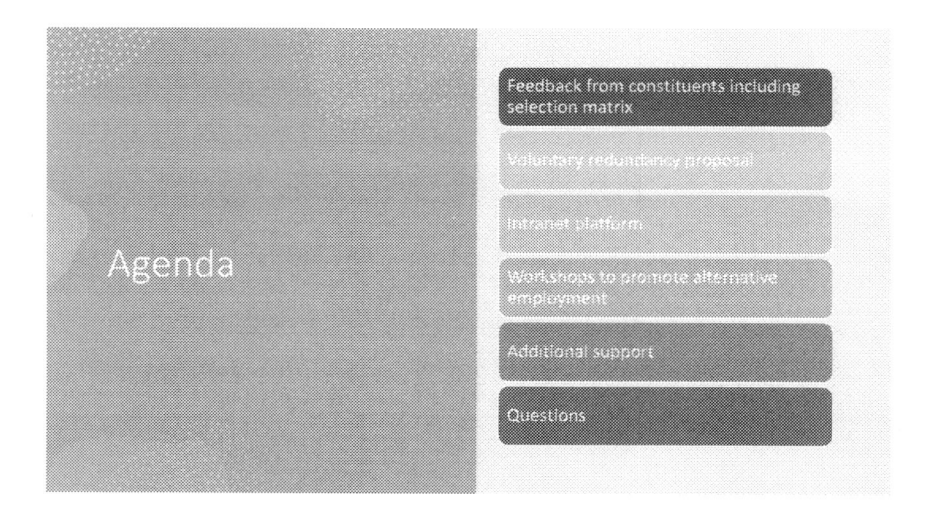

Agenda

- Feedback from constituents including selection matrix
- Voluntary redundancy proposal
- Intranet platform
- Workshops to promote alternative employment
- Additional support
- Questions

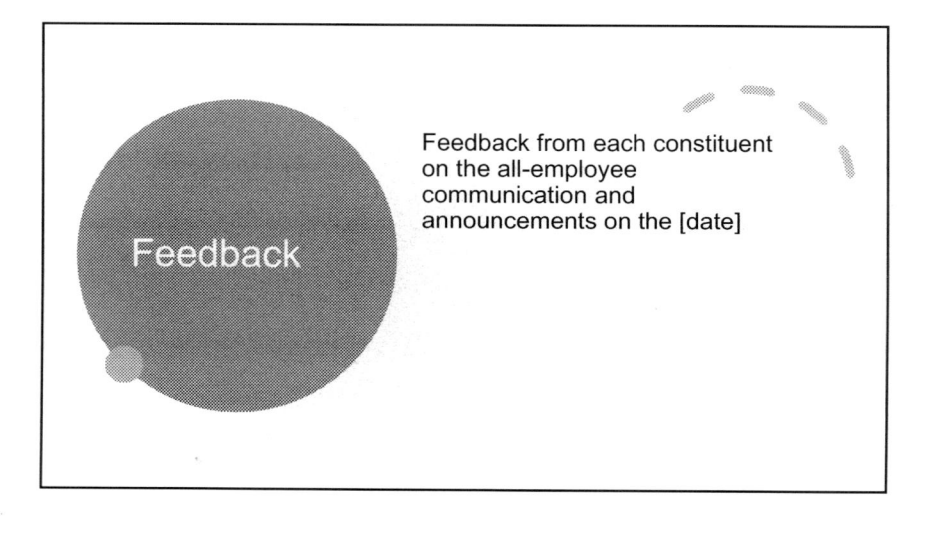

Feedback

Feedback from each constituent on the all-employee communication and announcements on the [date]

Voluntary Redundancy Process

[Launch date]

Voluntary Redundancy Objectives

 To provide an objective, and fair approach to (VR) selection which management teams will use as part of business area restructuring

 To minimise organisational disruption where possible

 To minimise the need for compulsory redundancies

 To reduce survivor guilt for our employees who remain

 To empower employees to decide to leave by their own choice

Terms

- There is no guarantee that VR will be granted.
- Expressing an interest does not amount to a resignation.
- Employees who are interested in volunteering are reassured that if their application is not accepted, the fact that they volunteered will not be taken into account when making any compulsory redundancies or in their future employment.
- When reviewing requests, business needs will take priority.
- Volunteers will continue to work until the date agreed by their line-manager.
- There is no right to appeal.
- Volunteers are invited from the following departments [explain the impacted departments, roles and locations].
- These terms have been agreed in consultation with your [trade union / employee representatives].

VR requests are invited from all employees within the following areas

[insert areas, departments and roles impacted]

Voluntary Redundancy Process & Timescales

Step 1:

Obtaining a VR quotation:

Contact: [email address]

Closing date for quotes [date and time]

Employees will receive their quotes within [24 hours]

Quotations are confidential

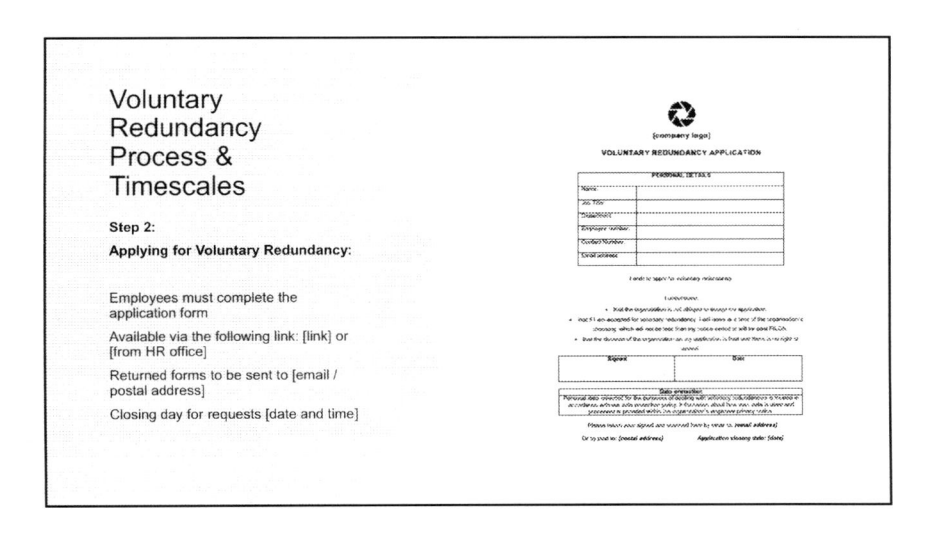

Voluntary Redundancy Process & Timescales

Step 2:

Applying for Voluntary Redundancy:

Employees must complete the application form

Available via the following link: [link] or [from HR office]

Returned forms to be sent to [email / postal address]

Closing day for requests [date and time]

VR Selection criteria

The Management and HR team will review each VR application, using the following criteria:

- The level of the employee's specialist knowledge, skills and experience. A VR cannot be accepted if the loss of the role leaves an unacceptable skill or expertise gap in the department which cannot be filled satisfactorily from existing resources.
- VRs will only be accepted if it prevents a compulsory redundancy.
- The total redundancy cost and, if applicable, any additional costs. The costs of the redundancy exercise should not outweigh the benefit.
- The potential redundancy satisfies the overall business needs of the department.

Outcome of applications

Step 3:

Verbally communicated outcomes

Communicated by employee's respective line manager by [date].

Written confirmation of provisional acceptance or rejection will be communicated by email [date].

If application is accepted, follow-up invitation to a consultation meeting to discuss any outstanding issues.

If application is not accepted, a letter to follow, making it clear what will happen next.

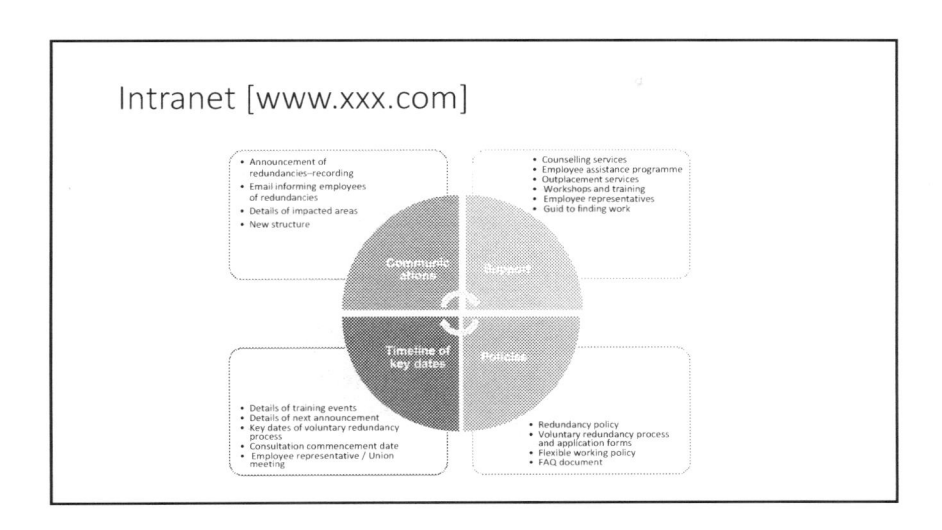

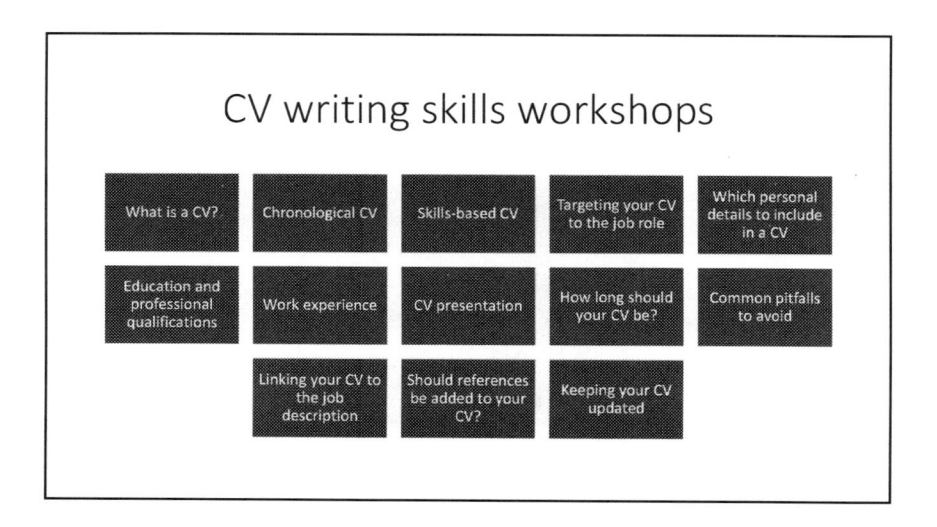

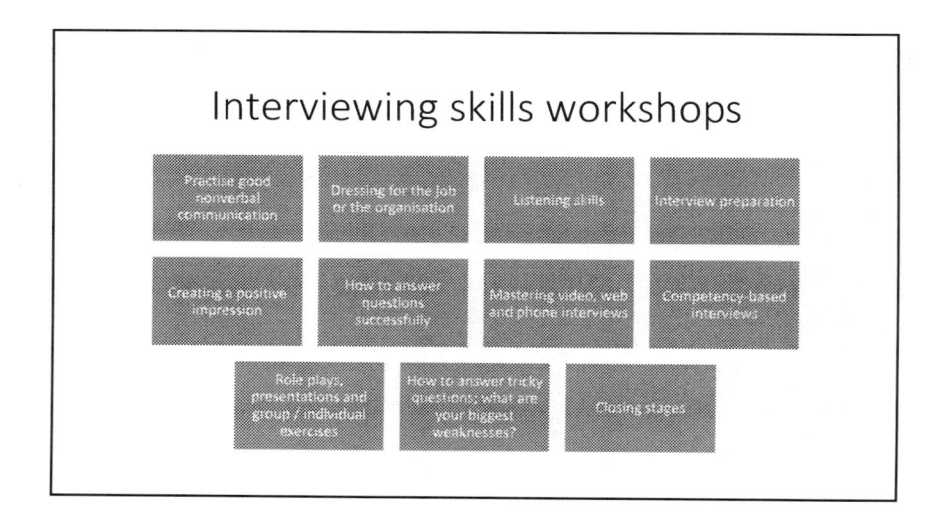

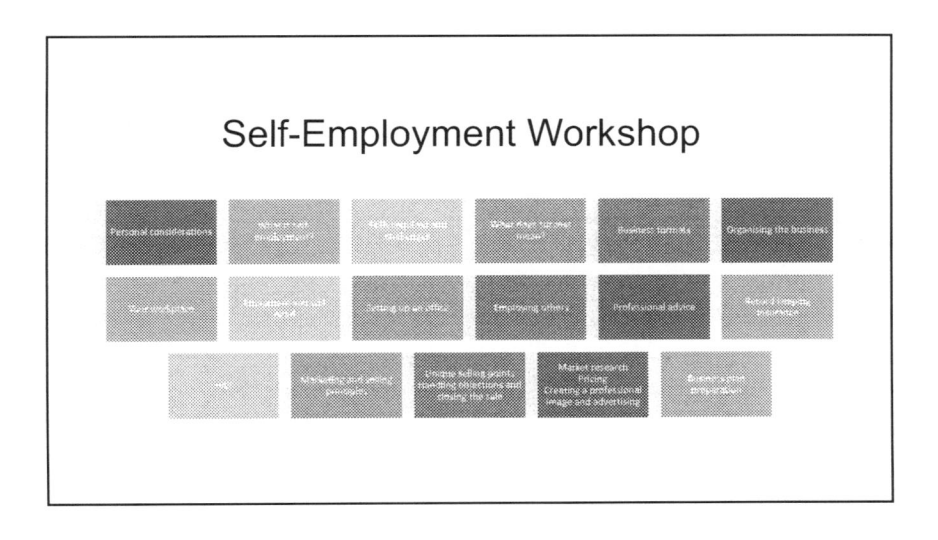

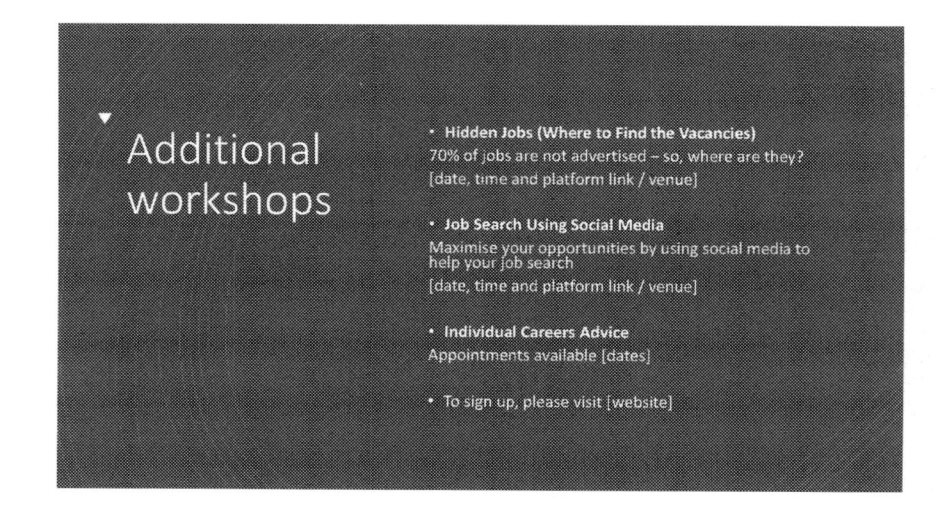

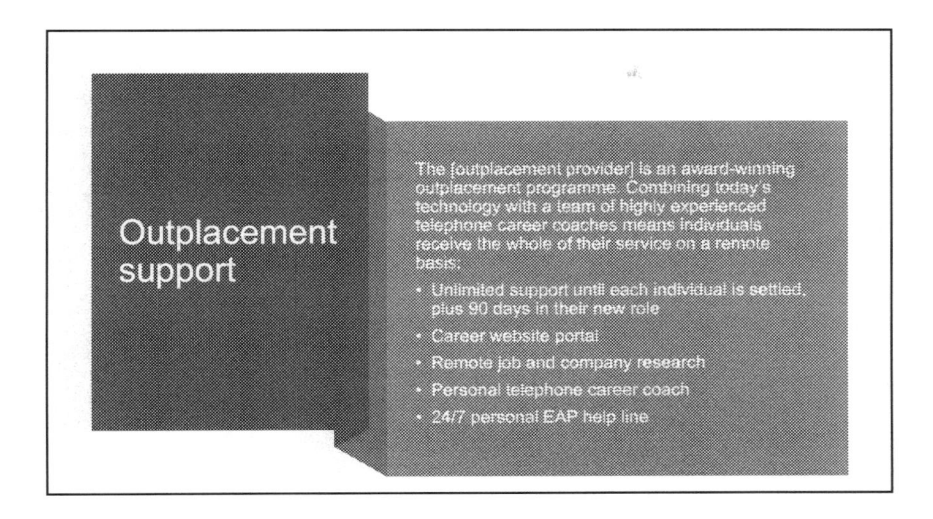

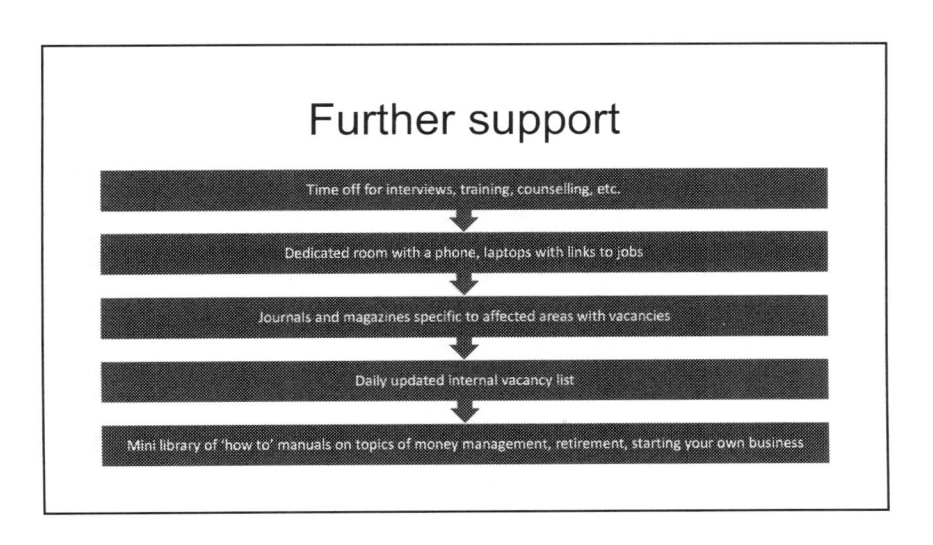

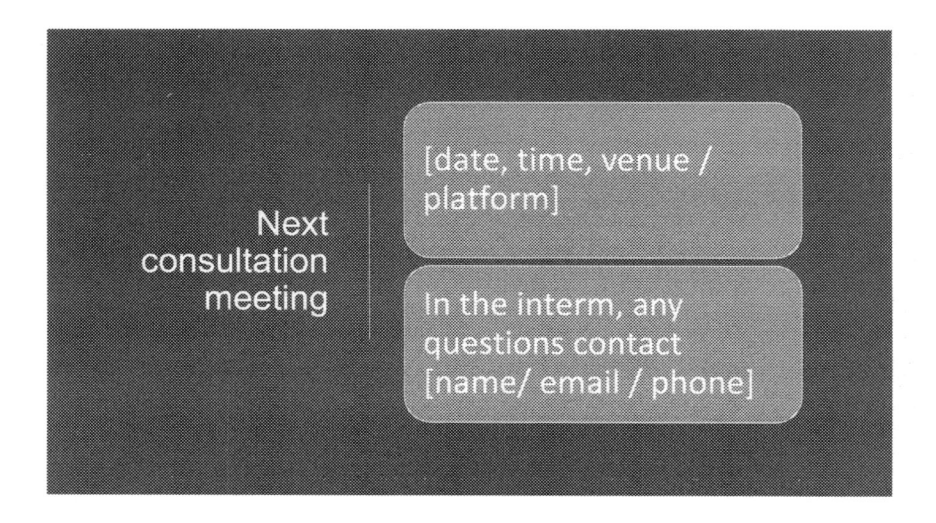

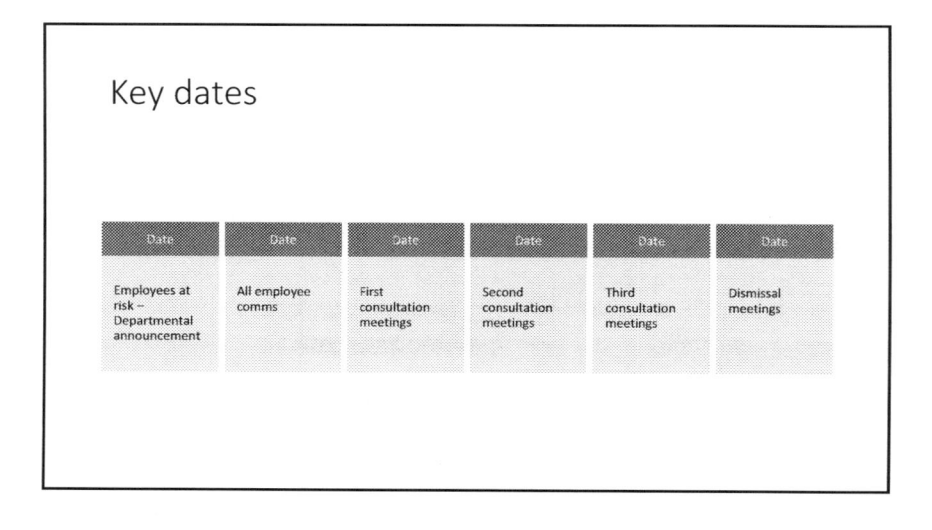

Questions

References

Ashman, I. 2015. The face-to-face delivery of downsizing decisions in UK public sector organizations: The envoy role. *Public Management Review*, 17, 108–128.

Baker, G., Gibbons, R. & Murphy, K. J. 2002. Relational contracts and the theory of the firm. *The Quarterly Journal of Economics*, 117, 39–84.

Becker, B. & Gerhart, B. 1996. The impact of human resource management on organizational performance: Progress and prospects. *Academy of Management Journal*, 39, 779–801.

Bergström, O. & Arman, R. 2017. Increasing commitment after downsizing: The role of involvement and voluntary redundancies. *Journal of Change Management*, 17, 297–320.

CIPD. 2020. *Information and consultation of employees (ICE) What, why and how* [Online]. CIPD. Available: https://www.cipd.co.uk/Images/ice-guide-full_tcm18-73473.pdf [Accessed 3 June 2021].

Cregan, C., Kulik, C. T., Johnston, S. & Bartram, T. 2021. The influence of calculative ("hard") and collaborative ("soft") HRM on the layoff-performance relationship in high performance workplaces. *Human Resource Management Journal*, 31, 202–224.

Guest, D. 1995. Human resource management, trade unions and industrial relations. *Human Resource Management: A Critical Text*, 1, 110–142.

Guest, D. E. & Peccei, R. 2001. Partnership at work: mutuality and the balance of advantage. *British Journal of Industrial Relations*, 39, 207–236.

Ichniowski, C. 1986. *The economic performance of survivors after layoffs: A plant-level study*. Cambridge, MA: National Bureau of Economic Research.

Kochan, T. & O'Sterman, P. 1994. *Mutual Gains Bargaining*. Boston, MA: Harvard Business School Press.

McCarthy, W. E. J. 1966. *The role of shop stewards in British industrial relations*. London: HM Stationery Office.

Petzer, M. 2019. *Developing effective interventions for mitigating the psychological impact experienced by redundancy envoys during redundancy situations*. PhD, Solent University.

Sako, M. 1998. The nature and impact of employee 'voice' in the European car components industry. *Human Resource Management Journal*, 8, 5.

10

ORGANISATIONAL SUPPORT FOR VICTIMS, SURVIVORS, SEMI-SURVIVORS AND REDUNDANCY ENVOYS

This chapter focuses on the promotion of employee well-being during a redundancy programme. Irrespective of whether employees leave the organisation or remain, employers need to act with compassion and ethics to ensure a redundancy programme is as painless as possible (Jacobs, 2020). This chapter provides recommendations of support that can be offered to each impacted group as underpinned by the Re-Focus, Re-Organise and Re-Build (RRR) strategy, Stage 7. This chapter proposes some recommendations for employers to support the workforce, although some of the key interventions have been underpinned throughout the book as part of the RRR strategy:

- effective and timely communication (Chapter 8)
- employee representation (Chapter 9)
- involvement and participation (Chapters 7–9)
- management training (Chapter 7)
- planning and analysis (Chapter 7)
- fairness and justice (Chapter 7).

DOI: 10.4324/9781003030416-12

Support for victims is evident in the literature (Flint, 2003); however, it needs to extend to organisational survivors, semi-survivors and redundancy envoys. Cameron et al. (1991) support this notion by stating that to ensure the success of a redundancy programme, the focus should be on victims as well as survivors, with specific support in place for each group. The decision by management to embrace employee well-being at work is likely to improve employee attitudes and productivity, which in turn can enhance organisational effectiveness and decision-making (Baptiste, 2008).

Support for victims

An important aspect of support is helping victims move through the change curve as discussed in Chapter 3, Figure 3.1. Support for victims will help them transition from shock and anger moving towards acceptance, which allows them to focus on their future (Davis et al., 2003). Interventions do not have to be limited to expensive solutions, and many services can be delivered in-house or through sources such as National Career Services or Job Centre in the UK. Helping victims to find alternative work or an alternative income stream, whether through self-employment or retirement will not only help the victims, but it will help lift the morale of their colleagues that remain in the organisation, as well as ease the guilt caused by implementing redundancies for redundancy envoys (Petzer, 2020). Various levels of support can be offered to victims including:

- voluntary redundancy
- financial support
- retraining and training vouchers
- CV writing workshops
- interview skills training
- self-employment workshops
- retirement workshops
- pension workshops
- financial portfolio management
- social media training
- where to find the 'hidden jobs'
- dedicated support 'space'

- collaboration with other industries for alternative employment
- Employee Assistance Programmes (EAP)
- counselling
- outplacement services.

Voluntary redundancy

Offering voluntary redundancies that include enhanced financial packages is a great strategy that can be deployed by organisations that have the available financial resources to promote such schemes. Despite voluntary redundancy still being a costly exercise, it does help in reducing resistance from trade unions and the number of compulsory redundancies required (Waters and Muller, 2004). As expressed previously, the selection and application process is critical in the success of a voluntary redundancy scheme to prevent the loss of critical skills.

From the organisation's perspective, utilising voluntary redundancy as a method to mitigate compulsory redundancies has a positive impact whereby suitable volunteers that are accepted by the organisation for redundancy, reduces the 'negative management aspect' for redundancy envoys. In addition, the employees who accept voluntary redundancy, do not regard themselves as 'victims' to the same extent as the 'victims' that leave the organisation through compulsory redundancy, but instead feel empowered by their own decision to leave the organisation. Offering voluntary redundancy therefore potentially helps mitigate the negative psychological impact on all impacted groups, with enhanced financial packages sweetening the deal just a little bit more.

Financial support

Building on the preceding argument of enhanced financial packages, it is worth giving this method of support more consideration. To mitigate the negative impact of redundancies, most organisations offer settlement packages; however, Labib and Appelbaum (1993) found that financial issues are a small part in the overall impact caused by job losses. Leana and Feldman (1988) have a contradictory view that severance pay, and extended benefits can have a big impact on reducing the stress levels of the victims. Severance packages also help with addressing the guilt experienced by redundancy envoys. Labib and Appelbaum (1993) warn, however, that a clear budget must be set for the implementation of a redundancy programme, whilst other authors advocate being generous to leavers (Mishra et al., 1998).

Retraining

Due to the fast pace of technological development, victims reported a need to retrain and acquire new skills to remain marketable (Labib and Appelbaum, 1993). Offering retraining programmes for victims can have a positive impact on reducing their stress levels and less stressed victims help ameliorate the impact on the redundancy envoy (Leana and Feldman, 1988) and thus the benefit is far reaching. To help support the notion of retraining, some organisations offer training vouchers or schemes to employees that are leaving. A training voucher entitles the employee to a specific amount that can be redeemed for a course of their choice at nominated training providers. Alternatively, some organisations prefer to retrain employees in-house to help develop new skills.

CV writing workshops

The offering of CV writing workshops is often favoured by employers. Many employees may not have applied or changed jobs in a long time and value the guidance and support of experts to provide assistance on how to write their CVs to be more attractive to employers. CV writing workshops typically include the following aspects as depicted in Figure 10.1.

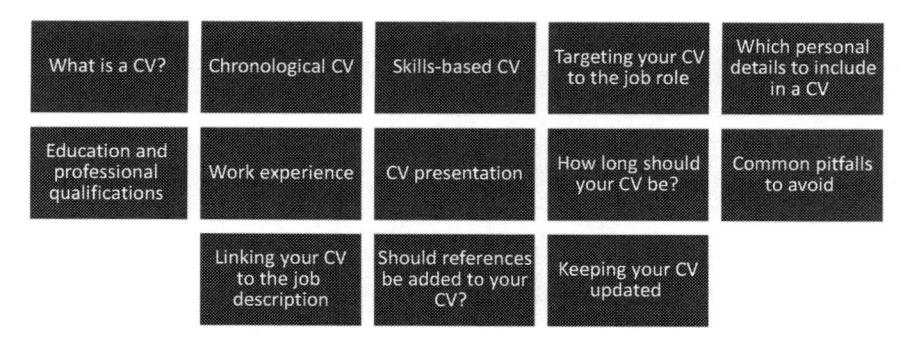

Figure 10.1 CV writing skills workshop content.

Interview skills training

On the same basis, helping employees to build their confidence when being interviewed is also very well received amongst victims. Interview skills workshops typically include contents as depicted in Figure 10.2.

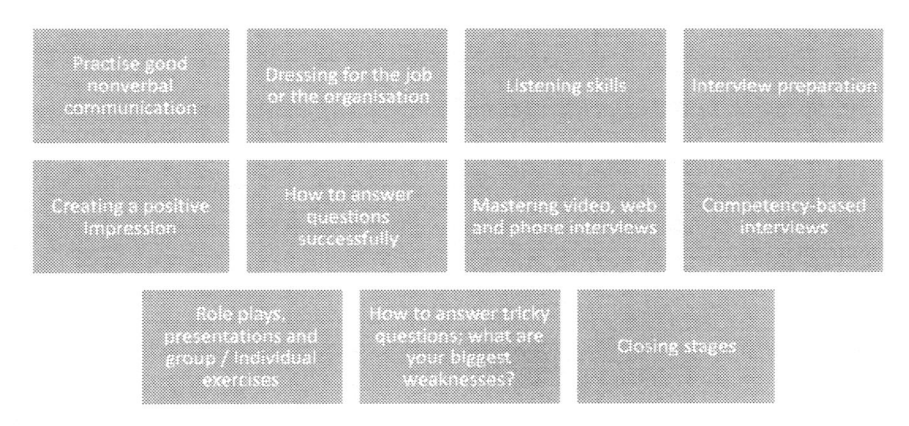

Figure 10.2 Interview skills workshop content.

Self-employment workshops

In previous redundancy programmes where I was involved, consultation with the employee representatives lead to an expression of interest from several employees who were interested in setting themselves up in their own business (Petzer, 2019). There are many success stories of employees who took a redundancy package and used their packages towards a business start-up that changed their lives for the better with some fulfilling lifelong

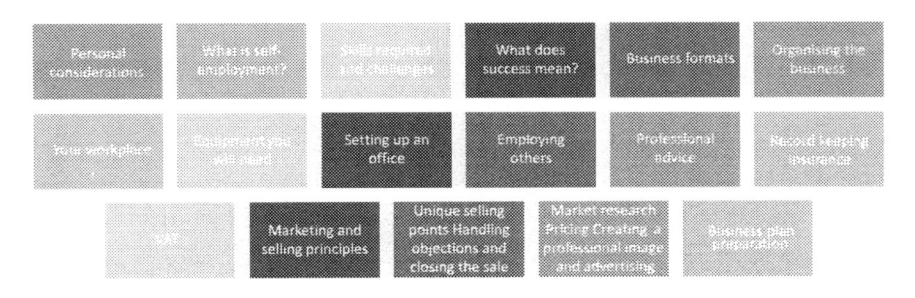

Figure 10.3 Self-employment workshop content.

dreams. By supporting these employees in providing education on what they will need to succeed, they could make more informed decisions on whether to apply for voluntary redundancy. Self-employment workshops typically include the following aspects as depicted in Figure 10.3.

Retirement workshops

Early retirement incentives mostly include increased retirement benefits such as extended medical insurance or a once of 'ex gratia' payment. These incentives have to be very carefully managed to ensure that the organisation does not loose talented employees. Caution regarding implementation is also supported by research that indicated that it was the most valuable employees who took advantage of incentives such as early retirement packages, resulting in loss of skilled and talented resources for the organisation (Bowman and Singh, 1993). On the contrary, if implemented with due diligence and based on the skills analysis as part of the RRR strategy discussed in Chapter 7, retirement workshops can be mutually beneficial for the organisation and individuals. Implemented responsibly, early retirement offers can provide the opportunity to limit compulsory redundancies, which support victims, drives empowerment amongst employees who choose this option and protect redundancy envoys from emotive discussions. Research has also indicated that implementing voluntary retirement packages as an alternative method of workforce reduction can reduce the negative impact on survivors (Iverson and Zatzick, 2007). To support employees who decide to opt for early retirement, a workshop is recommended, which typically includes the following elements as per Figure 10.4.

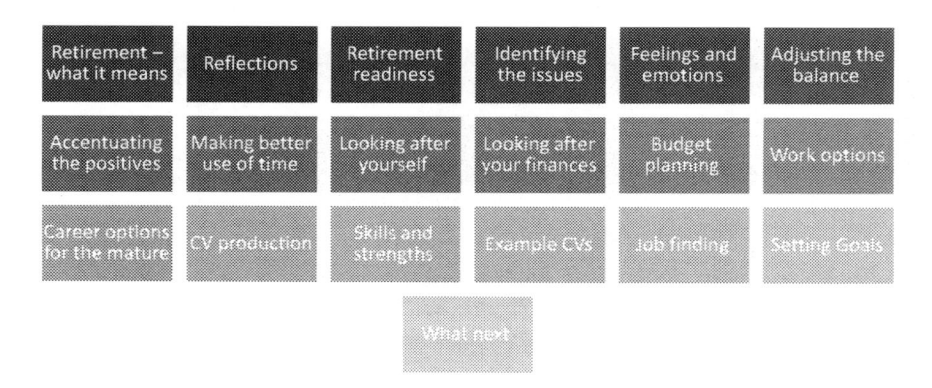

Figure 10.4 Retirement workshop content.

Pension workshops

Pension planning workshops extend the support for employees who opt to take early retirement offerings. Pension planning workshops are often available through the organisation's pension provider who typically cover a variety of related topics providing in-depth knowledge and financial guidance. Some providers include a combination of active retirement and pension planning contents in their courses such as this example below.

Managing change
> Identifying concerns
> Lifestyle, relationships, status, time, motivation

Building a new life
> Using time effectively
> Volunteering, leisure and learning opportunities
> Further employment

Maintaining health
> Mental, physical and social/emotional
> Holistic approach – practical steps

Money management
> Tax tips
> Budgeting – changes in income and expenditure
> Why you need income and capital
> Effects of inflation + life expectancy

Investing in retirement
> Banks, building societies, property, gilts, shares
> Understanding investment principles
> Managing and reducing investment risk
> Using cash to protect your investments
> Guaranteed investments

Personal health action plan
Income in retirement
> State pension and other state benefits/allowances occupational pension benefits
> Choices and decisions at retirement

> Selecting appropriate levels of income and cash, personal taxation, and changes in retirement

Legal issues and estate planning
> Why you need a professionally prepared will
> Power of attorney – who controls your assets?
> Long-term care – planning ahead
> Inheritance tax – planning ahead

Thinking about the future
> Making a start – an action plan
> Professional advice – what to expect

Financial portfolio management

Some of the biggest concerns for victims are the lack of future income and how to pay their bills and meet financial obligations. Employers can thus also support victims by providing guidance on how to claim benefits, how to obtain financial advice and general financial portfolio management. Many of these support mechanisms do not have to be an additional expense for an organisation. Free publications on the financial aid topics can be obtained from 'The Money Advice Service' – moneyadviceservice.org.uk. Some of the booklets they produce include:

- getting financial advice
- making the most of your money
- problems paying your mortgage
- income withdrawal
- your retirement options.

Social media training

Although for some employees, social media is part of daily life, they may have never used social media for the purpose of finding alternative employment. Providing training for employees on how to conduct job searches via social media is thus another helpful initiative to help victims find new roles.

Where to find the 'hidden jobs'

On a similar basis to using social media to find work, employers can offer victims training on where to find 'hidden jobs'. Short training courses can be outsourced or offered by in-house experts from the recruitment team. Typical course content includes the following modules:

- exploring your own network
- attending formal networking events
- digital networking
- leveraging LinkedIn and social media
- how to conduct job searches
- signing up for job posts.

Dedicated support 'space'

If employees are working on-site, whether it is a factory or an office location, think about the physical space they need whilst job hunting, employers can support victims by providing a confidential, physical space such as a dedicated office to make phone calls or attend counselling if they, for example, work in a warehouse of factory environment with limited privacy. If employees are working from home or on-site, allow them the freedom to conduct work searches, to ask questions and to make phone calls that will help them find new roles.

Employers can also offer support by pointing victims to useful websites specific for job hunting that are unique to their industry or the recruitment agencies that the organisation use to hire staff. Use knowledge pools to connect employees at risk of redundancy with specialist networks and give them the best 'insider' tips to find alternative work. This is not the time to aggressively 'monitor' their attendance, but instead show support and empathy.

Collaboration with other industries for alternative employment and outsourcing

Collaboration with other industries can be achieved through various means such as engaging with local job centres or connecting employees at risk of redundancy with organisations that are actively hiring. During the COVID-19 pandemic, whilst many industries were facing redundancies such as hospitability and transport, other industries were booming and recruiting, such as online retailers and building trades due to a surge in home deliveries and home improvements. HR can build partner relationships with organisations that are thriving, which may help individuals get new roles, but also save recruitment costs for the new employer, creating a win-win scenario.

Although securing alternative employment outside of the employer organisation does not necessarily mitigate redundancies, it does help to mitigate damaged psychological contracts for all the impacted groups.

'Outsourcing' employees to work as consultants is a strategy not often deployed (Tomasko, 1991); however, it is another opportunity to help victims or potentially save costs. Employees are kept on the payroll of the organisation, whilst delivering services to an external organisation, which is then billed for the service or employee time. Employees undertake this 'outsourced' role based on demand, which could include customers, contractors, suppliers, government agencies or trade associations. For some employees, this exposure may lead to the offer of permanent alternative employment.

EAP and counselling

Employee Assistance Programmes (EAP) provide comprehensive support to victims including one-to-one counselling sessions, either face to face or through telephone appointments. They also provide general advice with regard to managing financial difficulty, retirement and general areas of finding new employment. The range of services depending on the provider often includes performance coaching, legal services, training and personal development, self-help resources, employee well-being and work/life benefits.

The benefits of EAP services are noted in research that suggests that counselling services should be made available to employees when needed (Labib and Appelbaum, 1993). Although there is a cost associated per employee for using EAPs, the additional support it provides to employees, especially during tumultuous times, is immensely beneficial. It should also be noted that the support EAP provides lightens the pressure and responsibility on the organisation's redundancy envoys (Petzer, 2019).

Outplacement services

Outplacement services support employees who are being made redundant with finding alternative employment and offer a range of services from CV writing, career coaches, support with job hunting and interviewing skills. Research indicates that outplacement assistance can be critical to help reduce stress in the victims as they help to minimise the shock of the job loss but also support the employee in their efforts to find new alternative employment (Leana and Feldman, 1988; 1989). Another great benefit is that when organisations use the services of an outplacement company, it helps to alleviate the guilt experienced by redundancy envoys (Harrison, 1984, Tomasko, 1987). Labib and Appelbaum (1993) add that outplacement services such as financial advice, counselling and job search training may be a cost-effective option to support the victims of redundancies. Outplacement services can be offered to employees, tailored to their position in the organisation with employers having various options to choose from, depending on the budget available for such services. Most providers offer a bespoke programme for employees in senior positions, which typically include the following components:

- career assessment
- marketing preparation
- understanding the routes to market
- campaign support.

Employees seeking new employment typically receive a dedicated service that is unlimited until the individual is settled in their new role, irrespective of a specific time scale. Some providers offer support to individuals up to three months after they are established in their new role. An outplacement service normally comprises these key elements:

- career website portal
- personal telephone career coach
- remote job and company research
- 24/7 personal helpline.

Personal telephone career coach services typically include support service such as:

- leading-edge career information
- advice on career directions
- outbound career advice telephone calls
- unlimited inbound career help line
- company information and research resources
- trade and professional information.

Career website portals offer interactive online facilities such as:

- online career planning
- create and check CVs online interview audio files
- direct access to helpline advisers
- links to the best job sites
- downloadable career guides
- support and advice by e-mail
- 'how to' networking audio files CV and letter examples
- letter templates
- training and education links
- internet applications guide
- interview route planner.

Distance-based job and company research involves proactive, investigative support where job searches are undertaken based on the individual's personal circumstances, i.e., location, full or part-time job and salary requirements. Searches are conducted based on individuals:

- skills and experience
- areas of interest
- salary and geographical requirements.

Support for survivors and semi-survivors

The implementation of a successful redundancy programme relies on extending support to not only victims, but survivors as well (Cameron et al., 1991). Whilst typically victims receive support when exiting an organisation, such as financial packages and outplacement support, research indicates that survivors, on the other hand, receive very little organisational support (Gandolfi, 2006).

Counselling and outplacement support

The negative psychological impact on survivors was established in Chapter 3. Support for survivors will depend on individual requirements as the impact on each individual is unique. For some survivors, counselling may be beneficial to help process the period of change. This notion is supported in literature that posits that specific support should be made available to victims as well as survivors when it comes to counselling and outplacement (Cameron et al., 1991). Baruch and Hind (1999) agree that the provision of counselling to survivors during a redundancy programme is very important to help mitigate survivor syndrome.

Support for victims

Although this section discusses how to support survivors during redundancy implementation, it is worth noting that organisational support for victims, vicariously supports survivors. Helping victims to find work has a positive impact on survivors and redundancy envoys as it helps mitigate guilt experienced (Petzer, 2019). Research has also indicated that raising awareness of the benefits that victims receive and promoting good treatment and success stories have a liberating and positive impact on survivors (Noer, 1993). The use of outplacement service providers is also recognised to reduce the negative impact experienced by survivors when their colleagues who exit the organisation are supported through these means (Doherty, 1998). Supporting victims during redundancy thus have far-reaching positive implications for the organisation internally and externally as it helps limit reputation damage.

Training and development

Survivors often take on new responsibilities and increased workload as a result of employees leaving. They thus need support with training and how to manage the increase workload. A common pitfall of poor redundancy implementation is to place survivors in roles for which they have inadequate skills, which is likely to lead to failure, even in high-performing employees (Hitt et al., 1994). A recent study at SteelCo (McLachlan et al., 2020) supports the argument that employees that are redeployed require stability, development and career support (Clarke, 2013, McLachlan et al., 2020). Supporting survivors with training and development extends to more than just what is required during redundancy implementation, but also to what is required post redundancy implementation. The continued requirement for training and development is thus discussed in more depth in Chapter 11.

Redundancy envoys

Support groups for redundancy envoys

Research has indicated that one of the most successful support interventions for redundancy envoys is through support groups (Petzer, 2019). Discussions through support groups can alleviate some of the anxieties and fears that redundancy envoys experience during implementation (Morton, 1983). It is important to share experiences with others and by listening to the successes and failures of others, it is likely that greater objectivity will prevail (Boyd and Gumpert, 1983). In summary, to support redundancy envoys through redundancy implementation, organisations would benefit from setting up forums and social support groups (Clair and Dufresne, 2004).

Due to the level of confidentiality required during the implementation of redundancies, a 'safe platform' for redundancy envoys to share experiences are rather limited. A strong relationship between HR and management is thus important for both parties to provide morale support to each other during redundancy implementation (Petzer, 2019).

EAP and outplacement services

Weide and Abbott (1994) highlight that EAPs are not just there for victims, managers should also use them to get advice on how to deal with difficult or unfamiliar situations, thereby helping them to become more confident in dealing with redundancy implementation. As discussed earlier, the services offered by both these providers are comprehensive and should be promoted for redundancy envoys to utilise.

Training and development

The importance of training and development for redundancy envoys was discussed and included as part of the RRR strategy in Chapter 7, stage 4, Management training. This section here is thus an extension of the argument for the benefits of training and development for redundancy envoys.

When it comes to the communication of tough decisions, there is a clear requirement for training (Weide and Abbott, 1994). Managers are rarely shown or coached on how to break the news of tough decisions such as redundancies or dismissals, which therefore puts the case forward for managers and supervisors to receive training on critical communication and interpersonal skills. Weide and Abbott (1994) found in their study of 32 cases of homicide at work, that careful handling is required when giving news of redundancy or end of employment. It was found that in 80% of these cases, the homicide was either due to communication problems or something going wrong between the manager and the employee. This supports the need for management development programmes on how to communicate unpleasant news and how to resolve conflict.

Morton (1983) states that helping managers reduce their fears and anxieties when having to undergo the difficult conversations associated with redundancy related dismissal will help them appear more sensitive to the impacted employee. This will provide a win-win solution for the redundancy envoy, as well as the victims and survivors. Training can also help redundancy envoys to learn to deflect guilt (Pollan and Levine, 1994). Redundancy envoys should be trained on how to deal with emotional responses such as anger, crying, refusal to speak or leaving the building, wanting to talk to someone more senior, displays of aggression or acts of gross misconduct (Deems, 1995). This argument is supported by authors stating that organisations that are planning to run a redundancy programme should provide the necessary training and emotional support and at least raise awareness of the range of emotions that the redundancy envoys will experience themselves (Gandolfi, 2009). The training must incorporate the acquisition of skills that help managers address the concerns and needs of their staff (Labib and Appelbaum, 1993). Cameron et al. (1991) compliment the requirement for training by adding that managers should be given training on how to act during difficult situations such as during the consultation process and dismissal meeting.

Redundancy envoys need specific, focused management training, such as fine-tuning the process of delivering tough decisions, managing expectations and negotiating skills (Baruch and Hind, 1999). As change becomes more constant, so is the need for redundancy envoys to be resilient and able to cope with change, and where change-management skills will be advantageous for the organisation and employees. It is also important for a successful redundancy programme to ensure that the Human Resource Management function has the right skills and training to support the new organisation with the knowledge of how to deal with dismissals, minimal external hires and retrain the survivors (Labib and Appelbaum, 1993).

Outsourcing redundancy implementation

Research indicates that there is a direct correlation between previous redundancy experience and a reduced impact on redundancy envoys and it is thus recommended for organisations to consider outsourcing the responsibility of professionals who are experienced in redundancy implementations (Petzer, 2019). Clair and Dufresne (2004) equally found that the more organisational managers were exposed to redundancy programmes, the more frequently and regularly this led to the development of 'coping mechanisms' in itself. An ethical solution to employers may thus be to draw on the help of professional services to help with the consultation and dismissal of employees for reason of redundancy. This service is available from www.madeleinestevens.com.

This chapter summarises elements of support that employers can offer to each impacted group during redundancy implementation. Many aspects of mitigating the negative psychological aspects are represented throughout this book and not limited to this chapter. It is important for employers to continue to offer support post redundancy implementation, which will be explored in Chapter 11.

References

Baptiste, N. R. 2008. Tightening the link between employee wellbeing at work and performance. *Management Decision*, 46(2), 284–309.

Baruch, Y. & Hind, P. 1999. Perpetual motion in organizations: Effective management and the impact of the new psychological contracts on "Survivor Syndrome". *European Journal of Work and Organizational Psychology*, 8, 295–306.

Bowman, E. H. & Singh, H. 1993. Corporate restructuring: Reconfiguring the firm. *Strategic Management Journal*, 14, 5–14.

Boyd, D. P. & Gumpert, D. E. 1983. Coping with entrepreneurial stress. *Harvard Business Review*, 61, 44–&.

Cameron, K. S., Freeman, S. J. & Mishra, A. K. 1991. Best practices in white-collar downsizing: Managing contradictions. *Academy of Management Perspectives*, 5, 57–73.

Clair, J. A. & Dufresne, R. L. 2004. Playing the grim reaper: How employees experience carrying out a downsizing. *Human Relations*, 57, 1597–1625.

Clarke, M. 2013. The organizational career: Not dead but in need of redefinition. *The International Journal of Human Resource Management*, 24, 684–703.

Davis, J. A., Savage, G., Stewart, R. T. & Chapman, R. C. 2003. Organizational downsizing: A review of literature for planning and research/practitioner application. *Journal of Healthcare Management*, 48, 181.

Deems, R. S. 1995. *Fear of firing*. Franklin Lakes, NJ: Career Press.

Doherty, N. 1998. The role of outplacement in redundancy management. *Personnel Review*, 27, 343–353.

Flint, D. H. 2003. Downsizing in the public sector: Metro-Toronto's hospitals. *Journal of Health Organization and Management*, 17(6), 438–456.

Gandolfi, F. 2006. *Corporate Downsizing Demystified: A Scholarly Analysis of a Business Phenomenon*, Hyderabad, India, ICFAI University Press.

Gandolfi, F. 2009. Unraveling Downsizing—What do we know about the Phenomenon? *Revista de Management Comparat Internaţional*, 10, 414–426.

Harrison, C. E. 1984. *Managing staff reductions in corporations*: A multiple case study of program characteristics, outcomes and alternative strategies (reduction-in-force, outplacement, terminations). Web. Thesis publication, UMI Research Press.

Hitt, M. A., Keats, B. W., Harback, H. F. & Nixon, R. D. 1994. Rightsizing: Building and Maintaining Strategic Leadership and Long-Term Competitiveness. *Organizational Dynamics*, 23, 18–33.

Iverson, R. D. & Zatzick, C. D. 2007. High-commitment work practices and downsizing harshness in Australian workplaces. *Industrial Relations: A Journal of Economy and Society*, 46, 456–480.

Jacobs, K. 2020. Skills HR will need in 2021: Restructuring your business with confidence. *People Management, CIPD*.

Labib, N. & Appelbaum, S. H. 1993. Strategic downsizing: A human resources perspective. *Human Resource Planning*, 16(4), 69.

Leana, C. R. & Feldman, D. C, 1988. Individual responses to job loss: Perceptions, reactions, and coping behaviors. *Journal of Management*, 14, 375–389.

Leana, C. R. & Feldman, D. C. 1989. When Mergers Force Layoffs: Some Lessons about Managing the Human Resource Problems. *Human Resource Planning*, 12(2), 123.

Mclachlan, C. J., Mackenzie, R. & Greenwood, I. 2020. Victims, survivors and the emergence of 'endurers' as a reflection of shifting goals in the management of redeployment. *Human Resource Management Journal*, 31(2), 438–453.

Mishra, K. E., Spreitzer, G. M. & Mishra, A. K. 1998. Preserving employee morale during downsizing. *MIT Sloan Management Review*, 39, 83.

Morton, G. L. 1983. Helping managers and employees cope with work-force cutbacks. *Training & Development Journal*, 37(9), 50–54.

Noer, D. M. 1993. *Healing the wounds: Overcoming the trauma of layoffs and revitalizing downsized organizations*, 2nd edition. Hoboken: Jossey-Bass.

Petzer, M. 2019. *Developing effective interventions for mitigating the psychological impact experienced by redundancy envoys during redundancy situations*. PhD, Solent University.

Petzer, M. Don't shoot the messenger: The enigmatic impact of conveying bad news during redundancy situations and how to limit the impact. 2020 Applied Research Conference, 2020. CIPD.

Pollan, S. & Levine, M. 1994. Firing an employee. *Working Woman*, 19, 55.

Tomasko, R. M. 1987. *Downsizing: Reshaping the corporation for the future*. New York: AMACOM/American Management Association.

Tomasko, R. M. 1991. Downsizing: Layoffs and alternatives to layoffs. *Compensation & Benefits Review*, 23, 19–32.

Waters, L. & Muller, J. 2004. Voluntary and involuntary job redundancy: Hope or helplessness? *Academy of Management Annual Meeting Best Paper Proceedings*, CAR.

Weide, A. S. & Abbott, G. E. 1994. Management on the hot seat: In an increasingly violent workplace, how to deliver bad news. *Employment Relations Today*, 21, 23.

Part III

RE-BUILD

Re-building the organisation

11

RE-BUILDING THE ORGANISATION POST-REDUNDANCY IMPLEMENTATION

This chapter addresses the very important aspect of re-building the organisation, the last part of the RRR strategy; to 'Re-Build', focusing on recognition, ongoing development and investment, referring to Figure 11.1. Key aspects are addressed, including the importance of leadership, work redesign, training and development, relationship building, recognition and evaluation.

At this point we are well aware that the success of redundancies in reaping economic and strategic improvements remains contested in the literature (Sheaffer et al., 2009). It is also known that although organisations may report initial financial success, it is likely that long-term financial success will soon stumble once the root problems reoccur such as poor management practices and/or ineffective strategies (Mellahi and Wilkinson, 2005). To address these challenges, it is critical for employers to continue to invest in the organisation with enthusiasm to combat any survivor syndrome and to re-establish the business as a key competitor in the market.

DOI: 10.4324/9781003030416-14

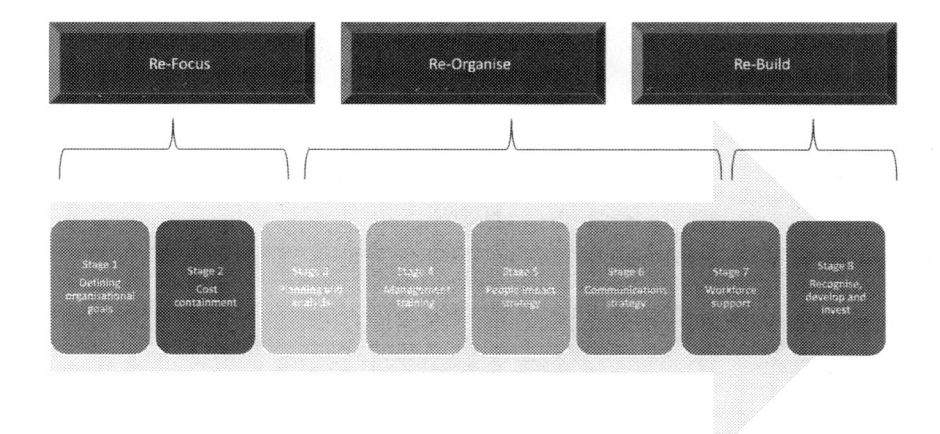

Figure 11.1 Eight stages of redundancy implementation.

Combating survivor syndrome

Addressing survivor needs is essential to the success of an organisation after a redundancy programme (Isabella, 1989). At this point, the organisation should be in a position where redundancies were implemented fairly and compassionately, which would have helped mitigate survivor syndrome and promote trust in leadership (Jacobs, 2020). Redundancy implementation is naturally an emotionally difficult and challenging time, which can pose a range of challenges to redundancy envoys in the aftermath of rebuilding the organisation.

Redundancies also have an impact on the organisation's reputation and external relationships such as customers, suppliers and the local community (Cascio, 2010), which all needs to be considered as part of the rebuilding process. Management is thus challenged to pick up the aftermath of declining organisational performance and decreased competitiveness (DeRue et al., 2008). The success of a redundancy programme in reducing costs will be measured after the event based on the financial output of the organisation and the stock returns created for investors (Cascio, 2002). As a result, the pressure is on management to strengthen and improve performance (Zatzick and Iverson, 2006).

This leads us to the question of how to address the known challenges caused by redundancies.

Leadership

Literature indicates that organisations that were successful at implementing redundancies had leaders who articulated a clear vision of where the organisation was headed (Flint, 2003). However, Hitt et al. (1994) warn that if the gap between the current and new vision is too large, employees could find it too threatening. It is thus important to implement change by taking the organisation on a slow and steady journey of continued involvement and participation. Charismatic leadership can help create this vision, which will encourage employees to make sensible compromises to their personal positions in the belief of a hopeful future for all. This can only be achieved if the leadership has the necessary integrity and established trust within the organisation. Employees need to know and feel that the redundancy envoys are aware of their needs, whilst the redundancy envoys need to know they can trust their workforce to protect the reputation and future of the organisation. High levels of goodwill, trust, innovation, propensity and procedural justice will reduce the desire for employees to seek new employment (De Clercq and Belausteguigoitia, 2017).

Leadership needs to be visible with a clear action plan on what the strategic goals are to achieve the intended objectives. Employees need to understand the vision, goals and objectives of the organisation to help them appreciate their role in achieving organisational success and create an ownership culture. The unknown creates fear and panic. Employers need to take measures proactively and have short-, medium- and long-term strategies in place.

To be effective, strategic leadership is required that allows for change to be continuous with management keeping employees onboard to achieve the new vision (Hitt et al., 1994). To facilitate and promote engagement, it is recommended to have regular updates on measuring and sharing the progress against clear organisational goals post-redundancy implementation. Hitt et al. (1994) also argue the importance of avoiding a culture that is focused on financial returns only, the focus should be on a balance of managerial actions and financial returns that is long term.

The presence of a strong, charismatic leader is pivotal during tumultuous times as this presence and leadership can positively influence the morale and engagement of employees. Hitt et al. (1994) advocate the positive impact of the presence of strategic leadership during redundancy implementations. In studies conducted by (Davis et al., 2003, Petzer, 2019), morale remained positive post-redundancy implementation due to open communication forums where employees could be heard with management taking proactive action to address issues. Correspondingly, management ought to communicate the organisation's commitment to employees (Mone, 1994). It is thus recommended to invest in rebranding or marketing specific to re-launch the new revitalised organisation, with its vision, mission and goals.

More than ever is important to continue with best practice strategies that helped the organisation transition through a successful redundancy programme, such as underpinned in the RRR strategy; effective communication, involvement and participation and engaging with the employee representatives. Employee accountability could be highly effective in driving performance, however, need to be associated with active employee involvement and participation (Hitt et al., 1994).

Work design and empowerment

In a post-redundancy environment, it is natural for managers to be concerned with organisational effectiveness and workforce performance. Designing jobs to allow for individual empowerment that drives motivation allows for improved effectiveness, despite the past turmoil caused by redundancies and the fear of future redundancies (Jalajas and Bommer, 1999). Effective job design will also help address the reality that often management supervision decreases after a redundancy, which means that working autonomously increases amongst survivors (Brockner, 1992).

As part of the redundancy programme, a new structure would have been established, which would allow for a change in roles and responsibilities. The new setup should reflect the changed roles, incorporate new processes with alignment to employee skills and responsibilities (Hitt, 1994). Due to the intense workload during a redundancy programme, many HR and line manager tasks are compromised. It is thus important to, as soon as possible, pick up on areas that may have slipped. Policies and processes may be revised to ensure continued cost savings such as a review of expenses policies, recruitment or training processes. To mitigate the negative aspect of additional workload, explore all opportunities to redesign roles that can help drive development and future promotions. Studies conducted by Hackman and Lawler (1971) and Hackman et al. (1980) posit that jobs that are well designed have a direct link to high internal motivation, high job and general satisfaction, as well as in quantity and quality of work effectiveness.

During the re-building stages, it is important to focus on job content as this is a critical motivating factor to drive long-term employee commitment, whereas the benefit of financial rewards alone is usually short-lived in the enhancement of performance (Hitt et al., 1994). The survivors of the organisation must be revitalised with clear definitions of their roles and responsibilities (Hitt et al., 1994).

Empowering employees has also been linked to higher effort, work performance and resilience during turbulent times (Spreitzer, 1995) and thus highly recommended to drive high performance in the aftermath of a redundancy programme (Hitt et al., 1994).

Training

Chapter 10 discussed the importance of supporting survivors with training and development. This argument is extended here with the focus on organisational survival. In the previous section, we discussed the redesigning of work and job content. Once it is clear who the survivors are, it is important to establish the training needs of the remaining employees to ensure the organisations strategic goals are met (Labib and Appelbaum, 1993). Hitt et al. (1994) support this notion that employees with core competencies must be identified, nurtured and developed.

Commitment can be shown through development opportunities and demonstrating the organisation's belief in a promising future by investing in sensible training. Quite often training budgets are the first to suffer from cost-cutting exercises, which can be a short-sighted approach. Bolster the organisation's confidence and motivation levels by investing in the workforce where possible. Hitt et al. (1994) agree that during tumultuous times of redundancy implementation, employees with strong leadership and management skills should be protected and mentored. Running post-redundancy workshops where lessons learned are explored will help with a collective approach to re-building the organisation and can provide closure to redundancy envoys who may have had a traumatic emotional experience. Lesson learned in workshops will also help to augment the principal competencies of the managers (Buono, 2003).

Offering retraining to employees post-redundancy programme has a positive impact on their motivation and loyalty, as they perceive they are being upskilled with highly valuable skills at no cost to themselves (Labib and Appelbaum, 1993). Training is also important when redesigning work to consider individual growth needs and individual strengths, rather than an impetus on organisational units and processes (Keidel, 1994). Training on lean management principles can also help survivors to learn how to work efficiently with 'less'.

Relationship building and development

Redundancies disrupt social communities as tacit knowledge in working relationships are damaged or removed when the organisation's knowledge inventory is reduced (Miller, 2002). In addition, implementing redundancies has a negative impact on organisational learning and hinders the organisation's ability to adapt to change due to damage caused to informal networks (Fisher and White, 2000). Therefore, it is important for organisational survival that the knowledge pool and organisational learning is re-established. Relationships can be re-established by focusing on team and group development and this will support the re-creation of 'updated' psychological contracts between employee and management, which is critical for the successful management of change and will reduce the negative impact of survivor syndrome (Baruch and Hind, 1999). To drive agility and organisational success, focus on hiring new skills and developing existing employees specifically in the areas of skill shortages, to ensure future sustainability (Hitt, 1994). Another method to help Re-Build trust post-redundancy implementation is the use of team-building activities (Buono, 2003). To develop employees in management and leadership roles, mentoring programmes would be mutually beneficial in building trust and demonstrating commitment from the organisation (Hitt, 1994).

Recognition

Isabella (1989) contends that the value of the survivors' expertise to the new organisation is often not understood or appreciated, and recognition is of key importance. Recognition can also take the form of employee development that is linked to performance (Labib and Appelbaum, 1993).

Although the availability of resources may be limited, employers must ensure that good work, orders won and employee commitment above and beyond expectations is recognised and rewarded publicly. This will help to build trust and belief in the ability of the business to reach its intended objectives and demonstrate the values the organisation want all employees to adopt.

Accordingly, there should be a reinvigorated focus on performance management. If reward cannot be instant, try to link objectives and bonus-related targets specific to outcomes that will ensure the sustainability and future success of the organisation by driving the right behaviours. Baruch and Hind (1999) argue that to recognise survivors adequately, a review of performance feedback and appraisal systems should take place as part of a redundancy programme. The performance appraisal system should be revised accordingly to ensure that performance is directly related to activities that support strategic changes of the organisation post-redundancy implementation (Butler et al., 1991).

In Isabella's (1989: 39) model of 'Employee Needs after Downsizing', she addresses the needs of survivors as crucial to organisational success. These needs include the importance of transforming the meaning of job security in the business, ensuring success is recognised, being understood and adequately rewarded, driving ownership for career self-management and fostering an innovative approach to loyalty and commitment to the new organisation. Applying Waldman and Spangler's (1989) reinforcement theory, when there is visible, immediate, positive reinforcement for good performance, people will continue to perform well.

Evaluation

As with any change programme, evaluation is key to measure success. Labib and Appelbaum (1993) recommend an evaluation six months after implementation of the redundancies to establish any lessons learned. On the contrary, other research has indicated that organisations require sufficient time to recover from a redundancy programme and as such evaluation should realistically only take place 12–18 months post-implementation (Petzer, 2019).

This chapter concluded with recommendations to address post-redundancy aftermath through effective leadership, establishing and communicating a clear vision, work redesign, investing in training and development, re-building relationships and post-redundancy evaluation. Implementation of redundancies and restructures will always be a challenging project, testing organisational performance and workforce loyalty. Although this book has hopefully provided some helpful suggestions and template examples for redundancy envoys to ease the process, caution should always be taken to protect the organisation's most valuable assets, their people.

Further support is available from www.madeleinestevens.com.

References

Baruch, Y. & Hind, P. 1999. Perpetual motion in organizations: Effective man-agement and the impact of the new psychological contracts on "survivor syndrome". *European Journal of Work and Organizational Psychology*, 8, 295–306.

Brockner, J. 1992. Managing the effects of layoffs on survivors. *California Management Review*, 34, 9–28.

Buono, A. F. 2003. SEAM-less post-merger integration strategies: a cause for concern. *Journal of Organizational Change Management*, 16(1), 90–98.

Butler, J. E., Ferris, G. R. & Napier, N. K. 1991. *Strategy and human resources management*. Cincinnati, OH: South-Western Pub.

Cascio, W. F. 2002. Strategies for responsible restructuring. *Academy of Management Perspectives*, 16, 80–91.

Cascio, W. F. 2010. Employment downsizing and its alternatives. *SHRM Foundation's Effective Practical Guide Series*.

Davis, J. A., Savage, G., Stewart, R. T. & Chapman, R. C. 2003. Organizational downsizing: A review of literature for planning and research/practitioner application. *Journal of Healthcare Management*, 48, 181.

De Clercq, D. & Belausteguigoitia, I. 2017. Reducing the harmful effect of role ambiguity on turnover intentions: The roles of innovation propensity, goodwill trust, and procedural justice. *Personnel Review*, 46(6), 1046–1069.

Derue, D. S., Hollenbeck, J. R., Johnson, M. D., Ilgen, D. R. & Jundt, D. K. 2008. How different team downsizing approaches influence team-level adapta-tion and performance. *Academy of Management Journal*, 51, 182–196.

Fisher, S. R. & White, M. A. 2000. Downsizing in a learning organization: Are there hidden costs? *Academy of Management Review*, 25, 244–251.

Flint, D. H. 2003. Downsizing in the public sector: Metro-Toronto's hospitals. *Journal of Health Organization and Management*, 17(6), 438–456.

Hackman, J. R., Hackman, R. J. & Oldham, G. R. 1980. *Work redesign*. Reading, MA: Addison-Wesley.

Hackman, J. R. & Lawler, E. E. 1971. Employee reactions to job characteristics. *Journal of Applied Psychology*, 55, 259.

Hitt, M. A. 1994. Rightsizing: Building and maintaining strategic leadership and long-term competitiveness. *Organizational Dynamics*, 23, 18–33.

Hitt, M. A., Keats, B. W., Harback, H. F. & Nixon, R. D. 1994. Rightsizing: Building and maintaining strategic leadership and long-term competitiveness. *Organizational Dynamics*, 23, 18–33.

Isabella, L. A. 1989. Downsizing: Survivors' assessments. *Business Horizons*, 32, 35–41.

Jacobs, K. 2020. Skills HR will need in 2021: Restructuring your business with confidence. *People Management, CIPD*.

Jalajas, D. S. & Bommer, M. 1999. The influence of job motivation versus downsizing on individual behavior. *Human Resource Development Quarterly*, 10, 329–341.

Keidel, R. W. 1994. Rethinking organizational design. *Academy of Management Perspectives*, 8, 12–28.

Labib, N. & Appelbaum, S. H. 1993. Strategic downsizing: A human resources perspective. *Human Resource Planning*, 16(4), 69.

Mellahi, K. & Wilkinson, A. 2005. Organizational failure: Introduction to the special issue. *Long Range Planning*, 38, 233–238.

Miller, K. D. 2002. Knowledge inventories and managerial myopia. *Strategic Management Journal*, 23, 689–706.

Mone, M. A. 1994. Relationships between self-concepts, aspirations, emotional responses, and intent to leave a downsizing organization. *Human Resource Management*, 33, 281–298.

Petzer, M. 2019. *Developing effective interventions for mitigating the psychological impact experienced by redundancy envoys during redundancy situations*. PhD, Solent University.

Sheaffer, Z., Carmeli, A., Steiner-Revivo, M. & Zionit, S. 2009. Downsizing strategies and organizational performance: A longitudinal study. *Management Decision*, 47(6), 950–974.

Spreitzer, G. M. 1995. Psychological empowerment in the workplace: Dimensions, measurement and validation. *Academy of Management Journal*, 38 (5), 1442–1465.

Waldman, D. A. & Spangler, W. D. 1989. Putting together the pieces: A closer look at the determinants of job performance. *Human Performance*, 2, 29–59.

Zatzick, C. D. & Iverson, R. D. 2006. High-involvement management and workforce reduction: Competitive advantage or disadvantage? *Academy of management Journal*, 49, 999–1015.

INDEX

Printed in the United States
by Baker & Taylor Publisher Services